20-Minute
Learning
Connection

by Douglas B. Reeves, Ph.D.

Simon & Schuster
New York · London · Singapore · Sydney · Toronto

Kaplan Publishing
Published by Simon & Schuster, Inc.
1230 Avenue of the Americas
New York, NY 10020

For bulk sales to schools, colleges, and universities, please contact:
Order Department, Simon & Schuster, Inc.,
100 Front Street, Riverside, NJ 08075
Phone: (800) 223-2336 Fax: (800) 943-9831.

Kaplan® is a registered trademark of Kaplan, Inc.

Designed by Richard Oriolo

Manufactured in the United States of America

January 2002
10 9 8 7 6 5 4 3 2 1

Library of Congress Cataloging-in Publication-Data

ISBN: 0-7432-1182-0
ISSN:

Contents

Acknowledgements

In my discipline of statistics, we learn about *a priori* and *a posteriori* probabilities. There is a lesson in such study. My *a priori* obligations include a debt of thanks to the grandfather I never knew, Sherman Vester Reeves, but whose 1906 teaching license I found in my father's office. Teachers in Green Forest, Arkansas at the dawn of the 20th century had their test scores on their teaching licenses. If one were to search for the genesis of high academic standards, the search might profitably begin in Carroll County. My grandmother, Laura Anderson Johnson, was a teacher and superintendent of schools. My mother, Julie Reeves, taught as a volunteer for decades, with her only compensation being the love and admiration of her students. My father, J.B. Reeves, devoted his last years of his life to the professorate, but those who knew him would argue that from his time as a field artilleryman in World War II until his last breath, he was a teacher to generations.

My *a posteriori* obligations are to my children, whose enthusiasm, love, and kind words are the lights of my life. Having said those nice things, I offer this plea: If you see four children laughing uproariously in the education section of your local bookstore as they point at this book, their names are Brooks, Alexander, Julia, and James. Please tell them to behave themselves and return to the self-improvement aisle where they belong.

Between the past and future lies the present, in which I wrote this volume. Maureen McMahon of Simon & Schuster is walking evidence of Stephen King's maxim that, "to write is human; to edit, divine." Rudy Robles provided encyclopedic knowledge of state standards and synthesized his knowledge in a manner so clear and concise that he will never find employment in Washington, D.C. Lori Duggan Gold provided a steady stream of connections to reporters and policy analysts who helped me distinguish the rhetorical chaff from the intellectual wheat. Abby Remer's creative and thoughtful voice preserved an emphasis on art, music, beauty, and enjoyment in a world in which standards are stereotyped as sterile and dull.

Special thanks are due to the hundreds of parents, teachers, and school leaders who took the time to participate in focus groups and personal interviews as part of my research for this book. I am particularly indebted to Charles Sodergren, a retired principal and teacher, whose extensive comments and perspectives as a parent, grandparent, and career educator were very helpful.

For reassurance at just the right time, challenge when I needed it, and love when I least deserved it, I am always indebted to Shelley Sackett. This mother, lawyer, teacher, and wonderful spouse makes books worth writing and life worth living.

dr
Swampscott, Massachusetts

Special Note to Academic and Professional Readers

Some teachers, school leaders, researchers, and professors may read the following pages and ask, "Where are the footnotes?" It is a fair question and it deserves a straight answer. This book is directed to a lay audience. In the interest of clarity, I have not provided the citations and footnotes that would normally accompany every allusion to research and each assertion of fact. For readers interested in my most recent writings directed toward a professional audience where the research is clearly cited, please consult the articles and book chapters that can be downloaded free of charge at www.edaccountability.org and www.makingstandardswork.com.

How to Get the Most Out of This Book

Here is the most important test question you will ever have:

A parent's best strategy to promote school success is to:

a) *Terrorize* children by threatening them with failure and loss of promotion to the next grade.

b) *Humiliate* children by comparing them to other kids with better scores.

c) *Exhaust* children by engaging in frantic last-minute test preparation.

d) *Build, nurture, and empower* children by giving them the skills to be confident and capable learners.

If the last choice appeals to you more than the first three alternatives, then this book is written for you. You will learn not only how to help your child meet academic standards and succeed on tests, but more importantly, you will learn how to help your child become a confident, capable, and empowered learner.

a busy parent

How Can You Make a Difference in Just 20 Minutes a Day?

Although we have not met, I believe I have a good idea of who you are and why you selected this book. You are a busy parent. Whether you work at home, at an office, or on the road, you manage multiple priorities and face many demands on your time. You want to be more involved in your children's education, but some days it seems as if the time required by your other responsibilities leaves little time for a focus on your child's schoolwork. You read the report cards and newsletters and often look at your child's schoolwork, some of which may be on your refrigerator door. You attend parent meetings and school events whenever you can. You read with your child, though not as much as you did during the preschool years. You have heard about academic standards and know that some of the tests required by the state and school district are very important, and you have a nagging feeling that your child should be better prepared. But at the end of a long day, you really don't feel like adding the role of substitute teacher to your long and growing list of duties. Am I getting close to your reality?

Practical Advice for Busy Parents

Your busy lifestyle is the norm, not the exception. Less than a third of children attending school today come from a home of the 1950s' television stereotype with a stay-at-home mother whose principal role is the management of family and nurturing of children. Far more typical is a case in which both parents are working outside the home or there is only one parent in the household, and that person must work to support the family. Even the parents who have chosen to stay at home and make the raising of children their primary goal have a far different routine than Donna Reed and her television counterparts. The caricature of the stay-at-home parent has given way to parents who are active in political, cultural, and social causes and for whom school activities are one of many other pursuits. The fact that these parents earn no money outside the home does not indicate that they are not working. These parents are subject to the same exhaustion, burn-out, and frustration as parents who rise at 5:30 every morning, get children ready for school, work a full day and more, and return home in the evening to potentially overwhelming demands for help from their children.

Here is the good news: If you can devote 20 minutes each day to helping your children succeed in school, you can make a profound difference in the intellectual development and emotional growth of your child. If you like the ideas put forth here, you may find that the amount of time you spend building confident, capable, and empowered children will be worth more than 20 minutes a day. But make no mistake: Twenty minutes a day, focused on the right questions and the most effective activities, can make a huge difference in the lives of your children and their success in school. We are not talking about aimless discussions and unproductive questions such as the exchange known to every parent:

"What did you do in school today?"
"Nothing."

Rather, we offer practical advice for kids and parents. Throughout this book you will find checklists, activities, even letters to school officials that have been written for you. While no one, least of all authors, can take the place of parents, we can save you some time and make your role in supporting school success somewhat less stressful and time consuming.

The path to student success is not without some challenges. Therefore, we will address the requirements for making some reasonable trade-offs and minor changes in family routine. Fair warning: This will involve a little less television and a little more reading. It will involve moving a few chairs and creating the space and time for an effective home learning environment. But our goal is joyful learning, not joyless boot camp. Even as an exceptionally busy parent, you can make 20 minutes into a powerful learning experience if you will commit to three principles:

First, be yourself. Find activities that you genuinely enjoy and with which you can model the creative energy that comes from intellectual engagement with your child. This book contains a wonderful variety of activities that directly support essential knowledge and skills for your child. Although the activities are arranged in the same order as the state standards, you need not go through them in that sequence. Find activities that are engaging, exciting, interesting, and fun for both you and your child.

The second principle that will make your 20 minutes most valuable is that you are supportive. Remember the last time you learned a new skill? Perhaps it was a computer program, a foreign language, or a musical instrument. No matter how talented and brilliant you are, learning new things takes some time and patience. No matter how motivated you are, learning requires some perseverance and emotional resilience. Some of the academic requirements for children in school today are as challenging for them as they were for you when you were struggling with and eventually acquiring complex skills. If you can recall the need for patience, understanding, and clarity during your own difficult learning experiences, then assume that those needs apply in exponentially large proportions for your child. An important part of your support is the clarity of your expectations. Two of the most important intellectual skills you will build with your child are reflection and self-evaluation. You will build those skills by regularly asking your child to revise and improve work, whether it is a letter to a relative or a recipe for dinner. Performing these activities will be most valuable if you encourage your child to take a moment to reflect and ask, "What did I learn and how can I do this better next time?"

Third, it is important that you are consistent. Find a regular time, perhaps immediately before or after your evening meal, for your 20-Minute Learning Connection. During this time, the television is off and the telephone answering machine is on. You are giving your children the gift that they need, indeed crave, more than anything else in the world: your undivided attention. The focus that you provide during these 20-minute activities will model the concentration and diligence that you associate with learning.

What Are Standards and Will They Last?

Academic standards have been the single most important movement in education in the last fifty years. Standards—simple statements of what students should know and be able to do—will continue long after every other contemporary educational fad has expired. While teachers and parents are weary of the "flavor of the month" educational reforms that come and go with the phases of the moon, standards have two qualities that guarantee their success: fairness and effectiveness.

Because so many educational movements have come and gone, it is reasonable to wonder whether standards will follow "new math" into oblivion. The enduring nature of standards rests with the fact that standards are the key to fairness, and fairness is a value that is timeless. Lots of trends come and go in education, but the simple requirement—that teachers, students, and parents should understand what students are expected to know and be able to do—is an enduring element of education both in the U.S. and abroad. Every state, and virtually every industrialized nation in the world, has some form of academic standards. The actual content of the standards varies, with some sets of standards emphasizing certain academic areas more than others. But the central idea of standards is consistent from Peoria to Paris, from Florida to Florence, from Los Angeles to London: School should not be an impenetrable mystery, and students have a right to know what is expected of them. Fairness will not go out of style.

Rather than exposing children to a demoralizing environment in which lucky students understand what makes the teacher happy and the unlucky just "don't get it," standards-based schools offer a clear set of expectations. With standards, students, teachers, and parents have the opportunity to know and understand what is expected of every student. Children have an innate sense of fairness. They understand that clarity is better than ambiguity and that consistency is superior to uncertainty.

The second essential quality of standards is that they are effective. When they are properly implemented, school standards have an impact on test designers, curriculum creators, teachers, and school leaders, as well as students. Far from transforming schools into joyless boot camps, effective school leaders use academic standards to make connections to the arts, extracurricular activities, and every other element of school life.

Thus standards are related not only to academic success but also to the emotional and intellectual welfare of children. Our desire is to help build confident, capable, and empowered learners. This means much more than drilling students in math and spelling facts (though that is still not a bad idea), and more than asking children to read aloud after dinner (though that is a wonderful family practice). Children become confident, capable, and empowered not only when they know the right answer on a test, but when they have the emotional resilience to persist in learning difficult concepts and when they persevere in the face of challenging, ambiguous, or seemingly impossible test items. Real student empowerment rests not in the futile effort to memorize the answer to every conceivable test question, but on the realistic prospect of developing strategies that can be used on every test in school, in college, and in the world of work and life beyond school.

empowered learners

Connections: Music, Art, Physical Education, and More

Although this book focuses on the most commonly tested academic standards—mathematics, language arts, social studies, and science—it is important to note that other areas of the school curriculum remain vitally important for your child's intellectual growth and development. Evidence from a number of research studies is consistent: Students who participate in the arts, physical education, and extracurricular activities consistently demonstrate superior academic and social skills. Thus, our focus on academic standards is not intended to diminish other athletic, artistic, and extracurricular activities that enrich the lives of children. In fact, many of the activities in this book combine academic and artistic, or academic and athletic skills.

Stress and Anxiety

Perhaps the most important message for parents is this: Stress and anxiety are communicable diseases. Children are not born with stress about school, homework, and tests; they *learn* that debilitating stress and anxiety are a part of school. Perhaps these destructive lessons are learned from schoolmates and teachers, but it is far more likely that such lessons are learned at home. No parent intentionally creates anxiety and stress for a child, but our conversations about school—particularly our discussions of tests—can have such an effect. This is very likely a reflection of the parents' own attitude toward school and testing. Take a few minutes to think about your own experiences and the stress and anxiety you experienced as a student. Most parents can objectively recognize that their school experiences had some good and bad elements. We are far more likely, however, to recall and transmit the parts of school that had the strongest emotional impact, and strong emotional impact in school is quite likely to be negative. The embarrassment over a failed exam, the humiliation as other students laughed, the feeling of despair and rejection when a teacher expressed disappointment—these memories linger far more than a hundred "smiley faces" that we routinely received on schoolwork. Thus, it is the parent, and no one but the parent, who adds balance and clarity to the school experience. The two essential ways in which effective parents add this balance include constructive and accurate discussions about school and the creation of learning opportunities that occur outside of school. The activities in this book are designed to support schoolwork and they will also develop students who are confident and capable. These activities have value not only because they are related to educational standards, but also because they will help to create a learning environment in your home. They will help you model the love of learning that every child must have and which every parent can nurture.

only a parent

The Most Important Teacher: You

The enormity of the task ahead can be daunting. After all, a parent might ask, "Shouldn't schools be doing this?" It's a fair question. In some cases, the schools can and should do more. But there is one thing that even the best schools with unlimited resources and brilliant teachers cannot do: They cannot be parents. Parents are the most important teachers any child can ever have. This doesn't mean that parents must be experts in every subject or masters of teaching techniques. But only a parent can give a child the ability to say words such as:

"I know that my mom and dad are proud of me."

"I mess up sometimes, but it's okay, because I know I can learn from my mistakes."

"I didn't do as well as I wanted to, but I know how to get better next time."

Only a parent can provide the emotional security and strength of character that build a child who is confident, capable, and empowered. Unfortunately, some parents substitute their own academic expertise for emotional resilience. Every time there is the "nuclear-powered science fair project" obviously done by a parent, the emotional consequence is not pride, but the absolute conviction by the child that "I'm not good enough to do this on my own." The activities in this book will show you how to create a learning environment in which you and your child learn together, make mistakes together, laugh together, and maintain a love of learning amidst all the chaos of daily life, as your child develops independence and confidence.

If You Don't Have Time for the Whole Book

A few readers are thinking, "I can't read the whole book—where do I start?" Although every page is here for a purpose, we recognize the limits of time and the need to focus on the essentials. Therefore, if your time is limited and you want the maximum value in the minimum time, we suggest that you focus on three areas. Start with Chapter 2 for the "why" of standards, then proceed to Chapter 5 for the "how" of standards. Then find an activity from the section starting on page 139 that you and your child will enjoy. Finish with a review of the appendices, where you can find additional resources that are directly relevant to your particular needs. Not every reader will be interested in the sections for students with special needs nor will everyone find the chapter on home schooling essential. We include those chapters because they represent significant and growing areas in education.

Learning Activities

At the end of this book you will find a variety of learning activities. You will find that these ideas have value, not only because they are directly related to the academic standards of your state, but also because they help to build the necessary thinking, reasoning, and communication skills your child needs in any school in any state. These activities will help you make family learning time a regular part of your routine.

A Special Note for Parents of Children with Special Needs

More than ten percent of students in school have a disability that influences their success in school. These disabilities range from differences in the way that they process information to profound physical and neurological challenges. These students are protected by a variety of federal and state statutes, the Individuals with Disabilities Education Act (IDEA) being the most significant legislation in this area. Parents of these students are often alarmed when a school official states that academic standards must apply to "all" students, sometimes adding sarcastically, "What is it about the word 'all' you don't understand?" Chapter 9 is devoted entirely to students with special needs. The bottom line, however, is the clear legal mandate that the individual needs of students must be taken into consideration in all matters involving standards, testing, and curriculum. Standards have great merit for schools, but there is danger in linking legitimate educational standards to the "standardization" of policies for students for whom the law clearly requires attention to individual needs.

It has been said that education is the "new civil right." This is true for students with special needs as well as disadvantaged families. The individualization of standards and testing requirements for students with special needs is not merely a nice thing to do; it is a legal requirement. Chapter 9 and the appendices provide sample letters and checklists for parents of students with special needs to ensure that you are empowered to protect the rights of your child and serve as an advocate on his behalf.

What about Changes in Standards and Tests?

Finally, the subject of standards and testing is changing on a daily basis. As this book goes to press, legislatures throughout the nation are being challenged to change tests and reformulate standards. The only thing that is certain is that tests and standards will continue to change. To help you keep up to date on the latest changes in standards and assessment for your state, we have created an Internet website with current information on the latest changes in standards and tests for your state. Just go to www.kaptest.com/crusadeintheclassroom and click on the name of your state for the latest updates on standards and assessment in your area. You will also find links to the state education department for your state where you can find the latest information on policy and procedures for education in your state.

The prospect of changes in standards, however, must not obscure this essential fact: While individual standards and particular testing policies may change, the fundamentals of standards are here to stay. Standards will endure because they are the most fair and effective way to educate children. While change may be a certainty in our world, it is also certain that the educational system will not retreat to the age of mystery in which a "standard" was whatever captured the interest of a teacher and "proficiency" varied from one classroom to another. Fads may come and go, but the imperatives of fairness and effectiveness will never vanish from the educational landscape.

communication

A Dose of Reality

My children are in public schools, including elementary, middle, and high school. My travels to schools throughout the world place me in contact with teachers, school leaders, and parents, hundreds of whom contributed ideas for this book. Each year I speak and listen to more than a hundred audiences, and thus far have worked in forty-nine states as well as Africa, Asia, and Europe. Whether these conversations take place in the United States or abroad, whether in an economically advantaged setting or a financially depressed area, there are remarkably common themes that I hear from parents, teachers, and school leaders. The number one issue is always communication. Parents want to hear more specific and more frequent information from the school; teachers want to have more immediate feedback from parents. Parents want to be welcomed into the classroom and insist that the individual needs and characteristics of their children be taken into account; educators and school leaders want parents to understand that today's schools are different from the classrooms of three decades ago. Most of all, parents do not wish to guess about the educational needs of their children. They want to know more than a list of subjects accompanied by a list of grades on a report card and demand to know what the expectations are and how their children can improve. This clarity and specificity is the essence of effective educational standards. I am also the beneficiary of a regular dose of blunt advice from Brooks, Alex, Julia, and James, children whose patience, love, and insight into educational matters are an unending source of inspiration and understanding. Thus, the following pages are not theoretical musings, but the result of daily contact with the real world of the reader.

Chapter 1

Making the 20-Minute Learning Connection Work for You

The Power of 20 Minutes a Day

As important as the role of parent is, many parents have multiple roles, including spouse, worker, employer, neighbor, volunteer, and parent to other children. When asked to find 20 minutes a day for educational activities in an already crowded schedule, an exhausted parent might respond, "I've been up since 5:30 this morning and have four phone calls to make, dinner to cook, and after that comes Cub Scouts and choir practice. And you want me to do more to enrich my child's education? That's the school's responsibility. I'm doing the best I can!"

Both the fatigue and frustration are understandable, and the recommendations we offer to parents are not a retreat to the 1950s or an appeal only to parents with unlimited reserves of time and energy. There is great power in 20 minutes a day. This is not merely a convenient figure taken out of the air, but rather an amount of time that is both validated by research and supported by the practicalities of the busy lives of families. In one study of student achievement, those children who completed 20 minutes a day of independent reading outside of school were 60 percentile points higher than their counterparts who did no such reading. While reading an hour or more a day is wonderful, the greatest gain in achievement occurred from just 20 minutes a day.

What can you do in 20 minutes? This book is full of activities that are directly related to the academic standards of your state. But consider the routines that any family can create in just 20 minutes a day.

In 20 minutes you and your child can . . .

- **Read aloud for fifteen minutes, and then describe what the story or news article was about for another five minutes.**

- **Write a letter to a grandparent, friend, or relative.**

- **Measure the ingredients for dinner.**

- **Explore the factors affecting recent weather patterns and predict tomorrow's weather.**

- **Draft and revise step-by-step instructions for the use of adult-defying devices such as VCRs and electronic games.**

- **Plan an imaginary trip to an exotic location using maps, weather data, and transportation schedules.**

This chapter considers the practical details of creating the place and the time for your 20-Minute Learning Connection. The habits you develop and the time you invest in making a learning connection with your child can fundamentally change the way you talk about school and, more importantly, the way your child thinks about learning. You can move away from conversations that are unproductive and threatening to discussions that are focused on interesting and engaging activities. You can move away from an inspection of the backpack and the dreary march through the daily homework toward learning for the sheer joy of spending time together, developing new skills, and contemplating new ideas. Of course, the 20-Minute Learning Connection does not replace homework any more than it will avoid death and taxes. But these moments will give your child the skills, enthusiasm, and knowledge to make homework and other academic challenges more accessible.

opportunity for reflection

"What Did You Do in School Today?"

Most parents have had the following unproductive conversation:

"What did you do in school today?" Nothin.

"Why did you get that grade?" I dunno.

The antidote to this conversational dead-end is not browbeating the child until, after parental cross-examination, the child confesses some activity during the school day. Rather, we must re-frame the conversation about school. Let us begin by asking different questions. Here are some conversation starters that are quite different from "What did you do in school today?"

"What did you learn in school today?"

"What happened in school today that was scary?"

"What happened today that made you happy?"

"What happened today that made you sad?"

"What happened today that made you feel great?"

By shifting the conversation from a narrative of news events to a focus on the child's own feelings, there is the opportunity for reflection and personal engagement. Without asking these sorts of emotionally relevant questions, parents risk waiting until they read a bad report card or receive an alarming call from school before learning about significant problems.

The Power of Expectations

In a famous series of experiments in the early 1960s, two different groups of teachers were given students who were similar with regard to prior learning and demographic characteristics. One group, however, was described to their teachers as the "smart" group, while the other was described as "slow." A year later, both groups of students were measured on a variety of academic and intelligence tests. Despite the similarity of these two groups, the teachers and their widely varying expectations had an enormous impact on student performance, with the students living up to—and down to—the expectations of their teachers. Parental expectations are even more profound in their influence on student achievement. There is a fine line between parental pressure and expectations, and the difference is not always clear. We all know of the parents who "expect" their child to become a doctor or lawyer, and any professional or educational decision short of the mark leaves the child feeling like a failure in the eyes of the parent. Far more common, however, is the reluctance of parents to articulate clear expectations of academic success. While most parents are quite clear in their expectations of behavior and integrity, the same parents are less clear about the "house rules" regarding reading, homework, and learning.

The older children get, the more ambiguous the academic expectations of parents become. While every kindergartner has a world of potential ahead, the impulse to rate, rank, sort, and label children is in full flower by late elementary school. The child with brilliant potential in first grade has, by the sixth grade, been determined to be someone who "just isn't a reader" or "just isn't very good at math." While many sixth graders can express ambitions to be a jet pilot, opera singer, astronaut, or brain surgeon, parents none too subtly scoff at such ambitions just a few years later. The skepticism is not always obvious, but the message is clear. Even the well-intentioned, "If that's what you want to do, then you will have to do a lot better in school" becomes "You've got to be kidding! You—a brain surgeon? Forget it." This destructive disapproval is a long emotional distance from the cheering parent on the sidelines at a basketball game assuring the twelve-year-old who makes one basket out of fifty, "I know you can do it!"

How do parents express their expectations for student success? Here are some positive practices you may wish to consider. Parents who expect their children to do well in school and in life value learning and model that value, just as parents who expect their children to have integrity and compassion model those values. In order to model a love of learning, parents should consider the following steps toward the creation of learning time and learning space in their home.

learning together

Time and Space for Your 20-Minute Learning Connection

Set aside a "learning time" of 20 minutes every day. Many families devote the time after dinner to this purpose. Among my fondest memories of childhood are the times after dinner when someone would ask a question, and the family would discuss the idea, read about it, and learn something new. These were not extended multi-hour discussions, but they were clearly opportunities to learn that were not related to the school day. The discussions, readings, and questions were the result of a love of learning and a passion for inquiry. There is another critical element to such discussions: They provide adults with an opportunity to take the views of children seriously. A child's day is full of reminders of the impotence of children compared to the power of adults. When a parent or other significant adult takes the time to listen, question, and learn together with a child, there is more than merely the acquisition of new information taking place. There is the development of a sense of value, the ability of children to take themselves seriously, and in time, to expect others to take them seriously as well. The time consistently devoted to learning and exploration should be appropriate to your family's lifestyle and it should be consistent. Many families identify one night a week in which other activities are not allowed to intrude, and they play games, read, discuss, and enjoy one another's company. Other families take just 20 minutes after dinner. Still other families carve out time first thing in the morning before the busy day begins. Whatever time you establish, consistency will be important. It is important that you not allow the ideal to be the enemy of progress. In other words, even if ideally you would like to have a two-hour after-dinner discussion that is free of interruptions and unfettered by the activities of children and parents, such a vision should not stop you from making the best use of 20 minutes any time during the day.

Every home should have some "learning space" that is the family equivalent of a library. This space need not be a room devoted only to learning, for few family homes have libraries or studies. Rather, the learning space is instantly created by the way it is used. Your learning space might be the dinner table, a desk in the basement, or any place set aside that meets three conditions. First, it is relatively free of distractions. This means that when the learning space is being used, the television is turned off and a sibling is not practicing the trombone in the same area. Second, there is abundant light. Third, it is easily accessible. If the table in the kitchen or dining room is to be used as the learning place, then it becomes the learning place as soon as someone sits down and opens a book, begins to write, or otherwise starts learning. If it requires fifteen minutes of clearing and setting up before learning can begin, then it is not sufficiently accessible. The learning place need not be formal or expensive, but it does need to be quiet, well lit, and easy to use.

Parents' Checklist:

❑ Create a "learning space" in your home that is quiet, well lit, and easily accessible.

❑ Identify 20 minutes of "learning time" for your family to stop their other activities and learn together. This might involve reading alone or aloud, asking questions, or investigating a puzzling problem. To start your journey, we have suggested a number of learning activities that are specifically linked to the academic standards of your state. You will find the list of standards and activities starting on page 145.

a learning space

Chapter 2

What Are Academic Standards and Why Do We Have Them?

Academic standards give every parent essential information about what children are expected to know and be able to do in school. Parents need not guess or speculate about the idiosyncratic preferences of teachers. More importantly, children need not worry about what it takes to succeed in school. With the proper implementation of academic standards, guesswork is replaced with clarity.

The Importance of Knowing the Rules

Any parent who has observed children playing games in the park or on the playground knows the following scenario well. Children are playing a game and a new child joins the fun. Within minutes, however, it is clear that something is wrong. Cries of "That's not fair!" fill the air. The sounds of playground glee are replaced by tears, anger, and the indignant wail, "I'm never playing this game again!" When the mess is sorted out, there are no villains, no cheaters, no schemers determined to deny the aggrieved party his due. Rather, the tears, anger, and resolution to play no more all stem from ambiguity about the rules. All parties to the dispute thought that they knew how the game was played, and all had strikingly different understandings of what the rules of the game were supposed to be. Our children know that it is impossible to play any game without knowing the rules. Without clear rules, our determined efforts are reduced to random guessing, and the errors that we make do not provide useful feedback to improve our performance, but only greater frustration, more anger, and a river of tears. Whether the game is a seemingly inconsequential contest in the park or a high-stakes test with important consequences for a child's future, it is impossible to play the game without knowing the rules.

clear rules

Standards: The Rules of the Game

Any discussion of games in the context of education invites cynicism. The careless use of this analogy might indicate that education, standards, and testing are nothing more than trivial games where strategy is elevated above moral, ethical, and educational issues. Nothing could be further from the truth. In fact, there are a number of elements of games that reflect not merely strategic considerations, but fundamental values, such as fairness. Thus, my reference to games in the context of educational standards is designed to force us to confront the fact that, while clarity and fairness are routine requirements in games ranging from the playground to professional sports, the necessity for clarity and fairness applies no less to every important endeavor, including education. While these values may have trivial implications in a game, they are at the very heart of understanding why standards are so essential. Standards provide students with clear, unambiguous statements of what is required of them. In other words, standards are the rules of the game in school.

As I stated before, academic standards are statements of what students should know and be able to do. Although there are, to be sure, numerous examples of standards that are poorly worded, vague, over-reaching, unrealistic, and otherwise unhelpful, we must consider the alternative. Without standards, what would students have? They would be left with the mystery, guesswork, and ambiguity that prevail in the absence of rules.

Whenever I ask grandparents and experienced parents to tell me about the lessons they have learned about effective parenting, I find a theme in their advice. "You have to be consistent," they counsel. "Don't confuse sympathy and understanding with weakness. You have to be clear." For added emphasis, they warn, "You won't always make the right decisions, but children must know that they can count on you, and that requires consistency and dependability." There is wisdom in the words of these elders. Because perfection in parenting is not an option available to most of us, we are left with making the best of our imperfection. One way to reduce the risk of the mistakes that we inevitably make is clarity and consistency. This certainly does not guarantee the popularity or even the rectitude of our decisions about parental discipline, but clarity and consistency certainly will increase the probability that our children perceive us as fair, predictable, and dependable.

In contexts as diverse as child discipline and playground games, the role of standards is clear. Rules are necessary for motivation and fairness. Why is the role of standards so controversial in education? The value of clarity, consistency, and fairness is clear in the context of discipline and games. When the third-grade soccer championship or the sixth-grade music competition is on the line, few people doubt the necessity of standards, for the rules are the guarantor of fairness. Why does a football field always have 100 yards or a chessboard always have sixty-four squares? The answer is obvious: Without such clear and consistent rules, few people would be willing to play the game. Clarity and consistency are essential if people of any age are to be motivated sufficiently to engage in an activity. These standards are necessary in order for contests of any type, from the trivial to the most serious, to be regarded as fair. The fundamental rationale for educational standards is the same: a commitment to fairness.

The Old Way: Grading "On the Curve"

There are some people who are very upset with the standards movement and who have led angry demands for the abandonment of educational standards. They see standards as a device by which schools are rendered joyless boot camps and the needs of children are sacrificed to the needs of corporate employers. We should, therefore, consider where classrooms and schools would be if we had no standards. Recent history (and, unfortunately, many present-day schools) provides the answer. Without standards, we have the bell curve. You know that your child's school does not have a commitment to standards when you overhear the following conversation among children:

"How did you do on that assignment?"

"I didn't get the question right, but I was better than Steve!"

It is untrue that this school lacks standards. The standard is Steve, or any other child to whom another student can be favorably compared. No one knows what is really expected, because no one knows what Steve can do from one day to the next. But they do know this: If they can just beat Steve, then the teacher will have someone else on whom negative attention can be focused. Am I overstating the case? Consider the following authentic conversation from teachers in the schools I routinely visit:

"How do you evaluate students?"

"The best paper gets an A, the worst paper gets an F."

"How do you know what student work is acceptable?"

"I can't really tell you, but I know it when I see it."

Astonishingly, some parents embrace grading on the curve because it appears to foster the competitive spirit. After all, they reason, the cream rises to the top. It's a tough world out there, so my kids must get used to the competition. Ironically, grading on the curve does not produce the superior results and competitive spirit desired by parents. Rather, it creates the worst of both worlds because it discourages the competent student and fosters complacency in the incompetent student. The

"Steve Standard" provides justification to students who produce schoolwork that is incomplete, inaccurate, and disorganized but that is not quite as wretched as Steve's scrawl. With equally bad logic, the "Steve Standard" demoralizes the student who worked exceptionally hard to complete a wonderful assignment, but despite its exemplary quality, it was one footnote shy of the work submitted by Steve. Whether Steve is a wonderful student or a terrible student, the "Steve Standard" represents the shifting standards of grading on the curve. It is an inherently unfair and inaccurate way to evaluate students.

Some parents have a ready rejoinder: "But I don't want my child to be just 'good enough,' I want her to be the best. Only by comparing my child to other children can I be sure that she is meeting high standards." The subtext of this reasoning is the unrelenting counsel of successful business leaders of the past few decades who have insisted that business managers must be graded on the curve. This logic receives reinforcement from the sports world where there can be, after all, only a single champion. Because grading on the curve has proponents in business and athletics, it might be useful to use terminology that more accurately distinguishes a standards-based system from the alternative. Rather than call the competitive system "grading on the curve," we shall label it more accurately: mystery grading.

changing rules

The Worst Evaluation System: Mystery Grading

Imagine two children playing in the park. Lois challenges Robert to a ball game. With pleasure, Robert accepts the challenge, confident that he has played ball games successfully in the past. Lois then takes the ball and runs past an imaginary line and exclaims, "That's one point for me—I'm ahead!" Robert catches on quickly, takes the ball, and runs past the line happily. "You ran the wrong way!" Lois shouts. "That's another point for me—it's two to zero, my favor." Robert starts to pick up the ball, but Lois provides a quick elbow to his solar plexus, takes the ball, and runs past the line. "Three to zero," she says with a smile. Robert is upset, but under control. Confident that he now understands the game a bit better, he delivers a retaliatory blow to Lois and takes the ball, crossing the line with a smile of victory. "Foul!" Lois cries. "That's an automatic point for me—it's four to zero!" Robert is a bright child. How long do you think he will continue to play this game? It is a testimony to Robert's good grace

What Are Academic Standards and Why Do We Have Them?

and self-control that he has not been dispatched to the principal's office after having let his aggravation with Lois get the better of him. But despite his chivalry, this much is certain: Robert will not play this game again.

When the awarding of points is a mystery and when the rules of the game appear to shift with the winds, then children will not continue to play the game. When victory involves guessing and no amount of skill or prior information is of any value, then the game becomes an idle pursuit and not a purposeful enterprise.

Is this analogy exaggerated? Ask students why they received the grade they did. Sometimes you will receive a well-reasoned and clear answer. One student might say,

> *"The requirements of the assignment were this, but I actually did that. Therefore, I failed to meet the requirements and received a low grade. Having received this valuable feedback and recognizing the error of my ways, I shall return to my desk forthwith, revise this assignment, and resubmit it to my teacher."*

If your child provides such a response, please return this book for a refund, proceed to the nearest radio station, and host a call-in show for perfect parents with perfect children in perfect schools. For most of us and for our children, grading remains mysterious. Even teachers who take the time to create clear and precise grading systems find that precision is an illusion, far clearer to the designer of the system than to the students who must perform under its mandates.

For the vast majority of students, grading remains a mystery dominated by the largely unknown personal preferences of the teacher. The student is placed in the role of the sorcerer's apprentice, weakly emulating the acts of the master, hoping that some of the magic will rub off. Systematic learning is impossible because teaching comes only from the inscrutable wisdom of the master teacher, and learning is a matter of fortunate insight rather than diligent work. It is no wonder that such a system is discouraging to the student who finds luck more important than skill. There is a better way. We can replace mystery with clarity. Students can replace guesswork with hard work. Parents can replace aimless searching with careful direction. In brief, we can have standards.

The Best Way: Know the Rules Before You Play the Game

The game played by Lois and Robert was unfair. The failure of fairness was not a result of the scheming of Lois, but rather the absence of rules. The fundamental requirement of fairness is the existence of clear and consistent rules—standards, if you will—that let the participants know what conduct is acceptable and what is not. We can only play the game when we know the rules.

This is hardly an alien notion to schools. During the first few hours of the first day of classes in most schools in the country, teachers discuss the importance of behavior, respect, and decorum in the classroom. Teachers do not display elaborate posters on classroom walls that contain the precise words of the Board of Education's disciplinary policy or the state criminal statutes. Rather, each teacher has a single piece of paper labelled "class rules," which lays out in simple and clear language the requirements of conduct for students. "Respect yourself and others," the rules typically begin. "Do not talk while others are speaking." "Raise your hand before speaking." "Be kind and help others." There is a long tradition of identifying the standards of behavior in classrooms with clarity and precision. These same qualities must be the goal of those desiring academic excellence.

clarity

What Standards Mean for Students

While the word "standards" conveys to some parents a threat of failure and an association with difficult academic tests, the actual implications of school standards are quite positive. In a standards-based school, students know what is expected and they routinely receive constructive feedback on how to improve their performance. The typical parent-child conversation after report cards are issued in a school without standards begins with the question, "How did you get that grade?" followed by the plaintive response, "I don't know." With standards, this unproductive conversation is replaced by these confident statements:

"I know what the teacher wants me to do."

"I know when I'm successful and when I am not."

"I know how to get better and I can do so tomorrow."

"I know what it takes to win and I know that I can be a winner."

"I can help someone else and still be a winner—I don't have to beat Steve to be a great student."

real achievement

What Standards Mean for Parents

It is stunning for me to hear some parents bemoan the standards movement as a new educational fad when the requirement for fair and reasonable relationships among teaching, learning, curriculum, and assessment are as old as Socrates. Although our children may think their parents went to school in the Lyceum, we need not recall ancient Greece to consider our own examples of standards. Think of your favorite teacher or coach. Did that person patronize you with constant pats on the head or make your success a matter of mystery and luck? Or did that favorite coach or teacher let you know that whatever else had happened in your life, you would be a success if only you worked hard, followed the rules, and met the standards that the teacher clearly identified? These favorite teachers did not make learning easy, nor did they make learning impossible. Rather, our favorite teachers and coaches made learning challenging, fair, reasonable, and rewarding. This is the essence of standards-based teaching and learning.

Now that they are vividly called to mind, these influential teachers and coaches offer another interesting quality. Your success was not accomplished when you simply defeated another student, but when you met the standard articulated by the coach. Chances are, that standard included not only personal excellence, but also a willingness to help your teammates. While rivalries within teams are natural, the team that is beset by constant competition within the team is seldom able to deal with competition against other teams. In fact, your success was elevated by your willingness to help your colleagues. When you helped other students, you discovered an important truth: Not only did their performance improve, but your understanding of the same subject soared when you had the opportunity to help others master the subject. You found that helping other students was not an entirely altruistic act, but rather was the result of a collaborative process in which you both gave and received valuable lessons.

Academic standards imply a very different environment in school than many parents may have experienced. If your educational experience involved grading on the curve, frantic efforts to please a teacher, and a certain degree of mystery about the nature of your performance, then it is only natural that you might expect your own children to have a similar experience in school. If you have been successful in school and in life, you might initially prefer that your children attend a school that closely matches your own experiences when you were a student. Nevertheless, the case we have made for standards is based not upon personal history or popularity, but upon the fact that standards are fair and effective. Even if a standards-based approach to student achievement is not what you experienced as a child, please give it a chance. Your children will thrive in an environment in which the rules of the game are clear and their performance is rewarded based on real achievement rather than merely on a victory over a classmate.

What Standards Mean for Teachers and Schools

Standards offer clarity, fairness, and effectiveness, so teachers should universally rave about the use of academic standards. After all, if the case for standards is so overwhelming, why would any educational professional object? In fact, the reaction to standards by teachers and school administrators has been varied. Some teachers enthusiastically endorse the idea of standards and emphasize that it is hardly new. "What you call standards," they remark, "is what I have called 'good teaching' for about twenty-five years now."

But many other educators are wary. They have seen a number of educational fads come and go, and they reasonably wonder if this is just one more trend that will evaporate when something more popular comes along. In addition, some teachers resent the fact that standards were oversold when they were first introduced. Some proponents of standards let their enthusiasm surpass their judgment when they gushed, "Standards will make teaching easy!" Of course, nothing makes the difficult and complex job of teaching easy. Most of the objections to standards come from the failure of those who wrote the initial drafts of state standards to express their expectations with precision. Many standards swing from one extreme to the other, either describing curriculum content in excessive detail, or describing expectations of student performance in such broad generalities that teachers are left with little constructive guidance. Some teachers object that the standards are too difficult and too numerous. Considering all the other subjects that traditionally have been in the school curriculum, the additional layers of academic content seem to be too burdensome given the limited amount of time students spend in school. Finally, there are teachers who sincerely object to any outside interference in their classroom. Their rejoinder to standards or other intrusions is, "Just leave me alone and let me teach!" In their judgment, standards easily could become standardization, and such an approach to teaching fails to recognize the unique qualities of each individual student. Only the teacher, they argue, can make the subtle judgments required to identify what is appropriate for each child, and standards designed at the state or school district level fail to take into account the individual needs that are known only to the teacher.

Many parents have heard these arguments and have interpreted them as arguments against all academic standards. Every argument but the last one, however, is actually a persuasive case against poor standards, and the logical response is not the abandonment of standards, but the continuous improvement of them. Those people who make the final argument characterized as, "Just leave me alone and let me teach," will object to any standard. Improvements would not be sufficient, for even the most clear and constructive standard would represent an intrusion into their classroom and their curriculum.

Parents naturally appreciate a teacher who wishes to take into account the individual needs of their children. Moreover, most parents would object to any policy that appears to "standardize" their unique children. A balanced approach to standards might look something like this: The freedom and discretion of teachers are honored, respected, and encouraged, provided that this discretion takes place within a framework. That framework is one of academic excellence and equity in which all students have clear and fair guidelines and expectations. Educators have broad discretion to consider alternative strategies for teaching reading to a student who appears to be slow to catch on to phonics; the teacher does not have the discretion to say, "Considering his difficult upbringing and poor neighborhood, we really can't expect him to learn to read this year." Teachers can be creative and have wide latitude to collaborate with their colleagues to determine the best ways to improve mathematics skills, but they do not have the discretion to say (as I have actually heard a teacher and administrator claim),

"Well, those kids don't need algebra anyway." In a balanced approach to standards, there is neither micromanagement by school administrators, nor aimless anarchy among teachers. Standards need not dictate the day-to-day, minute-to-minute agenda for the classroom, but standards do establish the expectations of what all students should know and be able to do. When teachers have creative supplementary strategies to help students meet those expectations, that creativity is respected and rewarded. When, however, teachers make decisions that take students outside of the framework at the expense of meeting standards, then they have supplanted the needs of the child with the personal preferences of the teacher. That, in a school committed to excellence and equity, is not acceptable.

an effective classroom

What Standards Mean for Daily Life in School

The best way for students and teachers to succeed in school and to meet academic standards is a consistent emphasis on the thinking, reasoning, analysis, communication, and love of learning that characterizes any effective classroom. The frequent claim that the path to meeting standards lies in mindless drills, rather than analysis and thinking, is wrong. In extensive research from organizations as diverse as the Education Trust, the Center for Performance Assessment, and the National Science Foundation, the evidence is clear: Higher test scores on standards-based assessments are more likely to occur when students and teachers engage in critical thinking, extensive analysis, and frequent writing. The appropriate application of academic standards encourages an increase in thinking, reasoning, and communication by students.

To be sure, standards are the cause of some changes in schools, and those changes can be uncomfortable for the critics of standards. There are elementary classes that devote many hours of prime reading time to craft projects and preparation for performances, few of which are related to the improvement of student achievement. Some secondary teachers announce that next quarter will be devoted to current events "rather than standards," as if the possibility of relating contemporary political events to the study of history and government is impossible. There are many traditional projects that consume large chunks of time and the only thing that sustains these activities is their popularity, not their contribution to student learning. What is lost by the establishment of standards? Surely not thinking, reasoning, or even the fun of interactive and engaging activities in the classroom. What must be abandoned or modified, however, are the projects that have persisted year after year based only on the personal preference of the teacher and popularity with students and parents. Perhaps the least attractive feature of the standards movement is that it displaces popularity with effectiveness.

Does this mean that the kids can no longer carve pumpkins in October or dress up like Pilgrims in November? Certainly not. We know that hands-on activities and dramatic reenactments are splendid ways for students to learn. But some of these activities require close reexamination and detailed modification. If pumpkins are to be the theme for a few days, then much more than carving and candy must be the order of the day. There are wonderful classrooms in which students read about pumpkins, write about them, measure them, weigh them, compare them, and explore them. The traditional Thanksgiving drama, in which two students speak and many others look on in silence, can be replaced by an activity in which many students participate in writing the play based on their own reading and research. The speaking parts can be widely shared among all students, and the predominant feature of the activity is student learning rather than parent entertainment.

reasonable preparation

Won't Standards Result in Teaching to the Test?

Some teachers and parents have linked standards and testing to the point that any suggestion that standards are the basis of classroom instruction leads to the allegation that schools are "teaching to the test." It is true that there are examples around the nation in which some misguided administrators have encouraged a regimen of test drills and memorization rather than deep study, analysis, and reflection. It is also true that there are some schools that have curtailed traditional classroom activities and field trips, and a few people have blamed standards as the culprit that turned their schools into grim, academic factories.

The very phrase "teaching to the test" implies something unethical, as if teachers had sneaked into the State Department of Testing, secretly copied the test, and then conducted drills in class in which students memorized the answers by chanting, "Number 1 is C, number 2 is A, number 3 is B..." In fact, what most teachers have done is to use the freely available models of the practice tests to let students look at sample items in order to become more familiar with the format of the test. Moreover, thoughtful teachers also have reviewed their own curriculum and made appropriate revisions. "If my students need to know about graphs and tables for a test in March, and I was not going to address those skills until April, then it would be much more fair to my students if I changed my schedule to give them those skills before they take the test."

The contention that ethical teaching requires that testing must be a mystery must be challenged as absurd and unfair. Can you imagine students in a musical performance sitting down to discover that the music before them is completely unfamiliar? Can you imagine the football coach who refuses to use a football in practice or take students near an actual football field because practicing under such conditions would be "teaching to the test?"

The most appropriate way to discuss the relationship of classroom teaching to the tests students take is not "teaching to the test," but "teaching to the standard." Teachers cannot anticipate every single item on the test, but they can provide students with a fair opportunity to do well on any test. The opportunity for fairness is best provided when students have received curriculum and instruction based on the standards, and when the test designers have used those same standards as the basis for creating the tests. When the context is driving, music, or football, this would be called common sense. When the context is academic performance, it is not only common sense, but also fair and effective.

The Most Important Teacher Your Child Will Ever Have

When I was discussing this book with a teacher and grandparent in a border community where Spanish was the predominant language, she suggested a title for the Spanish-language edition of the book. "There's no doubt about it," she said. "Your title must be *Los Primeros Maestros*." This is a play on words, indicating that parents are not only the first teachers, but also the most important teachers that children will ever have. Her insight speaks volumes to parents of every culture, because we are all the first and most important teachers for our children.

Parents teach children so many things that they will never learn in school, including integrity, values, and respect for oneself and others. Parents also teach children about their interest in learning. This is not the same as their interest in school. Our children see through the ruse of the parent who berates a child over a poor grade in reading but never picks up a book for pleasure. Our children notice our inconsistency when we exclaim our disappointment in their writing abilities but fail ever to take pen in hand ourselves to write a letter. The most important lessons we teach are those with our actions and values, not our lectures.

Parents' Checklist:

❑ **Read the standards appropriate to your child's grade.**

❑ **Find one activity that you can complete in 20 minutes that will help your child achieve standards.**

❑ **Talk with your child's teacher about standards. If the teacher's attitude is negative, ask if the problem is the specific wording of the standards, or if the problem is any effort by the state to influence classroom activities. It is important for you to understand the teacher's commitment or aversion to standards.**

❑ **Find the exact dates of state tests for your child. Mark them on the calendar so that you can limit distractions and interruptions during that week.**

❑ **Ask your child about standards. "What do you think you have to do this year to be a great student?" Then listen carefully for the response. Standards only have meaning when children understand them. The response you receive will be your guide to future activities and discussions with teachers, school leaders, and your child.**

---

ask your child

Chapter 3

What Tests Tell You — and What They Don't

Tests are part of life. Babies take the Apgar test within moments of birth in the delivery room, and the results of that test can lead to essential and immediate medical intervention for the newborn child. Before formal schooling has begun, children routinely explore the world around them by experimenting with language and behavior. They "test" the world dominated by adults and older children and make instant observations about effective and ineffective strategies to meet their needs. When the young child is the one doing the testing and when the results of the test are immediately used to benefit the child, it is a remarkably effective way to learn about the world. In a few short years, however, the word "test" gains a very different meaning. It is no longer a way of learning and exploring, no longer a mechanism for gaining new knowledge and meeting the child's needs. Tests are soon associated with anxiety, demands for performance, and the prospect of failure. Three-year-old children take admissions tests for preschool and their older siblings are subjected to tests that will determine their acceptance or rejection by special programs in kindergarten. Within the minutes or hours that it takes to administer these tests, the path is set. Perhaps the child will bear the label of "gifted and talented" or "special needs" or, heaven forbid, "normal."

Because the tests purport to have scientific properties, the labels bestowed on children are rarely challenged. The purpose of this chapter is to confront the common acceptance of these labels by providing some background on what tests can and cannot tell parents about their children. Once you know that tests are merely snapshots of knowledge rather than definitive pronouncements about student ability, both you and your child can examine test results for what they are—a momentary record of achievement, not a certain prediction of future failure or success. Whether the test in question affects the labeling of a child, the acceptance into or rejection from a special program, or simply the awarding of a grade on a report card, the way that parents talk with children about tests reflects a philosophy that can be either discouraging or encouraging. Only through a deliberate effort to change the talk between parents and children into learning conversations will we make the transition away from test terror.

conquering anxiety

From Test Terror to Testing for Learning

Parents who have witnessed the transformation of testing from innocent exploration to childhood terror may express their dismay at how much inappropriate pressure is placed on children, not knowing that their own comments have already signaled the parents' anxieties to their children about the importance of tests. There are few more powerful psychological forces than the fear of disappointing a parent. Perhaps you can recall a time in which you would have preferred physical punishment to that look of dissatisfaction from a parent who sent the message, "I am disappointed in you." Few spankings could have been as painful. While no parent ever intends to send debilitating and terrorizing messages to children, we sometimes cannot help it. The stress and anxiety of every examination we have ever taken can subtly and unintentionally become the test terror we transmit to our children.

Constructive Skepticism for Tests

Fortunately, history is not destiny. Parents can fundamentally change their children's perceptions of testing. This cannot be accomplished by casually dismissing tests as unimportant. Our children see through that ruse, knowing that tests are indeed important, but that we are seeking to protect them. As surely as children know if they won or lost the soccer match in the supposedly "fun and scoreless" games that masquerade as noncompetitive exercises, children also know when tests are important, but their parents don't want to talk about them. If we are to liberate our children from test terror, we will do so not with patronizing tales about the irrelevance of tests, but with a philosophy toward testing that can best be described as "constructive skepticism."

Perhaps the best way to understand constructive skepticism for tests is to consider the opposite. Rather than engaging in rational analysis of the test, some students fall prey to analytical paralysis, when the test taker is convinced that failure, inadequacy, and stupidity are the inescapable diagnoses from an unsuccessful test attempt. "After all," these children reason, "either you know it or you don't, and I guess I just don't know it." The results of such analytical paralysis are predictable: anger, fear, and the studied avoidance of test taking opportunities in the future.

Constructive skepticism for tests is strikingly different. The child with constructive skepticism understands that every test is a game. Most of the rules of the game are clear, but the moves of the other side are not always obvious. Therefore, some strategy, some knowledge, and yes, some luck is involved in the successful completion of the game. Supplied with constructive skepticism for tests, children know that their success on a test is not necessarily the mark of genius, but of capable gamesmanship. When confronted with a test question that is unclear and ambiguous, the child with constructive skepticism does not conclude, "I'm a failure and I can't do this." Rather, this empowered test taker says, "I'm as smart as the person who wrote this test, but the right answer isn't very clear. Now I know that "B" is dumb and "D" is impossible, so I guess it's "A" or "C." I'm going to make a smart guess and move on, because this game is just about over…"

Constructive skepticism does not involve anger or the presumption of failure as the inescapable result when the right answer is not immediately clear. Rather, constructive skepticism provides students with the emotional resilience to persist even in the face of ambiguity and uncertainty. It is not just the intellectual ability to narrow the range of possible answers to a test question; it is the emotional ability to remain engaged in the game of test taking long after other students have given up on that test question and perhaps on the entire test. When students feel a sense of failure, they tend to generalize it: "I'm not only a failure on the soccer team; I can't do *anything* right! I can't read, I can't do math, and I can't kick the darn ball into the darn goal..." By contrast, the child with healthy skepticism for the test at hand possesses the emotional resilience to say, "Okay, so I can't remember what a rhombus is. Big deal. This question is asking about sides of a polygon, so that means that the answer has to have sides. So it can't be a circle and it can't be an ellipse—it must be either a trapezoid or a rhombus. I'll guess that it's a rhombus and move on to the next question."

At this point, the student with constructive skepticism is still in the game, engaged in the next question, convinced that thinking, reasoning, and skill are the keys to success. The student without this sort of resilience has given up, with pencil held limply in hand while the head rests on the desk waiting for the torture of this test to end. Whatever tests the future holds for your child, among the many valuable gifts you can provide is the gift of resilience—the ability for your child to remain engaged in a test or other difficult challenge, even when the questions are ambiguous and the answers are elusive.

Some readers may be uncomfortable referring to tests as games, especially when discussing tests with their children. "This is serious," they reason, "and references to gamesmanship trivialize tests, school, and education in general." This is a legitimate concern and it deserves a serious answer. The references to games in this chapter have three purposes, none of which trivializes tests or education. First, references to games help children recall experiences that have been successful and enjoyable. This is a more constructive basis for a conversation between parents and children than a stern lecture about the life-changing importance of a test and the associated risk of parental disappointment should the child not score sufficiently well. Feelings of trust, confidence, competence, and fun are the foundations of happy children and successful students, and parents do better when they nurture those feelings. Second, references to games involve strategy that both children and parents understand. Because tests are never perfect and answers are not always free of ambiguity, knowledge alone is insufficient. Strategy—thinking about the point of view of the test writer, eliminating wrong answers, and dealing with the uncertainty and ambiguity present in every test—is not only a great thinking skill for children, it is also the key to emotional resilience. Strategy—gamesmanship, if you will—is the bridge from "I don't know the answer so

I must be stupid" to "The right answer may not be obvious, but if I work on this I think I can figure it out." Third, I have observed that parents (with the exception of the stereotype of the abusive "Little League Dad") usually approach the performance of their children in games in a constructive and encouraging manner that builds confidence, success, and emotional resilience. When children play games, parents applaud, encourage, laugh, and console—all qualities sadly lacking in many discussions between parents and children when the subject is testing, homework, and school. In the final analysis, the references in this book to games have one central theme: Our children are more than the sum of their test scores, and the role of parents is not to cram every conceivable answer into the heads of their children, but to build healthy, happy, confident, capable, and empowered kids who know that they are loved and accepted by their parents.

emotional resilience

Tests Are Important, But . . .

It is national sport to ridicule school tests. After all, many people believe it is common knowledge that children are over-tested, that tests are irrelevant, that tests are political tools misused by critics of public education, and that tests fail to tell the complete and accurate story of student achievement. While each of these allegations may contain an element of truth, a fundamental fact remains: tests are an important and continuing part of life both during the early years of school and continuing into college, technical education, and the world of work. Moreover, students who have the intellectual and emotional ability to perform well on tests will find more open doors for educational and professional success. No doubt about it: Tests are important.

Success in test taking involves not only knowing the material, but also understanding the emotional foundations for successful test performance. Many readers can recall an instance in which they were intellectually prepared for a test and, as soon as the test administrator uttered the words "you may begin," their minds went blank. Terror replaced confidence and mystery replaced the clear organization of facts and concepts that the student possessed only moments before the test began. To make matters worse, we knew of students who had scarcely prepared for the same test, but who appeared to breeze through the examination. Our recollections of the power of panic make a profound case in favor of recognizing the importance of emotions in test success.

The Power of Emotions

encouragement

While the prevalence of emotions over intellect may be perplexing to students, it is great news for parents. Although we may not always be able to provide the right answer on math or geography homework, every parent can provide extraordinarily powerful support for the emotional resilience and psychological endurance of their children. The power of emotions in test preparation is an essential element of parent support. This is why "Let me help you with your homework" is far less powerful than "You're a smart kid and I believe in you; I *know* that you can do this!" As parents, we want to help our children. It is only natural. It hurts to see them struggle. It would be instructive, however, to recall the first steps of our toddler. The parent cannot walk for the child, but can only hold out loving arms and offer earnest encouragement. "Come on, *you can do it*!" And they do. Our praise is genuine, enthusiastic, and encouraging. That praise, confidence, and encouragement set a standard in the minds of our children that is a difficult bar to reach in later years. "You can do it!" gives way to "Turn off the darn television and finish your homework!" "I believe in you" is replaced by "I just don't understand how you messed this up so badly." The emotional connection of parent and child has been replaced with one more layer of anxiety and stress.

Building Confident, Capable, and Empowered Children

Although few children enjoy tests, most children love games. They particularly enjoy games they can win. Think about it: Children's games, from Crazy Eights to Monopoly to a host of board and card games are typically a combination of knowledge, skill, strategy, and luck. Clever game designers know that part of maintaining the interest of children is the reasonable prospect of success. Parents help to build confident, capable, and empowered children every time they participate in an activity in which it is possible for children to succeed. This does not mean that parents deliberately lose and children win every time. Such games, children quickly learn, are boring and unrewarding. They know that the rewards that come too easily have little value. Part of building emotional resilience and persistence in the face of difficulty is the habit of trying again after a failure, full of confidence that success is a function of endurance, skill, and a little luck.

My youngest child, James, is on a basketball team. A ten-foot basketball hoop appears to be an insurmountable goal for a group of six- and seven-year-olds. During practice, the balls fly everywhere, it seems, but into the net. But once in a while— perhaps once every five to ten minutes—there is a "swish" of the ball through the net that keeps the enthusiasm of everyone in the room at a high level. There is a lesson here: We do not build capable, confident, and empowered children through the contrivance of easy tasks and low expectations. Whether the challenge is the ten-foot basket or two-digit subtraction, the prospect of success is what keeps the players engaged. They do not need the certainty of success every time, but they need to know precisely what the rules of the game are so that, when success comes, the delicious moment of victory can be savored for a moment before the players return to the game.

The game scenario has practical applications for how parents interact with children about homework and tests. Many parents tend to one of two extremes, in which one parent demands, "Go to your room and don't come out until all the homework is done!" and another parent hovers over the nervous student, correcting every error and focusing exclusively on every misstep. Can you imagine the same parents exploding with disappointment at every missed basket? Can you imagine these parents saying, after the ball goes into the basket, "Well, he made the shot, but he's no Michael Jordan!" On the contrary, these parents wait and wait, offering encouragement and perhaps a few sympathetic groans, and then they roar with approval and applause when a child—any child—makes a basket. When was the last time we roared with approval and applause for a homework assignment well done, a test question answered correctly, or a project completed on time? In some arenas, parental feedback is immediate, positive, and relevant to success. In other cases, parental feedback is infrequent, negative, and related to vague expectations of perfection that seem unreachable by the student.

The Confusion of Self-Esteem and Self-Confidence

Much has been written and said about self-esteem, with most of these words substituting rhetoric for evidence. The facts are clear: Self-esteem is important. When students, or for that matter, adults, feel a sense of self-worth, they tend to perform at higher levels. The issue is not whether self-esteem is important, but how this elusive quality is best achieved. Some parents believe that we build self-esteem through challenge and rigor, in the way that the movie stereotype of the Marine drill sergeants "build men" in boot camp through a mix of ridicule, shouting, and demands. Other parents, and an astonishing number of teachers, believe that we build self-esteem through constant affirmation of children, including reassurances that children are always great, wonderful, and terrific even when the children know that they are not always great, wonderful, and terrific. Both extremes are wrong. Parents must balance affirmation with honesty. We cannot tell a child that she made the basket when her own observation is to the contrary. It is equally unwise to tell a child that his performance is inadequate when the child just scored a point for his team.

Let us move the context from the playground to schoolwork. We should not tell the child that her paper is wonderful when she knows and we know that it is careless and inaccurate. We should not tell the child of her shortcomings because her paragraph of sixth-grade work falls short of Hemingway. Honesty, rather than excessively high or low expectations, best serves children. We build self-esteem with clear, honest feedback, not with impossible challenges or improbable reassurances. "This was great and I'm really proud of you!" is as appropriate as "You are really getting good at this! With a little more work you're going to be even better. I know you can do it!"

While the distinction may appear subtle, the difference between self-esteem and self-efficacy is an important one. Esteem alone is not sufficient. Humans must not only feel a sense of worth, but they must also have the bone-deep conviction that their efforts make a difference. In other words, their self-esteem is the result of their genuine worth and effort, not merely awarded by someone out of sympathy for an incompetent child. Anyone who has listened attentively to the conversations of children about the important adults in their lives knows that children have a profound and insightful understanding of the difference between sympathy and confidence. The patronizing compliments of adults can be withdrawn, but the capacity that children have to make a difference in their own lives is enduring. Thus, it is not merely esteem that our children must develop and maintain, but efficacy. In the words of Dr. Jeff Howard, president of the Efficacy Institute, "Smart is something you get, not just something you are." When students believe that they have the capacity for improvement, they are far more resilient and persistent than when they depend on another person for compliments, assurances, and affirmation.

The Limits of Tests

As important as tests are, it is essential that parents and children understand what tests tell us and what they don't. The best any test can do is to report the performance of a student on a particular set of questions on a particular day. Just as a blood pressure test does not represent a complete physical and just as blood pressure is subject to change from one reading to the next, so also test results do not represent a complete analysis of student ability, and those results can change radically depending on testing conditions and student preparation.

The most meaningful tests report not only a score, but also how to get better. This is one of the most significant advantages of student self-evaluation. Rather than submitting work to an all-knowing teacher who then awards a grade, the student who engages in self-evaluation must understand the difference between acceptable and unacceptable work. Rather than communicating only a letter or numerical grade, the most effective tests challenge the complacent student and encourage the discouraged child. On letter-graded tests, the complacent student might receive an A or a B and receive the message, "I'm doing pretty well, so there isn't much else to learn." The discouraged student might receive a low grade and receive the message, "That's as well as I can do, so I guess I'm just not a very good student." The best tests not only evaluate, but educate students. These tests communicate to parents about the performance of their children and also provide specific information about what students know and where they need to improve. Supplied with these insights, parents can help their children improve. Of course, these ideal tests are rare in most schools. Parents receive a score, and that's it. Rather than attempt to draw conclusions from a score alone, parents need to be advocates for tests that educate. In addition, parents must be careful to avoid "over-interpreting" a test score or grade.

Consider the case of the child who brings home a "C" on a test. One parent's frame of reference might be that a C is acceptable, if not great work, so perhaps it's best not to make a big deal out of it, and another parent might exclaim, "You obviously didn't do your best work on this test—what went wrong?" Both conclusions are unhelpful and probably inaccurate. The focus of the parent-child conversation should not be on the evaluation, but rather on the learning that did and did not take place. Rather than begin the conversation with evaluative statements, we should reframe every discussion as a learning conversation. It is always wise to begin with something positive, such as, "You did a great job on number 17—I didn't know you knew all of that! Tell me more about it." Then we must do what is one of the most essential, and rare, activities of parents: We must listen. Parents and teachers routinely engage in the fantasy that because they are talking, children are learning. While there is value to talk from parents and teachers, conversations are far more constructive when they are informed by the child's point of view. Thus, we begin with what the child does know and the places on the test where the performance was satisfactory. After giving the child an opportunity to elaborate on the good parts of his performance, we can then ask, "What do you wish you had done differently on this test?" This opens the door to a discussion of the questions that were blank or answered incorrectly. You might learn that the child ran out of time. You might learn that the child had failed to study. You might learn that the child does not understand fundamental concepts necessary to performance on this test. But my experience suggests that it is far more likely that you will learn that the child knew the material, but failed to understand the instructions. You might learn, for example, that the child was so confident that the haste to display her knowledge got in the way of taking time to read the instructions. You might also learn that the instructions were unclear and that many reasonable test takers, including you, might have had the same misunderstanding as your child. And it is possible that you will learn that the response was correct after all and that the scoring of the test was wrong. None of these learning conversations will occur, however, if we respond to the grade on the test rather than the content of the test.

focus on learning

Report Cards and Learning Conversations

Just as learning conversations should prevail in our discussions of tests and homework, so should the communication between parent and child about report cards focus on learning rather than evaluation. This is difficult. As I write these words, I reflect on the times I have reacted in haste to report cards, with joy at the "A" and with disappointment at lower grades, and in neither case conducting a learning conversation with my children. Taking a deliberate break from our natural reactions toward evaluation rather than education requires intellectual and emotional discipline, and those qualities can be in short supply when any parent, including a professional educator, first sees a report card. But the skill can be learned. Consider the physician who looks at your test results and exclaims, "Oh boy, are *you* in trouble!" And with those words, orders you to "work harder in the future" and then quickly leaves the room. The bewilderment, fear, and rage that might be our natural reactions to such a confrontation with a preoccupied physician are not unlike the reactions of children to typical discussions of report cards with their parents. We expect the physician to stop, think, reflect, and then not only to offer the results of medical tests, but to engage in a conversation about how we can improve. If there is ambiguity or if the results indicate a problem, the wise physician might order additional tests or conduct additional examinations before coming to a hasty and potentially inaccurate conclusion. Even a physician who reports that a patient is in perfect health might be expected to offer analysis, insight, and discussion of how such excellent health can be maintained. We owe our children no less than the wise physicians owe their patients.

Inappropriate Uses of Test Scores

Just as we expect the wise physician to have a sound basis for drawing a conclusion, so must the wise parent and teacher have a reasonable body of evidence for the determinations they make about children. Incredibly, single tests are used inappropriately to make instant decisions on a routine basis. When this occurs, parents must become advocates not only for their children, but for the cause of accuracy in tests and the analysis of test results. By far the most common error made in the use of test scores is the overgeneralization about children, teachers, and schools. Based on a single test, a child can be denied promotion, a teacher's effectiveness can be questioned, or a school can be labeled as a failing institution. Worse yet are the life-changing decisions made based on a single test. Such decisions are typically associated with "high stakes" tests such as high school graduation examinations, but in fact many tests with significant consequences for children occur on a regular basis and do not have the label or the publicity associated with high stakes tests. Such important tests in which a few hours can make an enormous difference in the education and life of a child include the assessments used to label children as gifted or learning disabled, tests that grant or deny admission to special learning opportunities, and tests that claim to predict the ability, aptitude, or interests of children.

Parents should be deeply suspicious of tests that claim to draw conclusions about children, particularly when those conclusions are linked to words such as "intelligence" or "ability" or "aptitude." There is a sorry history of such tests stemming back to the early years of the twentieth century when the test results were appropriated by the eugenics movement to support their racist conclusions. With the jargon, statistics, and confidence of testing experts, the nation was assured of the scientific "proof" of the genetic inferiority of people of Irish, Italian, and Jewish descent, particularly if they came from southern or eastern Europe. These absurd conclusions were based on the low scores of recent immigrants taking the "Army Alpha" tests during the early days of World War I. Interestingly, the same populations displayed much higher scores a generation later as their language skills and familiarity with cultural references in the tests improved. Such changes prove that those tests did not measure anything like "intelligence" or "aptitude" because such qualities theoretically are not subject to change. If, however, the tests provide only a snapshot of the present knowledge of the test taker, then the results can change with the active decision of the test taker to improve. While the reader may find the racism of the test advocates of 1917 to be shocking and unacceptable, there is no logical distinction between the inappropriate conclusions based on a single test then and the overgeneralizations based on a single test for children in the early years of the twenty-first century.

Defenders of the use of tests for important decisions frequently refer to the objectivity, reliability, and validity that experts have claimed for these tests. Although this is not the forum for a professional discourse on the attributes of testing, there is one concept with which all parents should be familiar: validity. In lay terms, a test is valid when we test what we think we are testing. While this may seem simple on the face of it, the element of validity in testing is quite inconsistent. Consider the driving test we require in every state. Success on a multiple-choice test would not be a valid representation of driving ability. That is why every prospective driver must also get behind the wheel and demonstrate to the examiner some degree of proficiency in driving. Similarly, pilots do more than pass a multiple-choice exam; they must complete their flight examinations with an equal number of take-offs and landings. If the driving and pilot examinations result in the granting of licenses to unqualified applicants, the public safety is at risk. Conversely, if these examinations result in the denial of licenses to qualified applicants, it is not only inconvenient, but probably will result in litigation by the person to whom a license is denied. Such a reaction is possible because the test taker knows the impact of each test and is aware of the link between the test and an adverse decision.

While the requirement for validity is the same in every test, whether the subject is driving or kindergarten placement, the quality of testing is very different. We routinely make decisions about the educational opportunities for children based on test results, and in many cases the link between the test and the adverse decision is unclear or even secret. Counselors, teachers, and administrators give or deny students a variety of opportunities such as special reading groups or enrichment programs based on their performance on a single test. Worse yet, sometimes the decisions are based on tests that were taken during the prior school year.

The defenders of such decisions sometimes maintain that the students in special programs do better than the "average" and thus such tests must have been valid. In this context, validity becomes a self-fulfilling prophecy. A student does well on a test and then receives extra instruction from teachers who have high expectations. They come home to parents who have been told that their child is superior. If there is a challenge in school for such children, they assume that they can work harder, ask for help, and ultimately succeed. That is, after all, what smart kids, gifted kids, successful kids such as themselves would be expected to do. Of course, this combination of strategy, encouragement, expectations, persistence, and self-confidence would serve any student well. The converse is true. When a test indicates that a student has a poor math aptitude or is unlikely to become a good writer, then the subsequent expectations of teachers, parents, and the students themselves will assure that the negative prediction is accurate.

Does this mean that we should abandon all tests? Of course not. It is the use of the tests and the inappropriate interpretation of their results that should be reformed. The distinction that must be drawn is between tests as information and tests as prediction. Tarot cards provide information because the names of the cards are clear to any observer; few people outside of the Psychic Friends Network, however, would argue that the interpretation of the tarot cards can become transformed into accurate predictions. Consider other measurements in life. The bathroom scale may be mathematically accurate, but the next step—interpretation and prediction—can take one of two markedly different paths. A reading of 180 pounds can result in the inference, "I'd feel better if I lost ten pounds and I know just how to do it," or "I'm fat and stupid and ugly and can never change." The test was the same and the numbers were the same. The difference in the two responses involves interpretation and prediction.

Although parents may not always be able to influence the content or results of tests, we can make a profound impact on the interpretation of those tests and can fight the predictions that might be inaccurately made based upon those tests. The first challenge is in our own conversations about tests, focusing on learning and information rather than on evaluation, interpretation, and prediction. If parents fail to model learning conversations with children, they cannot influence the self-talk by children that inevitably occurs when parents are absent. Self-talk is powerful and, in the absence of strong logical challenges, can seem persuasive to anyone, particularly a child. Cognitive therapists challenge the illogical conclusions of their patients by helping them to identify the logical errors and destructive consequences of their self-talk. We do not need a therapist, however, to help our children think through why they believe as they do about their own successes and failures in school. If we listen, we might find thought patterns revealed in such self-talk as "I'm no good at math!" The source of such self-talk is rarely a scientific examination in which the algebra gene was found to be missing. Rather, there was some test, some conversation, some announcement of student proficiency in mathematics, and on that tenuous basis, an inappropriate conclusion was drawn. Sometimes the parent's first response is to offer assurances to the doubtful child such as, "Sure, you're good at math," or worse yet, "You think you were bad? I had trouble in math as well." It would be more constructive if we ask, "Why do you think that?" And then complete the conversation in a way that children can challenge their own conclusions. This might require some gentle inquiry and lots of listening by the parent. While the encouragement, love, and high expectations of parents are undeniably important, we must also develop the self-confidence of our children by giving them the skills to challenge their own negative images that stem from inappropriate interpretation and predictions of their past performance on tests.

fair tests

Standards: The Path Toward More Fair and Meaningful Tests

Because the words "standards" and "testing" are frequently used in the same sentence, some people have associated bad tests and inappropriate usage of test information with the standards movement. In fact, the proper application of academic standards leads to tests that are more fair and educational than traditional tests that are shrouded in mystery. Standards-based tests are fundamentally different from traditional tests in that student performance is compared to a standard rather than to the performance of other students. An academic standard is a simple statement of what students are expected to know and be able to do. Because the standards are public documents, students need not guess about the expectations of teachers. Thus, with standards, tests are not a game of *Jeopardy* in which the student with the most encyclopedic memory of many disconnected facts is the winner. Rather, any student who meets the standard can be a winner. Student success in a standards-based environment is a matter of what you know, not who you beat.

Because standards-based tests reject the notion of comparing one student to another, the traditional bell-shaped curve is rejected as a method of analyzing student performance. When schools use the bell curve, they assume that there are a few students who perform significantly above the average, a few students who are significantly below the average, and the vast majority of students who are in the middle. The last group forms the "bell"—the large hump in the middle of the curve. Although the bell curve is widely used in statistics and has been a staple of educational evaluation for more than a century, there is just one thing wrong with it: It is an inaccurate way to describe student achievement. When educational evaluation is based on a comparison to the average—the middle of the bell curve—then we have another self-fulfilling prophecy. If the instrument used to evaluate children only allows for a few students who are very much above average, then the use of that instrument—not the nature of children being tested—establishes the proof of the bell curve.

Test designers have a clever way of avoiding any evidence that does not fit their theory. If, for example, all children get a particular question right, then some observers might be delighted at the obvious result of diligent work by teachers and students. But in a test dedicated to the bell curve, such a question is simply discarded. The "good" questions are those that clearly differentiate one student from another. Ironically, the technical term for such differentiation is "discrimination," a term whose connotation of unfairness might be more accurate than the statistical meaning of identifying differences among students.

There are some instances in which a bell curve approach to testing might make some sense. If there are scarce resources to be allocated—such as admission to a selective college or selection for a high-paying job—then some people argue that only a bell curve test can rank students from best to worst. This sounds great in theory. After all, isn't the ninety-eighth percentile always better than the ninety-sixth percentile? The answer is, not necessarily. In fact, on many tests, the difference between those two rankings might be the response on a very small number of questions and student mastery of the those questions may or may not be related to success in the college or job under consideration. In fact, the difference between those two might be random or, at the very least, not relevant to the decision at hand. Consider other examinations, such as those for firefighter or jet pilot. In both cases, it is not sufficient for one candidate to beat another candidate. Any successful candidate applying for these positions must meet demanding physical and mental requirements. If no one meets those standards, the examiners do not say, "You can't carry someone out of a flaming building, but you're above the average of the other candidates, so we will accept you." Moreover, if there are several qualified candidates, the examiners do not say, "You are both highly qualified candidates, but Mary knew a little more about particle physics than Joe did, and therefore we will select Mary for the job." The candidates meet the standards or they don't, and if more people meet a standard than are needed to fill a vacancy, then the appropriate decision is not to resort to irrelevant information. In the context of education, the ultimate objectives should be accuracy and fairness. When schools use standards, teachers are liberated from the ancient and inaccurate practice of grading "on the curve" and instead can speak the truth: The student is proficient or not proficient compared to a standard, and a comparison to the work of other students is not relevant to my decision.

Standards are hardly a revolutionary approach to education. In fields as diverse as music and athletics, educators have long used standards. When a student wishes to play in the orchestra or participate on the basketball team, the requirement is not merely to beat other students, but rather to play scales, shoot baskets, or otherwise meet a standard that the conductor or coach has prescribed. The rules of the game are clear, and students need not guess about the height of the basket or the number of strings on a violin. Chapter 2 provides more detailed information about academic standards and what they mean for your child.

What about Talent and Intelligence?

Some readers are thinking, "Wait a minute! In the real world, everybody can't be a winner. Besides, there are some things that just can't be taught, and those things include talent and intelligence. You can't teach a golfer to be a Tiger Woods or a violinist to be Joshua Bell." This controversy about the relative impact of "born" traits versus taught skills has been at the center of educational debates since Plato. The Greek philosopher believed that there were "men of gold" who ruled over the "men of bronze." Not much has changed in the more than two thousand intervening years, as many people assume that "some kids have it and some don't."

Consider the example of musical talent, a quality many people assume is "born, not made." The Suzuki method of musical instruction has influenced literally millions of students and parents on every continent on the globe. As a result of the influence of Suzuki training, students without obvious genetic heritage of musicianship have found places in symphony orchestras throughout the world. Although the debate over talent and intelligence continues, those who discount the primacy of teaching and learning over inborn traits are deliberately indifferent to the evidence. There are surely cases of the most exceptional musicians, mathematicians, and athletes who may have some genetic predisposition toward their chosen careers. Nevertheless, the experience of the legions of students who have benefited from the Suzuki method make clear that the existence of exceptional talent and intelligence in a very few cases does not negate the general principle that talent and intelligence of the many can be nurtured, encouraged, and expanded. As Dr. Howard said, "Smart is something you get, not just something you are."

constructive conversations

Talking with Your Child about Standards and Tests

Children attribute an unusually high degree of credibility to what they hear at school, and thus the potentially negative conversations surrounding tests and standards that your child may encounter must be the subject of serious home discussion. Parents, not the local rumor mill, must determine the appropriate way for each child to react to standards and testing. This is not an issue on which the final parental word is, "Because I said so!" In our discussions with children, we must seek to equip them to stand on their own in the conflicts of the classroom and hallway. Thus, the following "point/counterpoint" dialogues are designed to suggest ways for you to talk constructively with your child about standards and tests.

"Those tests tell you how smart you are. If you don't do well, it means you're a dummy."

"Tests don't tell how smart you are, but tests do tell you a couple of things. They tell you what you have learned and they also tell you how good you are at figuring things out even when the right answer isn't very clear. That's why it's a good idea to pay attention and study,

and it's also a good idea to sit down with me and look at some of your old tests. If there is ever a test where you don't do well, we'll just work on it a little more. You're smart—and if you don't do well on a test, it just means we need to think through what happened and figure out how to do better. I know you can do it."

repeat positive

"If I don't do well on this test I'll be ruined! I won't get to go to the next grade with my friends. I just know I'm going to blow it!"

experiences

"It sounds as if you're pretty nervous about this test. Tell me how you're feeling about it right now. (Pause.) It's pretty scary, isn't it? Now, tell me how you felt when you did a great job in school. Remember that time when you got a perfect score on the math test and when you were so happy about your geography test? Tell me how you felt then. (Pause.) When you feel smart and good and happy, what did you do to make yourself feel that way? Let's make a list. Maybe we can discover the things that you have done when you felt smart and good and happy and we'll figure out how to do those things again now. If you do those same things, I know that you'll do a great job. And you know what? Even if your pencil breaks, the wind blows your test paper away, and the teacher turns into a green-eyed dragon and breathes fire on everybody's test, I'm going to love you anyway. Do we have a deal? Let's start making that list. . ."

"I can't possibly memorize all these things. My teacher said that the standards were impossible anyway and that no kids our age could do them. Mrs. Johnson said the same thing in the car on the way to school today. There's just nothing I can do. I give up!"

"I don't know. I've heard a lot of people say that kids can't do things, like play soccer or go on the Internet or create plays and make up songs, and then the kids do a great job anyway. When you said that the standards were impossible, which standards were you talking about? (Pause.) Well, I haven't read them either, so do you want to look them up and see if they are really impossible or if you can do most of them after all? What's your best subject? Let's start there . . ."*

*The state standards for grades 6 through 8 are reprinted in the second part of this book.

"I don't want to meet the standards—I want to be me! All my teachers have said I was a great writer ever since first grade. Now they tell me that I can only write the same way, every time, with a beginning, middle, and end. I used to write funny stories with crazy characters and goofy conversations, but now they say I have to be more serious. I hate standards, and so does everybody else. I have a dumb assignment because the dumb standard says that I have to compare two different dumb things. It's just stupid, and I don't want to do it. I want to write my stories!"

"I love your creative stories, too. I've saved some of the ones that you've written in the past. They show me that you are an intelligent, creative, and passionate person. You really care about what you write. Did you know that there are other people, aside from me, who could be moved by your writing? Tell me about something that really makes you angry. It might be people hurting animals or each other. It might be about the environment. It might be something at school or in our community. It might even be something about me or that happens at our house. Take a minute and think about it, and tell me something that makes you angry and that you want to change. (Pause, and let the child think of several options—you might get a fairly long list from a middle school student.) That's great! This is something that makes you really angry and that you want to change. Now, here's what we're going to do. You're a great writer, and writers can change things with their ideas and words. Write a letter about this. You might write it to me, to the President, to your teacher, to the principal, to the newspaper, or to anyone who can make a difference on this matter that makes you so angry. Let's agree that your letter should be your very best work. That means that you'll probably need to make an outline first. Then you'll write a draft, then edit it for errors in spelling, grammar, and punctuation. Finally, you will write your final copy. Of course, if you want to write persuasively, you will have both passion and evidence, so make sure that you support your arguments with research and examples. Because this is your very best work, your letter will have a clear beginning, middle, and end. If your letter is to me, I promise that I'll write a personal response to you. If your letter is to anyone else, I promise that I'll mail it to the recipient. I'm really proud of you for caring so much about this. I can't wait to see your letter!"

Your Right to Know about Tests in Your Child's School

Testing need not be mysterious or filled with terror. In fact, federal law establishes a parent's right to know what tests their children are taking and what the tests are about. This right includes everything from the weekly spelling tests to psychological tests to diagnostic tests to high-stakes graduation tests. If tests are mysterious, it is because parents do not ask the right questions. A sample letter from a parent to school officials requesting access to test information appears on page 92.

Parents' Checklist:

☐ Ask questions about your child's day based on his feelings and emotions, rather than events.

☐ Find out what tests are given in your child's school and how they are used to make any decisions about your child. Enter each of these test dates on your family calendar so that you can help to provide encouragement and reduce anxiety for your child.

☐ Celebrate your child's school accomplishments with the same enthusiasm you found in her first steps or her latest victory in a game.

---

celebrate
accomplishments

Chapter 4

Parents' Questions about Standards and Tests

This chapter is the result of hundreds of encounters with parents in focus groups, interviews, casual conversations, and letters. My research included parents from a wide variety of economic, educational, and cultural backgrounds. Although the parents with whom I spoke frequently expressed the conviction that their concerns were unique, the themes of these conversations were remarkably consistent. Parents have heard many rumors about academic standards, and much of what they have heard is the cause of significant fear and apprehension. The most consistent and significant desire expressed by parents is for specific communication from teachers about what children need to know and be able to do. Parents want more than a report card and annual parent-teacher conference. Parents want to play a role beyond working at a table at the school carnival or operating the copy machine in the school office. Parents, in brief, want information that is accurate and relevant to their children.

Despite the differences among the parents interviewed for this chapter, all of them have one thing in common: They care deeply about the educational opportunities for their children. Whether the parent was a Harvard-educated attorney or a high school dropout, the message was the same: Parents want their children to have more opportunities than they had and they are willing to support schools that provide such opportunities. They also insist on fairness for their children and clear communication from schools. Parents detest jargon, slogans, patronizing speeches, memos, and notes that appear to diminish the importance of the family. At the same time, parents are leery of the implication that they are primarily responsible for the education of their children. Whether the subject of discussion was math homework, test preparation, or summer reading, many parents bristled at the notion that they were responsible for doing a job that the school was supposed to do. Finally, the parents with whom I spoke were deeply concerned about the impact of a single test on their child, and most parents saw more threats than opportunities in the high-stakes testing movement.

The questions and responses that follow are hardly exhaustive, but they represent a synthesis of the attitudes, feelings, beliefs, and concerns of parents throughout the nation. You might recognize some of your own questions in the dialogue that follows.

What Is the Fundamental Purpose of School in the Middle Grades—That Is, the Grades Between Elementary School and High School?"

Many parents are confused about the fundamental purpose of middle school. Is it to explore different subjects, or to build the self-esteem of adolescents during a particularly difficult time of life? Many professional educators and state policymakers have strong disagreements about the purpose of middle school. Over the past 30 years, considerable research has been devoted to the unique needs of adolescents and pre-adolescents. While reasonable people disagree on many of these points, my response to this question is as follows: First, the fundamental purpose of education in the middle years between elementary school and high school is to prepare students to enter high school with confidence and success. High school teachers are nearly unanimous in the belief that incoming students must have strong skills in reading, writing, mathematics, time management, organization, and personal discipline. Second, the desire for exploration of many different subjects is understandable, as adolescence is an inquisitive time of life. Nevertheless, if parents and educators must choose between exploration and the development of basic skills in reading, the latter should take precedence over the former. Third and most important, educational researchers and parents of more than one child are unanimous on one point: Children acquire information at different rates. Therefore, the curriculum of the middle grades should assume differentiation, not uniformity. Some students require one period a day to master seventh-grade reading skills, while other students need two or three periods. Students are not widgets in a factory to be moved about in a uniform manner, but individuals with needs that are variable. Effective schools provide a different schedule to meet the individual learning needs of different students, and parents should support the recognition, analysis, and curriculum changes that result from a recognition of different student needs.

reduce anxiety

What Should I Say to My Child about Standards and Tests?

This is a great opportunity to move your children away from test terror toward becoming confident and capable students. Start with a clear definition: *Standards are the things that you should know and be able to do.* Then identify some of the standards that your children are already meeting. Review just a few of the standards in this book and tell your child, "You are already doing this. You see, standards aren't always something new and extra that you must learn; you already know many of these things right now!"

It is difficult to have a discussion with your child about academic standards without also discussing the tests based on your state's standards. This conversation is about emotions, not just about facts. Some parents are tempted to say something like, "You'd better study hard or you'll flunk the test!" In fact, the primary emotion of fear is already overwhelming, and the role of the parent is not to add to that anxiety, but to reduce it. How can you reduce your child's anxiety? Avoid false reassurances such as, "It's no big deal!" or "I'm sure you'll do just fine, so don't worry about it." When, in the life of parents, has the statement "Don't worry about it" served as a useful reassurance? What children most need to know is that their parent has heard and understood their fears. It is better to say, "Yes, tests can be pretty scary. When you fear something, it's always better to talk about it than to pretend that it's no big deal. What is there on this list of standards, or what have you heard about the test that is the most scary for you?" The parent finally has the information that can take the conversation from a dialogue filled with fear to the realm of the confident and empowered child. You will know that you have succeeded in these conversations—don't expect the matter to be resolved with a single discussion—when your child starts saying things such as:

"I know what I'm supposed to do in school."

"If I don't know how to do something, I know that I can figure it out or I know where I can get some help."

"I may not get a perfect score on the test, but I know most of the things on there. And if I miss a few questions, it doesn't mean I'm stupid. I'll just continue to learn all I can and do my best."

These are the words of a confident and empowered child. Parents need not give their children illusions, as if the Test Fairy will come to their aid in time of need. Rather, parents must give their children facts: what the standards are, what the tests mean, and how children's own efforts will improve their ability to achieve standards and do well on tests.

Is This Just Another Fad?

Y ou have probably heard of educational terms that sounded like fads, from "new math" to "whole language" to "learning styles" to "brain research" and a host of other labels that seem to dominate the discussion of educational matters from one year to the next. How do you know that the term "standards" is not just another passing fad? First, let's remember what standards are all about. The label is not important, but the essence of standards is vital. Standards are just about fairness. Because standards express what students should know and be able to do, and because standards-based schools expect teachers to give children the opportunity to meet those standards, there is nothing new or fancy at work here other than a simple commitment to fairness. Standards will not go "out of style" unless the desire of parents and teachers for fairness becomes a passing fad.

Who Sets the Standards?

In every state except Iowa, academic content standards are established by the state. In Iowa, every school district sets its own standards. Thus, some form of academic standards exists in every public school in the nation. Indeed, whether or not the term "standard" is used, most private and parochial schools also have a clear set of academic expectations for students.

One frequent misunderstanding is that "national standards" govern the content of the academic disciplines. In fact, a few groups such as the National Council for Teachers of Mathematics, National Council for Teachers of English, and other academic and professional organizations have offered suggested standards that frequently are used as resources by state departments of education and local school districts. There is not, however, a "Federal Department of Standards" in Washington, D.C. where busy bureaucrats wake up every morning plotting new ways to remove the local authority of school boards. There are no federally established academic standards imposed on schools. Although the federal government has broad authority with respect to protecting individual civil rights in school—particularly with regard to discrimination on the basis of ethnicity, gender, or disability—the federal role in curriculum is strictly advisory.

The evidence of state and local control over the curriculum is best revealed in the wide variation in the academic content standards of the states. Some states, such as New York and California, have very specific academic expectations, and those academic requirements are linked to curriculum documents and test objectives. Other states, by contrast, have academic requirements that are much more vague, leaving the discretion to select specific curriculum and test objectives to local school districts.

Despite the differences among state standards, there are some important commonalities. The most important distinguishing characteristic of standards-based schools is the comparison of students to a standard rather than to the average of other students. Many states blur this distinction in their testing policies. Rather than refer to the percentage of students who meet a standard, some state documents continue to make reference to "percentile" or other methods of ranking students. It will take some time before every state policy maker and administrator applies standards carefully and accurately.

Do Standards Place Too Much Emphasis on Academics?

Many parents expressed the concern that standards emphasize academic subjects to the exclusion of extracurricular activities, the arts, and simple fun in school. Some of these parents have heard alarming news stories (and more than a few unsubstantiated rumors) about schools that have been transformed into academic boot camps. In these dreary places, students do nothing except prepare for tests all day long. Work sheets and mock tests have replaced music and art. A number of popular writers have fanned the flames of this hysteria, fueled more by anecdote than by evidence.

It is true that when standards have been established with care, some traditional activities have been replaced by lessons with a greater academic orientation. This does not, however, imply the elimination of holiday celebrations and the systematic removal of fun from the school day. Students in standards-based schools will, for example, probably continue to discuss current events, enjoy physical activities, and participate in performing arts. It does not hurt the cause of student enjoyment, however, when students learn more about measurement and biology in their physical education classes, improve their mastery of fractions in their music classes, and otherwise incorporate academic relevance into fun activities. Indeed, the activities in this book make it clear that fun, engagement, and academic standards are not mutually exclusive.

Why Can't School Just Be Fun?

One of the frequent concerns expressed by parents I interviewed was the lament that school is no longer fun. Parents have heard tales of multi-hour homework assignments and children who complained that "Monday is the worst day of the week" because school was so terrifying. Some of these parents assumed that the appropriate reaction to the state of affairs must be a reduction of the academic expectations for their children. Parents should consider that it is entirely possible that the difficulties the students are facing arise because previous teachers did not have sufficiently high expectations of them. When everyone is focused on making school fun, the teacher who insists that students learn something is accused of being demanding and mean. This reinforces the notion that learning is burdensome and that school is dreadfully dull. The problem compounds itself in middle school, high school, and even in college, when the expectation of rigor is abandoned and students are viewed as "customers" who must be satisfied by credits that are easy, fun, and worthless.

What about the Basics—Reading, Writing, and Arithmetic?

Some parents are concerned that an emphasis on the higher order thinking skills included in many academic standards will reduce an emphasis on the "basics"—that is, skills in reading, writing, and arithmetic. In fact, there is not a contradiction between the requirement for higher order thinking and basic skills. Students cannot learn to master the challenge of mathematical problem solving if they do not have arithmetic skills. Moreover, students cannot respond to the challenge of critical thinking in social studies and science if they are unable to read their social studies and science textbooks or write a lab report.

The controversy over basic education has been particularly acute in mathematics. Partisans of pure "problem-solving" believe that an emphasis on mathematical concepts is essential, and that the dreary "drill and kill" of traditional worksheets must be discarded in favor of an emphasis on thinking. Of course, most mathematics teachers and parents recognize the intuitively obvious proposition that problem-solving and math skills are inseparable. Even in an age of calculators and computers, students must have "number sense." This means that students not only must be able to compute that $9 \times 9 = 81$ but they must also be able to understand that the number 81 is comprised of nine groups of nine and comprehend the notion that there are many other ways to achieve a product of 81. For example, consider these three levels of mathematical understanding, using the same example that begins with the question, "What is 9×9?"

The lowest level of understanding is expressed by the student who grabs the calculator and punches the buttons: $9 \times 9 =$ receives the answer 81. The next level of understanding is the student who recalled from memory that the product was 81 and did not need the calculator for assistance. But neither of these levels of understanding approaches the sophistication of the student who not only understands that $9 \times 9 = 81$, but also understands that since $3 \times 3 = 9$, then 81 is also the product of $3 \times 3 \times 3 \times 3$. For this student, the study of exponents in a future grade will be intuitive and easy. He will immediately grasp that $3^4 = 81$ rather than perceive exponents as a new and foreign mathematical concept that must be memorized without understanding. In other words, students need both the basics and thinking skills. The two are complementary, not competitive concepts.

Similarly, we expect students to have a deep understanding of causes and effects in history and science. But these deep understandings will elude students who do not have the ability to read and understand the paragraph before them. Moreover, the thinking skills involved in understanding the interplay of politics, geography, economics and conflict will elude students who did not study the factual details of those subjects. Thus, anyone who contends that an emphasis on standards excludes a commitment to basic skills has not carefully read the standards. I have met with angry parent groups whose concerns about standards were allayed when presented with the actual words of the standards. The academic standards make clear that students must not only master thinking, reasoning, and analysis, but also must understand how to read, write, and compute, as well as know the content associated with the foundational academic subjects.

understanding

Will Standards Mean the Elimination of Music, Art, and Physical Education?

There is a legitimate concern expressed by many parents that the overwhelming emphasis in state tests and standards on mathematics and language arts will exclude music, art, and physical education in some schools. In most successful schools I have studied, mathematics, social studies, science, music, art, and physical education are an integral part of the academic life of the school. For example, students in music class routinely use melody, rhythm, and song lyrics as a bridge to better understand history, learn new vocabulary, and master fractions. Students in art class use the visual images of art to expand their vocabulary and enhance their ability to compare and contrast different images. Moreover, students in effective art classes are able to master the art of scale and ratio, measurement, and the relationship between different geometric figures. There are wonderful physical education classes in which students acquire a better understanding of measurement. When the coach has given students the choice to run a millimeter or a kilometer, and the students make the wrong choice, the lesson on metric measurement tends to remain with them for a long time. Moreover, I have seen effective physical education teachers conduct vocabulary relays and math relays in which students must not only run fast but also must understand vocabulary and mathematical information in order to continue the race. This is the ideal intersection of the academic, the aesthetic, and the athletic.

Many middle schools and junior high schools have attempted to offer so much to so many different students that they have forgotten their fundamental mission: helping students to enter high school with confidence and success. It is clear from my interviews with high school teachers that the most important skills middle school students need are reading, writing, time management, and organization. Because classes in physical education, art, and music all can help to build these skills, they are not frills, but essential to the preparation of students for high school. The essential nature of these classes, of course, depends on teachers who understand that every class contains an academic component and that they are not a "teacher of music, art, and physical education," but rather a teacher of children.

the ideal intersection

Does My Child Really Have to Meet All of the Standards?

One of the weaknesses of standards as they have been articulated in most states is the failure of prioritization. In fact, not every standard is of equal value. Some standards recognize the need of basic skills, including reading, writing, and arithmetic. Moreover, the standards recognize the need of students to analyze and understand a relatively narrow set of facts. But neither every fact nor every skill has equal value for the student. Thus, it is not accurate to say that children have to meet every single standard elaborated by the state. One method of distinguishing the more important standards from those that are interesting but less valuable is the concept of "power standards." Chapter 5 provides more detailed elaboration on this concept.

What Happens If My Child Doesn't Meet the Standards?

When children do not meet academic content standards, the most immediate response should be the opportunity for additional learning. In other words, the immediate consequence for the failure to achieve a standard should be neither a low grade nor the repetition of an entire year of school. Rather, the initial consequence should be the opportunity for additional learning. This recognizes what all parents know to be true: Students learn at different rates. Many states have implemented high-stakes tests that are associated with academic content standards and some of these tests have dramatic consequences. For example, in some states, students must pass a reading proficiency test in order to enter the fourth grade. In other states, students must pass middle school proficiency tests in order to enter high school. A growing number of states—twenty-six at this writing—have established high school graduation examinations, which must be successfully completed by students in order to receive a high school diploma.

In the best school districts, the student performance on these examinations is rarely a surprise. In fact, students have multiple opportunities to prepare for important tests. Parents also have many opportunities to know well in advance of the test whether their children need additional help. Unfortunately, many school districts have a reactive response to high-stakes tests. Remediation and opportunities for additional learning only take place after a student has failed a test. Worst of all is the fallacy of remediation in high school for problems that have their roots in elementary and middle school.

If you are concerned about the performance of your child on a high-stakes test, then the use the letter format on page 92 to inquire of your school administration what specific testing policies will affect your child. Once you have this information, identify the particular knowledge and skills that your child will be required to have. Then you will be able to identify the gap between what your child knows at this time, and what your child will need to know and be able to do when the test is administered.

Parents frequently make the same mistake as schools, becoming involved in a child's academic challenges only after a student is experiencing difficulty in school. The most successful parental involvement occurs long before a child has experienced academic difficulty. Therefore, if you are concerned about the performance of your child in an upcoming test, the time to become involved is now, not after you receive your child's score.

My Child Just Doesn't Get It. What Do I Do?

Lots of frustrated parents share your concern. Most of us attempt to teach our children in the same way that we learned. In other words, if we learned by having someone read to us or speak to us, we assume that our children learn the same way. If we learned by having instructions written out for us, then we assume that our children will benefit from our own written instructions. Fortunately, children have a way of emulating some but not all of our characteristics. One of the things that they may not inherit is your learning style. As a result, please do not assume that your child "just doesn't get it" simply because the child is not learning the same way that you did.

You can discover your child's learning style by identifying the circumstances in which your child performs at a very high level. For example, perhaps your child plays a game exceptionally well. Perhaps your child enjoys a particular story, chapter, or book so much that she is able to recall it with astonishing detail. Perhaps your child enjoys writing to a relative or receiving mail. These will give you clues about the ways in which your child acquires information, processes that information, and applies information to the task at hand. Of course, just because a person prefers one learning style does not mean that the rest of the world will always accommodate that need. Therefore, children need to be able to process information from written text, oral instructions, and the context of the world around them. By finding your child's preferred method of learning, you can capitalize on that strength and also be more attentive to building skills in those learning methods that do not come so easily to your child.

When you become frustrated with your child's performance, one of the most important things that you can do is to stop the common practice of giving your child a single set of instructions involving the performance of multiple tasks. The most common example is, "Clean up your room!" For some children, this instruction is clear. For others, we must be more clear by breaking down the tasks: "Take the clothes off the floor and put them in the hamper." Then, after the successful completion of that task, "Empty the trash." Then, "Let your brother out of the closet," and so on, until the task of cleaning the room is completed. The breaking down of complex instructions into individual tasks is essential in the academic context as well. The only way you can isolate the difficulty your child is having is by providing clear instructions in a step-by-step manner. You may find that the problem is neither an inability to comprehend your instructions, nor an unwillingness to act on them. The difficulty, rather, may be that your child, like all of us, prefers some types of instructions to others. It is also quite likely that there is a difference in understanding when your child hears instructions compared to when the same instructions are printed on a page and your child must independently read and respond to them. The difference between oral and visual strengths is not the only learning style you should consider. Some children who do not respond well to oral or written instructions can perform the same tasks well if they see a physical model of the expected result, watch a demonstration, or engage in trial and error. The point is not that one of these learning styles is "right," but rather that every person learns in different ways, yet all of us occasionally are compelled to acquire information in a manner that does not correspond to our strengths. By understanding the need to listen, read, or observe demonstrations, a parent can support a child's strengths and offer encouragement and practice to deal with learning styles that are less familiar and, in the past, less successful.

Another common reason for children having difficulties in school is the disconnection between previous learning and current expectations. For example, students are bound to have difficulty with seventh-grade math requirements, such as finding the area of a circle by multiplying the square of the radius of the circle by pi, if they failed to master multiplication and exponents in earlier grades. Students are not going to be able to create a three-paragraph essay in eighth grade if they were unable to write coherent sentences in earlier grades. One of the principal benefits of the standards movement has been the requirement that teachers communicate with one another so that, in the best standards-based schools, there is a seamless transition from one grade to the next. An eighth-grade teacher has confidence about what students learned in the seventh grade because the seventh-grade curriculum was not based on the personal preferences of the teacher, but rather on a coherent curriculum that led directly to the instructional needs of the eighth-grade classroom. It is fair to say, however, that this ideal, seamless transition from one grade to the next is the exception rather than the rule in most American schools. Moreover, many schools have high rates of student and teacher mobility so that it is impossible to assume that every child in every class had a common foundation of learning.

The final consideration with respect to children who are having difficulty in school should be evaluation for learning disabilities. When you have tried to analyze a child's learning style with few results, and when you have attempted to help your child fill in the gaps from previous grade levels, it may be that your child continues to have immense difficulties in school. In these cases, it is appropriate to request an evaluation of your child for a variety of learning disabilities. Some parents fear that if they request an evaluation of their child, a label with negative connotations such as "special education" may be applied to their child. It is essential to note that both federal laws and public perceptions have changed markedly in the past several years on this issue. If your child is among the eleven percent of students nationwide with an identified learning disability, it does not mean that your child is "stupid" or otherwise incapable of great performance. The fields of law, medicine, music, and governmental leadership include many men and women who have learning disabilities. Indeed, identification of and compensation for a learning disability are the keys to their success. It is also very likely that children who are evaluated will not have a learning disability, and that work by those children, along with parents and teachers, on academic and behavioral issues will help them reach their full potential.

request an evaluation

What If My Child Has a Learning Disability?

More than eleven percent of students across the United States have some sort of learning disability. We have made great strides in this country in diagnosing, understanding, and even valuing the diversity of learning styles that different students bring to class, and this includes learning disabilities. The notion of "valuing" a learning disability is not merely a politically correct posture designed to make students and parents feel good about a bad situation. Marcus Buckingham and Donald Clifton of the Gallup Organization, one of the leading polling and management consulting firms in the world, provide examples of how even the profoundly challenging reading disability, dyslexia, can result in positive effects for students and adults who recognize the disability and carefully plot strategies for dealing with it. Students with learning disabilities have clear legal rights expressed in the Individuals with Disabilities Education Act (IDEA). Moreover, the students frequently have rights that are protected by local district policy and state law.

Foremost among the rights of learning disabled students is the right to have the "least restrictive environment" for learning. This typically means that learning disabled students are sitting next to students in regular education classes with regular teachers. The students, therefore, must have accommodations and adaptations made for them, particularly when it is time for a test. The most frequent accommodations and adaptations include time, environment, reading, and writing. The adaptation of time is provided to students who process information slowly, but accurately, and thus taking more time on a test allows them to accurately express what they know. The adaptation of environment provides for a quiet and secluded test-taking environment for students whose learning disability limits their concentration. The adaptation of reading allows students who understand words, but cannot process words in printed form, to have tests read aloud to them. Finally, the adaptation of writing allows a student who can speak words, but cannot write them, to dictate test responses to an adult for the writing portion of the test. Of course, these are only some of the many adaptations that are available to students with disabilities.

It is absolutely vital that parents and teachers distinguish between appropriate accommodation and the reduction of rigor for a test. Many professions include members who are extraordinarily gifted and intelligent, and yet suffer from some learning disability. The gifts of these professionals would never have been recognized had their teachers and parents reduced rigor rather than sought the most appropriate adaptation for the needs of the students. There are instances in which parents and teachers harbor grave misconceptions about the distinction between appropriate accommodation and an inappropriate reduction in rigor. Such misunderstandings are usually revealed in the form of a statement such as, "She's in special education so I had to give her a B," or, "He has a learning disability, so even though he didn't take the test or complete the project, I had to give him a C." Such statements are at odds with both federal law and the best interests of the child. The focus of IDEA is appropriate consideration of individual needs. There is not a single sentence in the law or accompanying regulations that requires teachers to lie to parents about the nature of student performance. Indeed, the requirements for individual considerations in curriculum and assessments are not a prescription for "dumbing down" requirements, but rather a requirement for appropriate accommodations and adaptations. When those adaptations are offered to students, it is typical that the report card will indicate that the student "achieved standards with appropriate adaptations and accommodations." Moreover, when a student does not meet an academic standard, the appropriate and accurate report should reflect that "the student met these objectives in the educational plan and did not meet the other objectives in the educational plan." The path to improved performance by all students, including students with learning disabilities, is accuracy and honesty in assessment.

For more information on students with learning disabilities, please consult Chapter 9. accuracy and honesty

What If I Disagree with the State and Local Standards?

Standards are political documents. They represent the efforts of a group of people who have endeavored to identify what students should know and be able to do. Nevertheless, as with any product of any committee, the documents are typically flawed. One can accept the obvious notion that some standards are too broad, some are too narrow, and most remain "works in progress," and nevertheless grasp that standards are superior to the poorly described curriculum or pedagogical anarchy that preceded them. It is entirely reasonable, and even likely, that thoughtful parents may disagree with some of the standards. Perhaps you disagree with the quantity of standards, with their specificity, with their vagueness, or even with their content. For example, I have heard a parent exclaim, "I don't care if my children can write, as long as they can read!" This was in direct response to the requirement of the state academic standards that children must be able to write coherent paragraphs. While this parent has a legitimate right to express such a point of view and, ultimately, to remove the children from the state school system, the parent should not have the right to require teachers to have a different set of standards for those children than for other children.

In many districts, parents have an extraordinary degree of influence on what the expectations are for their children. Unfortunately, these expectations are often used to reduce expectations and rigor and, as a result, dumb down the curriculum. In the example cited above, I confess to a prejudice. The research is clear and unambiguous: Writing is an effective way for students to think, reason, and learn. The fact that some parents may wish that their children did not have to write is not a sufficient justification for the absence of the requirement. I have worked in other schools where parents have asked the rhetorical question, "Why do these kids need algebra anyway? They will never use it." These parents, too, deserve a thoughtful hearing, but do not deserve to have their advice govern the curriculum standards for the school, district, or state that must serve all children.

There are other circumstances, however, in which the standards genuinely have deep flaws that contradict the philosophical, moral, or religious beliefs of parents. In these cases, parents have an opportunity to make their concerns known. Parents can exclude their students from tests and from subjects of study that they find objectionable on religious or moral grounds. Most schools ask parents specifically for permission to discuss issues involving human sexuality, birth control, religion, and other sensitive subjects. Schools routinely offer an alternative area of study and alternative literature to respond to parent wishes.

55

How Can I Deal with Stress and Anxiety about Tests?

Stress and anxiety are undeniably important parts of test performance. Most readers of this book can recall an instance in which they were well-prepared for an examination, or other challenge, and nevertheless performed below their ability. The reason for their poor performance was the stress and anxiety associated with a circumstance under which they had to perform. Although parents cannot completely eliminate childhood stress and anxiety, they can mitigate the negative impact by giving students healthy coping skills. These skills include the "second look" view of any situation in which children feel unprepared or uncomfortable. If the first look at a test question or other challenge reveals the student does not immediately know the answer, some students will simply assume that the challenge is impossible, emotionally shut down, succumb to the pressure at hand, and give up not only on the question before them but on the entire test. Other students, by contrast, have the ability to take a second look at a question or challenging circumstance. The second look of the student is comparable to the runner's second wind. This boost of energy occurs when students are able to use strategy, rather than mere recall, to address the question or challenge at hand.

Although parents need not conduct a test preparation academy from their home, they can give their students the ability to maintain and expand their repertoire of second look skills. Examples of second look skills include the following:

Two-pass technique—This technique suggests that students focus first on the questions to which they know the answer. Because every question typically has the same point value, students can generate the greatest yield on their investment of time when they focus first on those questions to which they immediately know the answer. After they have made the first pass going through all questions on a test, students can return to the beginning of the examination and devote additional energy to those questions that are ambiguous or more difficult. In most cases, students are well served to eliminate one or two obviously wrong answers, then guess the answer to these questions and quickly move along to the next challenge.

Outlining—Whenever students are faced with an essay question, there is a direct relationship between the amount of time spent outlining an answer and the time saved in creating the final answer. When students immediately launch into writing the final answer, they frequently produce an aimless and disorganized essay. When, on the other hand, students take the time to outline an answer first, they have the ability to produce a crisp and well-organized essay. Moreover, the very presence of the outline makes it clear to the teacher that the student understands the question and has taken the time to provide a detailed and well-organized response.

Process of elimination—In some cases, the right answer is not clear. Sometimes this is due to the difficulty of the test item. In many cases, however, this is due to the deliberate ambiguity of the test items. This is particularly true in the case of national standardized tests in which the test writers have determined that there must be a wide variation in the "difficulty value" of the test items. That is, some items are constructed in a manner so that many students will get them correct, and other items are constructed so that very few students will get the correct response. In the latter category, the cause for such a few number of students finding the correct answer is as likely the ambiguity as it is the difficulty of the question. In such cases, the students with the ability to persevere and take a second look at the question will find that, despite the difficulty or ambiguity of the question, they can at least eliminate one wrong answer and therefore have a higher probability of guessing the correct response. There is a great deal of mythology with respect to guessing on tests. In most cases, however, guessing strategies need not be mysterious at all. On many examinations, there is no "guessing correction factor" and therefore students should always guess if they do not know the right answer. On other tests, students are penalized for every wrong answer. In those cases, it only makes sense to guess if the student can eliminate one or two wrong answers. Consider these examples:

> Mary is taking a test without any guessing correction factor. It is a multiple-choice test with four possible answers: A, B, C, and D. After reviewing her work, there are still eight questions that she just can't understand. Should Mary guess? Absolutely yes. If she just marks "A" for each of those eight questions, she has a one-in-four chance that "A" is correct, and thus she is likely to get two out of the eight questions correct. That is an extra two correct answers that she otherwise would have missed if she just left them blank.

> In our second example, however, the rules are a little different. Bob is taking a similar test, with four possible answers. But for each question Bob

misses, he will be penalized $\frac{1}{3}$ point. Bob also has the same chance of guessing correctly that Mary had, and indeed, he answered two out of eight questions correctly. But what about the other six questions? Because Bob lost $\frac{1}{3}$ point for each of those six, he was penalized two points ($\frac{1}{3} \times 6$), and thus he gained no advantage guessing.

What if Bob was able to eliminate two possible wrong answers? In other words, he is not guessing among choices A, B, C, and D, but only among choices A and B, because he determined that C and D were not possible right answers. Now Bob has a 50/50 chance—it's either A or B—of guessing correctly. With eight questions, he probably will get four correct. He will be penalized $\frac{1}{3}$ point on the other four, for a total of $1\frac{1}{3}$ points ($4 \times \frac{1}{3}$). Because Bob could eliminate two possible wrong answers, it was a good strategy for him to guess.

The suggestions offered here are essential elements of educational and psychological strategy. One of the most powerful forces operating in the life of the empowered child is emotional resilience. Children with the ability and willingness to persevere in the face of seemingly great odds have the gift of emotional resilience. This lifelong ability has importance that extends far beyond test taking and academic pursuits. We routinely see parents encourage the skill of perseverance and emotional resilience in athletic competition. "You can do it!" the proud parents exclaim. The same level of perseverance can be encouraged through parent support for the resubmission of student work after the first draft did not meet the standard, encouraging more than one attempt at an essay, and encouraging one additional try for success at the mathematics homework. This encouragement is the source of emotional resilience that will be as valuable in algebra class as it is on the soccer field. In the future, this sense of empowerment, perseverance, and resilience will serve your child well in college, in relationships, and in any professional endeavor.

What If My Child Is Not Ready for a Test?

It is relatively uncommon for children to say with confidence, "I'm ready for this test and I'm going to ace it!" More often than not, we have created a sense of fear and loathing for tests, including those tests for which students are reasonably well-prepared. Parents have an important role to play here. First, parents have an obligation to help students be prepared for tests. The first step is simple: Mark test dates on the family calendar. When it is clear that Thursday is a test day, then Wednesday is not the ideal evening for a movie or an appeal for a later than usual bedtime. Most teachers—particularly at the secondary level—confirm that the difference between the superior students and the vast majority of their students is more a matter of time management and organizational skills than intellect. While parents cannot take tests for their children, nor should they, parents can give students the gift of organization and that includes a calendar, appropriate focus on test preparation, and a consistent theme that performance on tests is improved with preparation and hard work. Parents must obliterate the notion that prevails among many children that, "either you've got it or you don't —studying doesn't make much difference." In fact, the harder they work, the better they will perform in school and most other areas of life.

Consider the typical exchange between parent and child: "Do you have any homework tonight?" When the response is in the negative, parents need to ask a few more questions. The absence of homework might be genuine. On the other hand, the absence of homework, particularly in middle school and in upper elementary school, might be due to the fact that there is a test the next day. Students of every age should maintain a calendar with important dates on it. This is one of the key lifelong time management skills that everyone must master. The skill and discipline of maintaining an accurate and up-to-date calendar and task list not only separates successful students from unsuccessful students, but also distinguishes people in the professional and business world from one another. When there is a test the next day, the result need not be endless anxiety, trepidation, and fear. Rather, there must be a systematic approach to test preparation.

The systematic approach to test preparation includes the following steps. First, students must outline exactly what the test entails. Sometimes it is clear, such as all the traditional spelling tests in elementary school. At other times, a chapter test in a book will provide a clear and accurate preview of the test that students must face in the classroom. At other times, however, the content of the test may not be so clear, and some questions must be asked. If this inquiry takes place at half past nine o'clock the evening before the test, there are few alternatives other than an investigation into the mysteries of the backpack and notebook. If, by contrast, this inquiry takes place several days before the test, there is an opportunity to give the student responsibility for asking the teacher for help and for seeking additional guidance from other sources.

Second, students should prepare a sample test. One of the most effective learning exercises is for students to create a test. For younger students, acting as a teacher is a fun and engaging way to learn. For older students, such an activity may lack pure enjoyment, but the intellectual advantage is nevertheless very significant. In addition, when students practice creating and taking a test, they have not only provided themselves with a cognitive edge over their peers, but they also have provided themselves with an emotional safety net. By facing the unknown in friendly circumstances—the family room or bedroom—the student has the opportunity to endure natural test jitters in an environment that is far less consequential than in the classroom the following day. Moreover, it is my experience that students generally ask themselves far more difficult questions than those posed by the teacher.

In a Technological Age, Why Should Kids Take Paper and Pencil Tests?

It is a common parlor game for people to fantasize about the future. For years we have contemplated a world in which pencils and paper would become obsolete. The "paperless office" has been a concept considered by business people for years. Alas, the reality of our daily lives flies in the face of our fantasies. In fact, both students and people in the world of work must be able to create visual images, words, sentences, and paragraphs using pencil and paper, white boards, chalkboards, and a host of other media. In addition, the use of pencil and paper to slowly and carefully express ideas offers students the ability to think through problems without necessarily resorting to the guesswork involved in a multiple-choice question.

It is true that twenty-first century students must achieve a degree of technological literacy. Nevertheless, we also expect students to achieve a high degree of thinking, reasoning, and analysis. Those skills are best reinforced when students must take pen or pencil in hand, express an idea, communicate their thinking, and subject their reasoning to the critical review of others. Although computers clearly will play a role in the classroom and the future of today's students, technology does not replace the need for students to communicate clearly, accurately, analytically, and yes, legibly, in written form.

appropriate help

How Can I Help My Child with Homework and Projects Without Doing the Work Myself?

The subtext of this question is quite revealing. Every parent has observed instances in which the work presented to the teacher is clearly the product of a parent rather than the student. Such projects reveal far more about parental ambition than they do about student ability. The problem is that parents do not like to see their children become frustrated, angry, and ultimately disengaged from school. So how much "help" is appropriate and when do we cross the line from appropriate coaching and assistance to the inappropriate substitution of our own efforts for those of our children?

Parents are best served when teachers provide clear expectations for student performance. Some teachers are also clear about the nature of acceptable help and the instructions will clearly say, "Ask a parent or friend for help on this part," or, "Do this part all alone—don't get help from anyone else." Unfortunately, this level of clarity and specificity is the exception rather than the rule. One method that is particularly helpful when students are doing projects is the use of a scoring guide (sometimes called a "rubric" in educational jargon). When there is a clear set of teacher expectations, parents are able to help students not by doing work for them, but by asking students this critical question: If you were the teacher and you were grading this assignment using the scoring guide or rubric that the teacher provided, what grade would you give?

The cognitive scientist Benjamin Bloom made a tremendous contribution to the field of education when he recognized that the abilities to synthesize and evaluate information were essential for the intellectual development of children. When parents ask students to evaluate their own work, they are challenging students to engage in the advanced skill of evaluation, something too frequently left only to the teacher. If the teacher has provided a clear scoring guide or rubric—particularly a scoring guide that is expressed in student accessible language—then students can place themselves in the role of the teacher-evaluator and ask themselves how they would evaluate their own performance.

Too frequently, however, students merely do their best work, or do the work in the minimum amount of time given the exigencies of an upcoming television program, and assume that the teacher will evaluate the work in his or her own mysterious wisdom. This common practice of reserving evaluation responsibilities exclusively for the teacher denies students the opportunity to evaluate and learn. Make no mistake: This is not an exercise in making children feel good about themselves or engaging in unwarranted self-congratulatory smiling faces affixed to non-proficient work. Rather, the practice of evaluation and reflection requires thoughtful criticism, evaluation, and in many cases, rewriting, correction of errors, and the improvement of the quality of work. When parents insist that students engage in evaluation, they are doing far more than helping students on an individual homework assignment. These parents are giving their children the lifelong skills of reflection and evaluation.

a sense of accomplishment

How Much Homework Is Reasonable?
How Much Is Too Much?

In the early elementary grades, students revel in sharing school work, stories, and projects with parents. It hardly seems like "homework," but rather is a chance to share a daily sense of accomplishment. Some practice and reinforcement on basic skills, as well as a review and revision of school work, might require fifteen to twenty minutes each school night. As students enter the fourth and fifth grades, teachers are mindful of the need to prepare students for the homework demands of middle school. Most upper elementary teachers require about thirty minutes of homework each evening. In the middle grades (usually sixth through eighth grade), students should expect about ninety minutes of homework each evening. It is important to note that these are averages. Before you conclude that your child has too much homework because of a project that requires four hours to complete, it might be useful to note whether the project was assigned three weeks ago. If that is the case, don't be surprised if, the night before the project is due, you hear the claim that "My teacher gave me five hours of homework!"

If the averages noted above are consistently exceeded, then it might be reasonable to have a conversation with the teacher about how the student can better use classroom time to finish work and how the homework burden can be made more reasonable.

In addition to the quantity of homework, parents should attend to the quality of homework assigned by teachers. Are students building skills, conducting independent research, reading for understanding, and building confidence? These are the characteristics of effective homework assignments. If, on the other hand, students are bewildered, unfocused, bored, or completing worksheets on skills they have already mastered, then the value of the homework assignment is subject to question. The best way to approach the teacher is not with a complaint about "too much homework" but rather with the request that homework be challenging and meaningful. "I understand your desire to instill discipline through daily work," you might say, "and I want to be supportive of those habits as well. Perhaps we could work together to find assignments that will be best suited to my child's needs."

The most important contribution that parents can make on the homework front is to make it a priority, with a consistent place and time for the completion of daily work. When no homework has been assigned, the place and time remain available for learning activities in this book as well as those that you and your child create. In this way, you have a regular commitment to learning at home that will sustain your child whether or not homework has been assigned by the teacher.

What If I Can't Help My Child with a Subject in School?

I have a confession to make. I studied and taught mathematics, and yet sometimes I find my own children's homework in that subject baffling. Even more embarrassing, I have given my children the wrong answers when I violated my own rules and helped them too much with their homework. If these mistakes can be committed by a former teacher and professor, how much more likely is every parent to make them? If you have ever felt intimidated by your children's homework, you certainly are not alone.

Even if you can provide the answer, this is rarely the most appropriate way for you to help children. When your children ask for your help, here are some steps that will produce better results than insisting they do everything themselves, or doing their homework for them.

First, ask the child to make an attempt. In some cases, this means breaking the problem down into steps. For example, if there is a multi-step story problem in mathematics, and the child does not know how to frame the answer to the problem, an appropriate step toward solving the problem might be creating a picture that accurately describes the problem. This is particularly effective coaching because many children understand visual images of a problem better than they do the words of the story problem. This also makes the point that the key to answering a problem successfully is the accurate understanding of the problem, not merely asking the parent for help.

Second, ask the child to solve a single part of the problem. If, for example, the problem involves a complex series of geography questions, and the child does not have all the answers, encourage the child to answer only one or two of the possible problems. Every time we break a large and complex problem down into its component parts, the problem becomes more approachable. This gives your child not only excellent task and time management skills, but also reduces the anxiety associated with the majority of complex and difficult problems.

Third, it is entirely legitimate for the child to write down these words: "I don't know the complete answer—I tried, but this is as far as I got." The child then makes a good faith attempt to respond to the challenge at hand. This demonstrates to the teacher that the child considered the problem, thought about the problem, and genuinely did not know the answer. This is far more important information for a teacher than when a child merely leaves a piece of paper blank or turns in nothing at all. In such cases, the teacher is unable to distinguish between work that has been ignored and work that was attempted, but completed unsuccessfully. Moreover, this builds a skill too rarely discussed in the context of homework and academic achievement: the skill and habit of intellectual honesty. Leaders in professions, businesses, and academic institutions can all attest to the rare circumstances under which the words "I don't know" have been uttered. Nevertheless, the courageous people who say those words are often well regarded by their peers. When leaders express this trait, it becomes clear that honesty, rather than bluffs, is the acceptable code of conduct.

explore your options

What about Extracurricular Activities?

The research involving extracurricular activities is unambiguous. When students are participating in extracurricular activities such as sports, music, leadership, service, drama, debate, and a host of other wonderful activities, their academic achievement improves. Although these activities do take some time, and occasionally they even take time away from homework and academics, the overall research is not even a close call. Attendance and grades improve when students are busily involved in extracurricular activities, and the most effective schools seek to encourage every student, not just the most talented athletes and the most gifted musicians, to participate in activities beyond the classroom. Parents are well advised to encourage their children to participate in extracurricular activities. Moreover, schools must challenge themselves to give recognition to the most inclusive extracurricular activities in addition to the most exclusive extracurricular activities.

As valuable as extracurricular activities are, involvement can be carried to an unhealthy extreme. I know of children whose days begin with 7:30 chess club, followed by a full day of school, followed immediately by science club from 3:30 to 4:30. Religious school follows from 4:45 to 6:00. Eating a sandwich in the car, the child barely makes the 6:15 piano lesson. Basketball practice starts at 7:00 p.m. sharp and the child arrives home, exhausted, about 8:30 p.m. The cycle will repeat itself tomorrow, with soccer practice in place of basketball practice, a violin lesson replacing the piano lesson, and student council replacing science club. A reasonable rule might be, "one sport at a time" or "no more than one private lesson per week."

What If My Child Is Assigned to a Bad School?

The first question that must be considered is what makes a "bad" school. More often than not, parents evaluate schools the same way that real estate agents do, with a review of test scores. It is more than ironic that the same parents who seek out schools with high test scores express shock when those schools demonstrate that they take tests seriously. Moreover, it strikes administrators and teachers as deeply distressing when parents choose a school based on its academic excellence, and the same parents immediately try to change the policies of the school, expressing discontent that it is "too serious" and requires too much work for their children.

It is essential to identify what choice parents have in your school district. There is a national trend toward giving parents greater choice with respect to the assignment of students to different schools, but this is by no means a universal characteristic. Frequently, students are assigned to a school and parents have no choice within the public school system. Chapter 6 provides step-by-step procedures for exploring your school choice options.

Conclusion

When you are confronted with uncertainty, there is no substitute for information. While opinions and rumor abound, solid evidence and reliable information are frequently scarce. Because you want to have information that is directly relevant to *your* needs and the education of *your* children, there is no substitute for direct personal inquiry. You may be more comfortable with letters than with personal meetings or telephone conversations. However difficult the initiation of communication may be with the teachers and administrators at your children's schools, or the leaders at the district office, this challenge is worth the effort if you are able to begin the process of open dialogue, respectful communication, and accurate information.

seek reliable information

Chapter 5

What Your Child Is Expected to Know and Do in School

The academic standards at the back of this book can seem intimidating to parents, students, and teachers. You may experience many common apprehensions as you ask these questions: How can one child possibly do all that? How can a teacher possibly cover all of that material? What were these people thinking when they wrote all of these expectations for my children? This chapter puts the list of standards into focus by identifying some of the most important expectations for your children.

Before we begin, consider the most important question: What would parents be doing to help their children if we had no standards at all? We would probably do our best to build skills in reading, writing, and mathematics. We would help our children to understand that school is important, that diligence is a worthy character trait, and that perseverance in the face of difficulty is the way that one learns to master difficult tasks. In other words, if you simply followed your instincts as a good parent, you would impart to your child many of the most important elements of academic standards. With standards to augment common sense and good parenting, you need not guess at the details. You will understand what every student is expected to know and be able to do to become a successful student.

The inevitable question arises: Does my child have to master every standard in order to be successful? The straight answer is no. The details of academic standards—particularly with respect to social studies and science—represent more content than many teachers and parents understand. That even successful students have not mastered 100 percent of this material should be no surprise. In addition, each of you will find important information—perhaps things you learned in school—that appears to be missing from this chapter and from the state academic standards. This presents every teacher and school leader with a paradox: There are simultaneously too many and too few standards. The standards that exist require more time than is available in the school year; the standards that exist omit some subject matter that many parents and teachers find interesting or even vital. This paradox simply establishes what most parents are forced to admit rather early in the lives of their children: Perfection is not an option. The use of standards in school is no exception to this maxim. Therefore, use the standards as a guide, not a straitjacket. If you follow your instincts and help your child build academic skills in reading, writing, and mathematics, and if you consistently model and reinforce the development of sound character traits, your child will be successful in school.

Reading

Chances are that you began reading to your children while they were still babies By your early efforts, you were building a love of books, an understanding of the power of stories, and the belief that words on a page have meaning. In addition to reading, you probably provided plastic books on which your baby chewed, drooled, and even appeared to "read" as the vivid images captured the attention of the infant. As babies become toddlers and new words seemed to spring from their lips every day, reading together becomes a magical experience. Even before they know letters, very young children associate words with images and thus can fill in words in the picture books that parents are reading. When I ask parents about their favorite times of learning together with their children, these early days of eager discovery, quick mastery, joint experience, incredible wonder, and lots of laughter are the times recalled most fondly.

By the ages of four and five, the association between print and words is clear to most children, and they appear to "read" because they have memorized certain symbolic patterns. These so-called "sight words" help give children confidence, and therein lies one of the early misunderstandings about what it means to become a successful reader. While we naturally celebrate the ability of children to memorize symbols and their meaning, we also must understand that reading is more than the memorization of symbolic patterns. In order to become successful lifelong readers, we must build on the initial skill of memorization and add the following critical elements: decoding, comprehension, summarization, conclusions, and predictions.

As children enter adolescence, they naturally express a desire for more independence. Bedtime stories and long hugs give way to a peck on the cheek and a brief "good night!" Nevertheless, the fundamental need of middle school students is comparable to that of students in elementary school: Kids need to be competent, successful, and appreciated by the important adults in their lives. There is much in the lives of adolescents that seems out of control. Their bodies change, relationships are unstable, and emotions are out of control. One of the few things that offers stability to the adolescent is the mastery of academic skills, including reading. Parents who nurture and reinforce these skills provide reassurance, consistency, and stability to the teenager for whom these attributes are in very short supply.

successful reading

Literacy: Still the Most Essential Skill

Many parents and teachers of middle school students make the faulty assumption that reading proficiency is a certainty for fifth and sixth grade students. After all, they reason, children should have learned how to read and write in the first grade. Although it has been a few years since parents have heard their middle school children read a bedtime story, their ability to read directions, signs, and labels surely must indicate that literacy isn't a problem for these students. Such an assumption is fundamentally flawed for three reasons. First, many parents and teachers misunderstand what "good reading" really is. Many adults listen to a first grade child read aloud and exclaim, "My, what a good reader you are!" When the same child is identified a few years later as reading below grade level, the parents and teachers respond, "The test must be flawed. She is an excellent reader! In fact, she was able to read stories aloud without making a single mistake." Unfortunately, the oral pronunciation of words is not all of what "reading" really means. At the middle school level, students must be able to read long passages of 200 to 800 words silently; then they must be able to accurately recall and summarize the ideas, events, and people that were described in the passage. Good reading is much more than reading aloud.

The second reason that the presumption of "good reading" is potentially flawed is that students in elementary school tend to focus on fiction, while the reading requirements in middle school tend to be nonfiction. In one analysis of third grade reading I conducted last year, the ratio of fiction to nonfiction reading was 90 to 1. In middle school, however, students must be able to read nonfiction passages, including text on subjects such as social studies and science, in which students may not have a personal interest.

The third reason that parents must double-check their assumption that their child is a "good reader" is that the higher students progress in elementary school, the less detailed is the assessment of reading skill by teachers and school officials. Kindergarten and first grade teachers tend to keep detailed records of student progress in letter recognition and vocabulary development. These educators frequently maintain records that show which letters and words the child understands and where they will place particular emphasis in the weeks ahead. Teachers in the upper elementary grades discard such detailed record-keeping as their curriculum demands grow. Thus, a very bright and capable student can receive excellent grades, speak with confidence and assurance in class, impress most of the adults with whom he is in contact, and yet enter the sixth grade without the ability to read, comprehend, or write at a sixth grade level. In the upper elementary and early middle school grades, the discipline of reading gradually becomes a study of literature. Students and teachers discuss stories, characters, plots, and settings. Most of these discussions take place in groups, and there is little accountability for an individual student to read and understand the text. Indeed, the clever student can participate actively in a literature discussion, asking good questions and reflecting on the comments of classmates, without ever having read the text that is being discussed. Parents must therefore be willing to suspend their understandable confidence in their own children and ask the pointed question, "Can they really read and understand the pages of middle school textbooks?"

Whether or not reading is a problem for your child, there are two simple things that every family can do to improve the reading comprehension skills of every student. If your child is a superior reader, these ideas will elevate her skills to a higher level. If your child needs help in reading, you can quickly identify the areas where help is needed and build skills on a daily basis. Neither of these ideas will take more than 20 minutes of your time. First, have your child read aloud. The necessity to read aloud with clarity and confidence is important well beyond elementary school. Middle school students rarely get practice in the skill of oral reading, yet the development and maintenance of this skill is essential for their classroom success in middle school, high school, and beyond. Reading aloud can be a wonderful family activity and the selection of reading material can range from plays, in which each family member takes a part, to texts selected in turn by each member of the family In my family, we lingered around the dinner table for a few minutes every night and each person at the table, including children and adults, would read a paragraph. Sometimes it was an article about outer space, while other evenings it was a story. Often it was a brief article from an encyclopedia, usually hauled out to settle an argument. During certain seasons of the year, religious texts were read that were consistent with our family tradition. Whatever you select, these brief minutes will allow your children to develop confident reading skills in a safe and loving environment. If they make a mistake, the result will be your gentle encouragement rather than the snickering of classmates. If there is a serious problem in reading ability, you will learn about it firsthand and not be fooled by the awarding of a B in English class.

The second way families can improve the reading comprehension skills of middle school students is the "instant book report." Traditional book reports provide superficial summaries and evaluations of books and, at the middle school level, are written once every two or three months. The instant book report takes 20 minutes, with ten minutes of reading followed by ten minutes of writing. The child can select any text, although the parent may wish to alternate the genre between fiction and nonfiction. After ten minutes of silent reading, the child closes the book, takes out a piece of paper, and writes a brief summary of the text. If this is an activity that you do regularly, you also may wish to ask your child to compare the text of today's reading to the text that she read a few days ago. While the child is writing, the parent can read the text so that the actual reading passage can be compared to the child's summary.

These two reading strategies, reading aloud and reading silently before producing a written summary, are simple but powerful ways for parents of middle school students to get at the heart of what "good reading" really means. Because the number of students assigned to each teacher in middle school is significantly greater than was the case in elementary school, few middle school teachers have the time for this sort of individual attention to students and detailed analysis of reading ability. It is up to you, the parent, to provide this, and it only takes 20 minutes of your time.

Books: Just so Twentieth Century

This book, as with most of those published in the twenty-first century thus far, is written on a computer. Much of the research that I conduct comes from Internet searches and electronically published journals. If computers and electronic communication are to be the future of the written word, why should parents invest money and time in old-fashioned books? You might as easily ask why you should attend a live symphony orchestra concert when there are so many fine compact discs available. Why should you write a thank-you note with pen in hand rather than send an e-mail? The answer to these questions is that there are intangibles to the heft of a book and the resonance of the symphony hall, and to holding a letter that someone else took the time to write that are absent when technology, no matter how elegant or sophisticated, replaces physical contact.

There is, of course, an important role that technology will play in the future of our children. There are some wonderful computer programs that are successfully used to help children develop skills. As I write these words, my seven-year-old is explaining the nature of pulleys and levers to his five-year-old friend using illustrations from a clever science program. As with many education matters, this is not an "either/or" proposition. We can nurture a love and respect for books while encouraging an understanding of appropriate uses of technology. Our priorities, however, must be clear. My observation is that there are many more students who can troll the Internet than who can write a sentence with appropriate grammar, spelling, and punctuation.

the most effective strategy

Writing

Although most educators and parents properly place an exceptional emphasis on reading, we dare not neglect the importance of writing. It is also essential to recall that language development does not proceed in a neat linear fashion in which we first perfect speaking skills, then polish reading skills, and only then proceed to writing. In fact, as students improve their writing, they also improve their ability to read, particularly with regard to the advanced skills of comprehension, summarization, and prediction. Student proficiency in writing also is associated with improved student achievement in mathematics, social studies, and science. In fact, of all the strategies that teachers and parents can use to boost student achievement, improved formal writing is the single most effective strategy that provides benefits in every other area of the curriculum.

Some parents may question whether writing is really that important when state academic tests and college admissions tests are typically multiple-choice exams. The answer is not that there is some magic in a number two pencil, but rather that writing—particularly formal nonfiction writing—requires students to think, reason, analyze, and communicate. Those skills will help students deal with multiple-choice tests and every other challenge that they face in school. Indeed, the best teachers I have observed do not see writing as a trade-off with multiple-choice tests, but rather combine these two testing methods. They routinely require students not only to choose the correct response, but also require written explanations of why one response was chosen and another possible answer was rejected. Such an approach transforms multiple-choice tests from a guessing game into a challenging and engaging intellectual task.

Some parents and teachers regard writing with pen or pencil as an ancient craft, soon to be displaced by computers. I respectfully dissent. If we think of writing not merely as a means of communication, but also as a means to enhance thinking, reasoning, analysis, and communication, then writing will not "go out of style" until thinking goes out of style. Moreover, children and adults who are able to convey in handwritten form their deep emotions and sentiments such as sympathy, appreciation, and encouragement, will find that they have a far more profound impact on those with whom they communicate than if they are brought up to rely solely on a word processor. Technology will replace neither emotions nor the need to communicate them. Thus writing, including the ability to write legibly and without the aid of a computerized spell-checker, remains an essential characteristic of the educated child.

Rewriting: The Key to Improved Writing

Think of the things your child does well. Perhaps she plays soccer. Maybe he plays the violin or piano. She might be a great swimmer. Every child has something in which enjoyment and skill coincide. Now consider how that skill was developed. It never—not once—occurred with a single effort. Many soccer balls were kicked far from the net before that first glorious goal. A fair amount of screeching preceded the successful completion of "Minuet in G" on the violin. The first attempt at the G-major scale probably omitted the F-sharp. Skills are never developed in one-shot endeavors. Children know intuitively that practice makes perfect and that the remedy for failure is additional practice. Why then, is so much written schoolwork submitted on a one-shot basis? The habit of writing a rough draft, submission to a parent or teacher for correction, and rewriting, is not merely a habit for writing; it is a habit of mind that displays perseverance and character.

developing skills

The Basics: Spelling, Grammar, Punctuation, and Legibility

Some of the best support for the proposition that the basics of English communication are important in every academic and vocational setting has come from several unexpected sources. The president of an urban electricians' union, for example, addressed an audience of technical school students and parents and provided a passionate defense for the literacy requirements. "Successful members of this union must be able to read and write instructions. Mistakes in writing can mean putting yourself and others at safety risk. We require people to be good writers." Many high schools have conducted focus groups of former students who were invited to share their responses to the question, "What do you wish you would have had in school?" With remarkable consistency, students in universities noted that they were required to write not only in English class, but in history, music, economics, and every other discipline. They needed more formal writing, they admitted. Individuals in technical schools and the world of work similarly expressed their concern that they were required to write on a regular basis and that they needed additional training to do so. Whether the former student was a dispatcher in a truck stop or an undergraduate in the Ivy League, the consistent theme was a request for more writing. Of course, none of these chastened high school graduates requested more writing during the course of elementary, middle, or high school classes. The role of teachers and parents in this and many other areas is not to give children what they want, but what they need. Writing is, in brief, a skill that they need, but rarely request.

It is important that parents and teachers are specific about what "writing" really means, for too often students have been left with the impression that aimless reflections in journals fulfill the requirement for written expression. Whatever merit journal writing may have, the self-absorbed and frequently scatological reflections of teenagers do not develop the formal writing skills that students need. They need to write paragraphs with topic sentences and essays with a clear beginning, middle, and end. They need models of good writing and clear criteria for what constitutes acceptable and exemplary composition. In any other area of skill development, specificity is essential. Children would laugh at the notion that they should be creative with regard to where the soccer ball should go. Thankfully, they do not find the need to be creative with regard to the tones to which the violin is tuned. Yet, there are remarkably creative and gifted soccer players and musicians. The strict application of structure, in other words, does not remove creativity, but rather creates a clear framework within which creative expression can occur.

The overwhelming majority of writing by students in elementary and middle schools is in the form of a creative narrative. While this genre of writing is important, it is not sufficient. Specifically, students must be able to write for several purposes. First, students must write to inform. That is, they must describe an object, sequence of events, person, or situation with clarity and accuracy. Second, students must write to analyze. Typically, analytical writing involves the comparison of two different events, people, or activities. When students write analytically, they carefully explain similarities and differences between the objects of their analysis. Third, students must write to persuade. Effective persuasive writing is not an expression of personal preference, but rather an argument supported by evidence, examples, and illustrations. Although the labels of these types of writing may vary from one class to another, students must understand differences between creative writing and description, analysis, and persuasion. Middle school students can be asked to compare different books and describe the characters, settings, and plots of novels. It is particularly important for students in middle school social studies and science classes to be able to express a conclusion and support it with evidence. My interviews with secondary school and college faculty members reveal that the single greatest deficiency among their students is writing, and in particular, nonfiction writing in the form of description, analysis, and persuasion. College students who persist in the illusion that a successful argument begins with the words "I feel" have, at some early point in their academic career, been denied the opportunity to learn the craft of writing.

Mathematics

The controversies involving mathematics education have mirrored the phonics vs. whole language debate. Typically, the terminology of the math wars includes "problem-solving" and "number operations," with advocates of the "new, new math" preferring the former over the latter and traditionalists taking the reverse point of view. While few thoughtful people doubt that problem-solving is a useful skill in mathematics, it is baffling to me that anyone would think that skill in solving mathematical problems can be developed without an understanding of calculation. Conversely, no mastery of the times tables replaces the necessity to read a story problem and write a clear explanation for a solution. The debate between these extremes implies a dichotomy that is illogical. Students must have both the ability to read and write about mathematics, as well as a sound grounding in the fundamentals of arithmetic.

One common source of friction is the use of calculators. Indeed, calculators are commonly used in math classes, based on the "obvious" proposition that students would be foolish not to make use of the best technology at hand. Evidence reported in the *Wall Street Journal* (December 15, 2000, p. A1) indicates that students who make frequent use of calculators in class perform at much lower levels on state tests than students who use calculators only two or three times a month. This is no surprise to the parent or math teacher who has witnessed a child instinctively reach for a calculator when asked to multiply three times three. Worse yet, if the student hits a wrong key and the screen says that the answer is 25, she may have been conditioned to place more confidence in the calculator than in her own understanding that three groups of three cannot conceivably yield a product of 25. This is not merely an issue of discipline and the "basics." Some of the most sophisticated mathematics at the secondary school and collegiate levels require students to be able to estimate. Their ability in "mental math," and their confidence in making a judgment about what a likely answer might be, is an important input into some statistical and financial equations. In sum, calculators do not replace the need for the disciplined thinking in mathematics any more than word processors replace the need for thoughtful analysis in an English class.

building sound skills

If You Are Intimidated by Math

It is possible, even likely, that your own experiences in mathematics were not favorable in school. Moreover, the format, content, and sheer size of mathematics text-books can be intimidating. Nevertheless, there are many things you can do to help your children develop sound mathematical skills. In addition to the many activities suggested at the back of this book, there are four common household themes that will build the math skills of your children. These include games, money, time, and measurement. Children love games, and keeping score is normally part of this family activity Parents may be tempted to take on the scorekeeping duties in the name of accuracy or speed. This is a missed opportunity. My experience is that if one child is keeping score, every other child at the table will be doing the same thing, keeping an eagle eye out for errors. When the parent keeps score, children may passively accept the calculations. Money offers an exceptional opportunity to build mental math skills. If children are paid an allowance or compensated for chores, parents should make a point of providing money in different denominations and combinations. Middle school is a wonderful opportunity for budding entrepreneurs to mow lawns, baby-sit, sell popcorn and soft drinks, or engage in other creative ways to make money and, of course, keep careful track of the income and expenses of the enterprise. A regular review of the business records creates opportunities to practice the arithmetic involved in subtracting expenses from income to yield profit, and to introduce questions that involve common middle school chal-lenges such as percents, decimals, fractions, and ratios. The power of these authentic situations is that they give genuine value and meaning to the field of mathematical problem-solving. These situations are no longer the academic questions of a textbook, but real-world situations that have relevance to your child's activities. How well does Pepsi sell compared to Dr. Pepper? How did sales change from week to week during the summer? If I charged a flat fee for the lawn job, how much did I make per hour?

Time is a theme that governs many households, yet the predominance of digital clocks prevents many children from learning to tell time or to solve problems regard-ing the intervals between different time periods. Daily reinforcement of these skills can occur with questions such as, "What time is it now, and how many minutes before school starts?" Finally, the theme of measurement offers abundant opportunities for the building of math skills in the kitchen, the yard, home construction jobs, or marking off athletic fields. Because measurement refers to space and volume, these lessons cannot be learned by reading a chapter in a math book about measurement. Students learn about measurement by measuring, by observing the impact of measurement mistakes, by making corrections, and by learning the carpenter's rule to "measure twice, cut once."

Science — a spirit of inquiry

As intimidating as mathematics may be, the science curriculum can be even more baffling to many parents. The traditional curriculum of weather, dinosaurs, and volcanoes has been replaced by an early emphasis on the physical, chemical, and biological sciences. Both state standards and school texts can present remarkably sophisticated challenges for students. Despite these challenges, there are several things that parents can do that will improve the scientific thinking of their children.

Parents can encourage a spirit of inquiry, helping children to understand that science is not just about providing answers, but also about asking questions. Real scientists are not just smart people who have all the answers. Even very famous scientists, such as Galileo, have been spectacularly wrong about many of their theories. Science advances through the process of generating a theory, developing alternative hypotheses, and then systematically testing those hypotheses. For science to advance, we must disprove hypotheses. This means that for every gain in scientific knowledge, some very smart scientist was proven wrong. This does not diminish the credibility or importance of scientific work. Indeed, the researcher's aphorism is, "We learn more from error than from uncertainty." This is a good rule in the lives of students as well. When they don't know the answer, testing an idea—even if such a test proves their previous conceptions to be untrue—is better than proceeding in ignorance.

Scientific observation can occur in the home every day when children pose the hypothetical question, "What will happen if I do this?" If we announce the answer, we deny our children the opportunity to generate a hypothesis and then test it through systematic observation. Children are full of "why" questions that are directly susceptible to the generation of hypotheses and systematic testing.

- **Why do some years have 365 days and other years have 366 days?**

- **Why is it colder in January and hotter in July in the Northern Hemisphere, but the other way around in the Southern Hemisphere?**

- **If I drop a penny and a baseball from the top of a ladder, which one will hit the ground first?**

The list is endless. The key is not for parents to attempt to become walking encyclopedias, but to build a spirit of inquiry and testing in which children are not afraid to generate thoughtful guesses and then test those guesses. Real scientists, and thoughtful students, are not afraid to routinely write the words, "My hypothesis was not supported by the evidence." This approach to learning values evidence over alchemy and thus is not only a sound intellectual trait, but an opportunity to build sound character as well.

Social Studies

The amount of content in social studies curricula can be overwhelming. Spanning the subjects of history, geography, civics, and economics, social studies texts can add many pounds to your child's backpack and nevertheless omit many important subjects. Despite the bewildering array of complex ideas in the subjects involved in social studies, parents can reinforce some fundamental understandings that every child should have.

The first and most important principle to understand is that advancement in social studies is directly related to student proficiency in reading and writing. Make no mistake: If your child needs help in reading and writing, then you and the teachers must devote time to these areas as a priority. Of course, it is possible to use reading texts that include history and government. There is, however, no substitute for absolute proficiency in literacy as an antecedent to the study of social studies. I have never heard a secondary school teacher say, "I wish that more students knew the capital of South Dakota," but I have heard hundreds of them say, "I wish that more students could read my textbook."

Government and Civics

At the end of the Cold War, President Gorbachev of the former Soviet Union famously said to General (now Secretary of State) Colin Powell, "General, you will have to find yourself another enemy." While Americans who grew up in the 1940s and 1950s rejoiced at the diminution of world tensions, and the reduction in the likelihood that our own children would face the prospect of nuclear war, the demise of the Soviet Union also changed conversations in schools and homes. For the last decade, we rarely talked about the difference between democracy and authoritarian forms of government with the same urgency that we did when our own form of government seemed to be threatened. These are distinctions that remain important and are among the fundamental concepts that students must know. If you can take your children to see any democratically elected body in action, it is worth the trip. If you live near the state capital, watch the legislature in session. Better yet, arrange to have your child serve as a page in one of the legislative chambers for a day. If distance from the capital prevents such an excursion, then take your children to a meeting of the school board, county commission, or city council. The concept of representative democracy is fundamental and every child should understand that one of the distinguishing parts of our heritage of freedom is the ability to vote, selecting men and women who do the public's bidding. Of course, parents who wish to encourage good civic behavior by their children must vote, and you may wish to consider taking your children with you to observe this most fundamental civic right and obligation. There can be little doubt in the aftermath of the presidential election of 2000 that every vote has an important influence on the future of the nation.

History

History has been the subject of the most hotly debated state standards. Part of this controversy stems from the idiosyncratic manner in which history has been taught in schools, with the principal source of differentiation being the personal preference of the teacher. Some teachers devote weeks to the building of scale models of the Coliseum as a substitute for the study of ancient Rome, while others devote the month of November to an historically inaccurate drama inevitably focusing on Pocahontas and John Smith. Other classrooms devote weeks to Custer's Last Battle, while others linger for months on the Civil War. Few, however, stop to ask what the study of history is all about and many leave students with the conviction that it is simply "a bunch of facts" that are regurgitated on demand. If the teacher deliberately avoided the fact-based approach to history, then students would have the impression that history is a series of disjointed dramas and personal stories. The presence of social studies standards offers the beginning of some coherence to the study of this discipline.

Let us first put to rest the "facts vs. themes" controversy. Students need to learn historical facts. It is preposterous to assume that students can apply higher order thinking skills to history, geography, and economics without understanding that the Civil War preceded Vietnam, that the Balkans are not the Baltics, and that there is rarely a singular cause for an historical or economic effect. While not every date is of equal importance, a sense of sequence in the broad sweep of history is essential if students are to have an appropriate context for their understanding of historical events, political decisions, and cultural artifacts of the time. The words of the song, "Battle Hymn of the Republic" have a profoundly different meaning for students who have studied the words as part of their understanding of 19th century history.

Parents can reinforce this understanding of historical context by talking about family history. Family trees and time lines can lend context that many children do not understand. If your children have parents, grandparents, or great-grandparents who fought in a war, then encourage serious family discussion about those events. For today's students, Vietnam is simply one more piece of history, as removed from their reality as the World Wars of the last century, or the many conflicts of centuries long past. If you can add profound family context to these events, the lessons learned by your children will have value far beyond a few paragraphs in a textbook. Every community has historical landmarks and most have museums. Although the events commemorated in those monuments may not be the focus of your school's textbooks, there is nothing to match the visual impression of personal observation. If your family has the resources to take a vacation, then plan to spend a week or more in the nation's capital. Let your children see the Constitution, the Declaration of Independence, and the words of Lincoln beneath his majestic statue.

adding context

Foreign Language, Music, and Art

Although this book focuses on the core academic areas of language arts, mathematics, social studies, and science, parents are wise to reinforce their children's pursuit of studies in foreign language, music, and art. At the very least, study of a foreign language will help to build English vocabulary, and at best will improve your child's understanding of other cultures. Much of the world's classic literature first appeared in languages other than English, and by opening the door to the study of other languages, you will provide a lifelong gift with which your children can explore other cultures and lands. Even a slight familiarity with another language allows your children to recognize the value of courtesy when they are guests in other nations.

The study of music is one of the most important disciplines for children. It is not necessary for your child to become a concert pianist or to play first chair in the saxophone section of the school band. The study of music, however, will improve your child's understanding of mathematics with the study of rhythm and notation. The study of songs will build your child's vocabulary and reading skills. The occasional performance will build confidence and presence.

The study of art allows your child a creative outlet that can be successfully combined with many other disciplines. Because vivid images are one of the best ways for children to acquire understanding and knowledge, the study of art should include not only the creation of original pieces of art, but trips to the museum and the observation of the art work of the world's great artists. The connection between art and written expression is particularly important. A wonderful way to build your child's skills in analytical writing is the comparison of two pieces of art. Moreover, students can illustrate their creative and nonfiction work with vivid illustrations that reflect their words.

Behavior

No discussion of learning at home is complete without addressing the issue of behavior. Veteran teachers frequently complain of the extent to which behavioral education has been transferred from parents to schools, and teachers readily acknowledge that schools are ill-equipped to begin teaching respect, teamwork, and integrity in a classroom for six hours a day if those values were not taught before a child's schooling began and reinforced before and after the school day.

Although every family has its own code of behavior, these differences need not obscure some fundamental obligations that people, including school children, have in a civil society. Parents may differ about the need to call adults "sir" and "ma'am," but every parent has an obligation to instill in children a respect for the authority of teachers and school leaders. No amount of parental guilt due to absence and no amount of parental recollections of unsatisfactory relationships with their own parents justifies the wholesale abandonment of behavioral training. Even more shocking than the abandonment of parental attempts to instill codes of civil behavior in children is the frequent support of student behavior that is disruptive, rude, and dangerous, as if the school had an obligation to conform to the behavioral code of the children, rather than the reverse.

In addition to encouraging a fundamental respect for adult authority, parents can build sound behavior in their children by insisting upon good organization in everything from the toy box to the dresser, closet, and backpacks. The adage, "A place for everything and everything in its place" may not conform to the adults who routinely display messy desks and ridicule their more organized colleagues. Nevertheless, secondary school educators routinely speak of students who fail not because of poor intellectual skills, but due to lack of the most fundamental organizational skills. The teachers assumed that children would learn these skills at home, while parents assumed the children would pick up these traits at school. Meanwhile, school lockers resemble toxic waste dumps, completed homework assignments are lost in a backpack full of trash, and bright students flounder because they lack simple organizational skills and habits.

The most important consideration with regard to building strong organizational skills is to establish the fact that good student organization is a skill, not an inherited genetic trait. Writing assignments in a notebook, making daily lists of things that must be done, and putting away books and toys are not matters encoded in DNA; they are skills and habits that are taught, learned, practiced, and developed over time.

What to Do When You Can't Do it All: Power Standards

Having reached the end of this chapter and not yet confronted the list of standards at the end of this book, the skeptical reader might be tempted to exclaim, "Twenty minutes a day? He's got to be kidding! I could devote hours every day to the reading, writing, mathematics, science, music, and art, and never even get to the behavior and organizational stuff. Attempting to make a difference in 20 minutes is sheer fantasy."

Your skepticism is understandable. Moreover, this perception of standards and school curricula as overwhelming burdens is shared by many teachers and school leaders who know that even the most diligent teacher may not produce students who know and understand every single standard. Nevertheless, the plain fact remains that your time does matter and that 20 minutes a day makes a world of difference. Without question, the homes in which independent reading routinely takes place probably have other characteristics, including access to books, caring adults, quiet space, and time. Nevertheless, the evidence is clear. Student achievement can dramatically improve without transforming school and home into a joyless test prep center. Rather, the ideas in this book, implemented incrementally and balanced between academic and behavioral objectives, serve to have a clear and dramatic impact on student success.

Given the overwhelming number of standards and the many activities in this book, a fair question to ask is, "Where do we start?" The concept of "power standards" provides one mechanism for parents, teachers, and students to choose wisely among many available alternatives. The notion of power standards suggests that the choice is not necessarily based on popularity, but on impact. Power standards must pass three thresholds. First, they must have endurance. In other words, some information memorized for a particular test is liberated from our neurons within nanoseconds after the completion of a test. While the knowledge that Pb is the chemical symbol for lead may be of use when the *Jeopardy* category is Chemical Symbols, it is not a piece of knowledge that has endurance. While the scientific method endures, memorization of chemical symbols and, for that matter, the dimensions of the stegosaurus do not.

The second criterion for power standards is leverage. This chapter has already highlighted a skill that provides students with leverage, that is, it has impact on many different subjects. When students write more frequently, particularly when that writing includes formal submissions with rewriting based on teacher feedback, student achievement improves not only in writing, but in mathematics, social studies, and science.

Another example of leverage is the skill involved in creating tables, charts, and graphs, and the understanding necessary to draw inferences from the graphic representation of data. This requirement not only appears in the mathematics standards, but also in academic standards for science, social studies, and language arts. Time invested in the development of a skill with leverage will pay dividends in many different academic areas.

The third threshold that power standards must cross is that they be necessary for success at the next level of instruction. Whenever I have challenged teachers to narrow the focus of their curriculum and omit a chapter, activity, or unit, they frequently respond that "everything I do is important" and besides, "The children will need this information for the next grade." When I ask the same teachers to provide advice for a new teacher who has the responsibility for students in the next lower grade, the story changes. While the sixth-grade teacher may insist that "everything I do is important," the seventh-grade teacher is quite willing to provide a very brief list of requirements for sixth grade. The sixth-grade teacher is similarly willing to provide clarity and focus for a suggested fifth-grade curriculum. In contrast to the lists of standards and test objectives that include scores of items and extend to several pages, the lists of requirements for the next lower grade that I routinely receive from teachers rarely exceeds a dozen items and seldom exceeds a single page. Part of this phenomenon may be the very human characteristic that it is easier to give advice than to take it. The inescapable conclusion, however, is that teachers and parents know that hasty and superficial coverage of massive amounts of curriculum is not as effective as thorough student knowledge of the most important elements of the curriculum.

While reasonable people may differ with regard to the ideal curriculum, no parent wishes students to be in a classroom where reading is not valued. Few parents would find competent the teacher who provides writing requirements only on rare occasions. In other words, while reasonable people may disagree about the universe of standards, most parents and teachers can apply the three criteria—endurance, leverage, and readiness for the next grade—and quickly arrive at a consensus on the most important pieces of information that are the non-negotiable. These are the areas of knowledge and skill that students must absolutely, positively have in order to be successful. This might mean that the scale model of the Coliseum gives way to improved reading instruction, that the eighteenth annual dramatization of Pocahontas yields to the need to master fractions, and the recollections of summer vacations are supplanted with a better understanding of the Constitution. In brief, power standards help teachers and parents make choices in the real world of limited time.

What's Worth Fighting For

Although it may appear that the burdens of standards are staggering, there are only a few areas on which parents must absolutely insist both with regard to student work at home and the curriculum in school. Those areas worth the assertion of parental authority include thinking, reasoning, and communication. If you find that students are only being asked to complete drill sheets rather than engage in deep and thoughtful analysis, it is essential that such practices are challenged with the evidence that the path toward greater student achievement lies not in mindless test preparation, but in extensive analysis, reasoning, and writing. If you find that students are taking exclusively multiple-choice tests and rarely if ever are required to write, then it is essential that such practices are challenged with the evidence that more frequent student writing not only builds thinking and reasoning skills, but also improves student performance on multiple-choice tests.

Although parents may not win every issue of contention over curriculum and testing, these discussions with teachers and school officials will make clear that the obligation of the parent is not merely to support homework and reinforce the skills required by the school. Sometimes the most important obligation of the parent is to provide complementary skills in those areas that the school is short-changing. If writing is underemphasized, then it is important that parents pay particular attention to writing requirements as part of your 20-Minute Learning Connection. If math calculation is underemphasized in the name of improved problem-solving techniques, then parents must make up the shortfall with an emphasis on the development of sound basic skills in addition, subtraction, multiplication, and division. If the discussion of literature takes precedence over the development of reading comprehension skills, then parents must give children the opportunity for independent reading—both aloud and silently—at home. Most importantly, parents must ensure that students can understand the text before them and write a brief summary that is accurate and complete.

When parents are proactive as advocates for their children, then they not only help future generations of children, but also immediately and decisively intervene in the educational lives of their own children.

be a proactive advocate

Chapter 6

Before School Begins: Planning for School Success

The 20-Minute Learning Connection begins long before children enter school. Part of the success of parent planning is a commitment to being proactive rather than reactive when dealing with school issues. This chapter addresses the strategies parents can use to maximize their influence on their children's educational opportunities.

Much of the recent discussion about parent choice in schools has been focused on the politically volatile issue of school vouchers. Although only a very few school systems in the nation offer publicly funded vouchers that parents may choose to use for a private school education for their children, there is frequently a great deal of choice that parents can and should exercise with regard to the educational opportunities for their children.

Choosing Schools

In some school districts, a parent's request for school "choice" is welcomed as an indication of positive involvement. Even some large urban school systems pride themselves on the claim that more than 90 percent of parents and children receive their first choice of school. In other school systems, however, choice of school is something exercised only by the administration, with boundary lines, program assignment, and bus schedules, all matters that are announced to parents, rather than decisions that invite participation and comparison among alternatives.

If you wish to get the straight story about parent rights and choice in your district, it is important that you ask the right questions. Figure 6.1 provides an easy guide to the specific questions you should ask school administrators in your district about your rights as a parent. Don't settle for a form letter or impromptu policy statement by a harried administrator. Ask the questions and write down the answers.

FIGURE 6.1
What Are My Choices?

School Administration Telephone Number:_____

Name of Administrator:_____

Introduction:

"Hello. My name is _____ and my child is a student in this district. I would like to ask some questions about the choices of schools available to my child. Are you the right person to talk with about this matter?"

If "no": "Thanks very much. Who should I speak with about this?"

Name:_____

Phone Number: _____

If "Yes": "That's great. Do you have a moment so that I can learn more about this?"

"Does the district have a voucher program that provides funding for private schools?"

❑ No

❑ Yes

❑ Details:_____

"Does the district have any charter schools?"

❑ No

❑ Yes

❑ Details:_____

"Is my child required to attend the school nearest to me, or may I select any of the public schools available?"

❑ Your child must attend local school. That is:_____

❑ Your child may choose any school.

❑ Your child may go to another school, but must deal with certain restrictions.

❑ Your child may go to another school, but families living close to each school have first priority, and people outside of the boundaries of that school are only permitted to enroll if there is space available.

❑ Additional details:_____

If no choice at all: "I understand that you are saying I have no choice of schools at all. Is that correct? So that I understand this clearly, are you saying that there are no situations in the school district at all in which students are attending a school other than their official assigned school? Could you please tell me about these exceptions to your normal policy?

If choice is available: "That's great. Is there a written policy that governs the choices that I have as a parent? Would you please send me a printed copy of that policy?"

"Just one more question. Where can I find information about the different schools? Is there an accountability report or other document that will provide detailed information about the enrollment, teaching staff, and academic programs of each school in the district?"

"Thank you very much."

Although most public school systems are far from a genuine market system in which consumers can make informed choices from among a variety of alternatives, there is frequently much more choice available than parents recognize. Although only a tiny minority of school systems offers publicly funded vouchers and only a few school systems offer charter schools that may appeal to some parents, virtually every school system with more than one school will provide some level of parent choice if the matter is pressed. The purpose for the inquiry is not necessarily to engage in political advocacy for vouchers, charters, or other forms of school choice. Rather, the purpose for your question is simply to ensure that you have the best possible information with which you can make a reasoned judgment.

choose wisely

Making the Best Choice

Once you have determined that you have some level of school choice, it is important that you choose wisely. The label of the school tells you very little about the quality of the curriculum and teachers. For example, some charter schools are among the very best in the nation; some charter schools have been abject failures. The label "charter" does little to assure a parent of educational quality. Rather, you must make specific inquiries about the curriculum, teaching, and leadership of the school. Sometimes these inquiries may be uncomfortable, as many schools have a history of operating free from parental scrutiny. Many other schools welcome parent questions and provide easy-to-understand accountability information for parents or any other member of the community. Regardless of the ease with which you acquire this data, the following questions will serve as a useful guide for your conversations about schools, curricula, teachers, and leadership.

Your inquiries must be specific. First, you'll want to know what the academic expectations of the school are. The assurance that "we are standards-based" or "we follow the state standards" is not sufficient. You deserve a direct answer to this question: "What is my child expected to know and be able to do at the beginning of the school year and at the end of the school year?" You should receive a specific list of the knowledge and skills with which your child should enter and leave each grade level. Anything less than a straightforward response to this inquiry is evidence that the school is "standards-based" in name only, and that curriculum anarchy prevails. The extent to which individual teachers can choose to make extraordinary departures from the curriculum is stunning to many parents. Some teachers offer little or no science, while others emphasize science to the exclusion of essential literacy programs. Some teachers invest extraordinary amounts of time in student performances, often with the enthusiastic encouragement and support of parents, omitting large amounts of academic requirements. A great number of teachers emphasize arts and crafts more than academic requirements. Kati Haycock, president of the Education Trust, recently observed that in classroom after classroom she witnessed more coloring assignments than reading, writing, and mathematics assignments. You must ask, "What is my child expected to know and be able to do?" The principal and individual teachers must be able to answer this question clearly and without hesitation. If the response is unclear to you, academic expectations will be the subject of mystery and ambiguity for your child.

Another important part of your consideration of curriculum is testing and assessment. Curriculum without testing is wishful thinking. All the elegant lesson plans, detailed curriculum documents, and heavy textbooks in the world have little impact if there is not a systematic method of determining the extent to which students are learning what is expected. Do not settle for unspecific assurances such as, "We do regular testing." Ask to see the results for the past two years of the state and district tests that are related to the academic standards and curriculum requirements of the school. Determine for yourself whether students in this school are learning what school leaders believe that students are learning.

Second, you want to know about the teaching qualifications of the staff. Teachers typically receive certifications for specific subjects, particular groups of grade levels, or both. While certification is no guarantee of quality, the evidence is over-whelming that students taught by noncertified teachers perform at significantly lower levels than students under the tutelage of certified teachers. Many school systems have emphasized reductions in class size. Unfortunately, they have filled some classrooms with well-intentioned, but untrained, people. You must insist that your child be taught by a certified teacher. In addition, the educational background and experience of the staff should be examined. Advanced degrees and extensive experience is no guarantee of quality, but you may wish to consider carefully whether your child should be in the classroom of a teacher with little or no experience.

Third, you want to learn about the leadership of the school. In some schools, the principal operates autonomously, with little or no oversight. In other schools, a collabo-rative decision-making body includes teachers, parents, and administrators. Sometimes these committees operate differently in practice than the theory with which they were originated. The best way for you to address this is to ask when the next meeting of the decision-making committee will be and plan to attend the meeting. Does the group make substantive contributions to the decision-making process? Do some groups dominate the discussion? Do parents have a real voice on matters such as curriculum, instruction, and policy? Finally, ask this specific question: "Can you give me an example of how parents have influenced the curriculum and instruction policies of the school?"

There is no doubt about this fact: You have a right to make these inquiries. Information about curriculum and teacher qualifications is not secret. If you receive anything less than completely forthcoming information, then you should make a written inquiry to your district superintendent. Figure 6.2 provides an example of how you can make these inquiries in a courteous and businesslike manner.

FIGURE 6.2
Inquiry Letter to School Superintendent

(name), Superintendent of Schools

(district name)

(address, city, state, zip)

Re: Information concerning _____ school

Dear (Dr./Ms./Mr.) _____:

On (date) I met with the principal of _____ school. The purpose of my meeting was to learn more about the curriculum, teaching, and leadership of the school my children may attend next year. I still have some questions about these matters and I would appreciate your assistance in responding to them.

With respect to the curriculum, I am particularly interested in the specific academic expectations of my children and how those expectations are assessed. If there are specific curriculum standards that every child is expected to meet, I would like to see them. In addition, I would like to know if there are district or state tests that address the extent to which the school has met those academic expectations in the past. I would also appreciate seeing the results from those assessments for the past two years. Please let me know if there are differences among the curriculum based on choices made by each teacher or if the curriculum is the same for each teacher. If there are differences, please elaborate on those differences.

With respect to the faculty, I would like to know about the subject matter and grade-level certification of the staff, their educational backgrounds, and teaching experience. If some faculty members have particular interests or areas of expertise, please share that information as well.

Finally, I am very interested to learn about the leadership of the school and particularly about the manner in which parents are able to participate in school decision-making. If there is a governing or advisory body in which parents participate, I would like to learn more about the operations of this group and when its next meeting will be held.

Thank you very much for your assistance.

Sincerely,

(your name)

be courteous but persistent

Choosing Teachers

Parent choice of teachers is a delicate subject. Reasonable people may disagree on the matter. Those advocating parent choice see it as a way of encouraging parent involvement and ensuring that parents have a vested interest in supporting the teacher and encouraging their child to succeed. Certainly most parents believe that they know their children better than anyone and are therefore best equipped to determine which teachers and educational programs are best suited for their children. Those opposing parent choice of teachers see this practice as an inequitable device in which activist parents get better teachers for their children than parents who do not have the time, ability, or interest to attempt to influence school administrators. Moreover, some administrators fear that parent choice is more of a popularity contest fueled by rumor than a choice based on professional abilities. In addition, some administrators worry that teachers might make unwise educational decisions in an attempt to be popular with parents. Finally, there is the concern that since teaching ability and popularity never will be equally distributed among various teachers in a grade level, some classes might be overburdened with too many students in a quest to meet the demands of parents.

Whatever the policy of your local school, it is important that parents take the time to understand the extent of their ability to influence the assignment of students to the classroom. Even if there is an official policy against parent choice, parents are entitled to ask questions about the differences among teachers with regard to certification, education, experience, and educational practices. While some of this information may be obtained through public documents, other matters, such as the educational practices of individual teachers, will only be revealed through interviews and observation.

When you make your initial inquiries about teachers, you will likely be told, "All of our teaching staff are excellent. Besides, we all have state standards, so you'll find that pretty much every class is the same. That's why we handle teacher assignment." You should be courteous but persistent in pursuing your inquiries. After you have learned the basics—certification, education, experience—you will need to dig deeper. Talk with your child's prospective teacher, preferably in the classroom. Plan to spend more time listening than talking. This is not the time for you to articulate your educational philosophy, but rather the time for you to determine what the philosophy and practices of the teacher will be. This is a difficult but important consideration: Your time is better spent finding a school and teacher that conform to your philosophy than attempting to convince a school and teacher that they should change their philosophies to agree with you.

Here are some things to notice as you enter the classroom:

❑ **Student work:** Is student work prominently posted around the room? If so, is there clear and specific feedback on what work is acceptable and what work needs improvement? Does every paper, including poor work, have a "smiley face," or does the teacher provide encouraging but clear guidance on how to improve? Are there samples of exemplary work that represent the educational target for students?

❑ **Class rules:** Are there high standards of behavior that are clear and unambiguous? Does the appearance of the classroom indicate that students take good care of their personal property and school property?

❑ **Teacher's desk:** Does the teacher set an example of organization and neatness?

❑ **Availability:** Were you welcomed into the classroom at any time or was your entry into the classroom restricted to specific pre-announced times? Were other parents actively volunteering, participating, and improving the learning environment?

Following is a list of things you should discuss with the teacher. It is absolutely important to take the time to listen to the responses without interruption. You want to solicit clear and unambiguous answers. You might need to draw the teacher out with some encouraging phrases such as, "Please tell me a little more about that."

❑ **What should a child know and be able to do at the beginning of the school year? In other words, what preparation should a successful student have before coming to your class?**

❑ **What should a student know and be able to do at the end of this school year? Please be as specific as possible.**

❑ **How do you assess student progress? May I please see an example of one of the tests you routinely use to assess student progress? What is the consequence when a student does poorly on a test? Can you please provide an example of a time when you changed the curriculum based on your analysis of the assessment results of the class? If my child does badly on a test, how soon will I be informed? Are there reports of student progress other than the report card?**

❑ **Please tell me about your favorite things to teach. Are there certain areas for which you provide extra emphasis based on your personal interest and knowledge?**

❑ **Are there some areas that you are not as comfortable teaching? Are there certain areas that you tend to emphasize less as a result?**

❑ **As a parent, how can I be most supportive of my child's education? Are there particular things that the parents of students in your class should do?**

❑ **Please explain your homework policy. How much homework should students normally have? What is the consequence when a student fails to turn in homework?**

❑ **What is your policy with regard to parent volunteers in the classroom?**

☐ **What is the practice of the school and your class with regard to extracurricular activities? If these activities occur during the regular school day, do students make up for lost instructional time? If so, please explain.**

☐ **May I please see a copy of the report card form? Please explain how grades or other marks on the report card are determined. Is there a written grading policy? May I please have a copy of it?**

☐ **What happens when students learn and complete their work at different levels of speed and proficiency? What assistance is provided to students who are slower or less proficient? What enrichment is provided to students who are quicker or more proficient? If enrichment work is provided, could you please show me an example of such a task?**

While these questions are certainly not exhaustive, they provide the basis for a continuing conversation and mutual understanding between parent and teacher. Even if there is absolutely no parent choice with regard to teacher and class assignment, this conversation will allow you and your child to begin the year with greater clarity and less ambiguity. Such a conversation also makes clear to the teacher that you are genuinely interested in the education of your children and that you are willing to be helpful and supportive of the teacher.

When You Need to Change Teachers

Many teachers are wonderful. They are dedicated professionals who work extra hours, take a personal interest in every child, and who are remembered by generations of students who were lucky enough to be in their classroom. Students in these classes may not come home every day having had fun, but they always come home having been challenged to do their best. Many teachers are solid practitioners, perhaps a little cynical because of their treatment at the hands of administrators and school boards. These teachers have had a few run-ins with parents, and those experiences left the teacher wondering whether the parents really wanted to support education or just wanted a babysitting service for their child. These teachers can provide a solid education for your children, but they are not the exceptional educators who will inspire a child to excellence. A few teachers are truly incompetent. Their classrooms are out of control, perhaps dangerous. Sometimes they scream; sometimes they are silent in the face of belligerent behavior that appears to be tacitly approved by their silence. They play favorites and the incomprehensibility of their evaluation system makes it impossible to tell how grades are awarded. Some of these terrible teachers embrace every new fad, sometimes to the exclusion of educational basics; others have learned nothing since they left college, perhaps decades ago. They rarely ask students to write, and the teacher's own writing is full of errors in grammar and spelling. Their personal understanding of the subjects that they teach rarely extends beyond the textbook, so that if there were errors in the science or social studies text, they would be unlikely to notice.

In the course of thirteen years of education, from kindergarten through the completion of high school, your children will probably have more than fifty different teachers, assuming one or more teacher for each elementary grade and six or seven teachers for each middle school and high school grade. Of these fifty teachers, some will be wonderful, some will be solid practitioners, and perhaps a very few will be incompetent. If that is the case, you have an obligation to intervene. In some cases, such as with an unclear grading policy, the situation may improve with a simple request. In most cases of a true incompetent, however, no amount of cajoling or complaining will change the fact that the person in the classroom is not equipped to do the job. Whatever the inconvenience, you will be less aggravated and your child will be better educated if you insist on a change. You may be able to change to a different teacher within your school or it may be necessary to change schools. In extreme cases, where the district and school administration are extremely uncooperative, it may be necessary to change to a different public school system or to find a charter or private school that will meet your child's needs. The impact of this disruption is negligible when compared to the impact of a lost year of learning.

If you request a change of teacher, you must have your facts straight. Present to the principal a written request, identifying the specific objections you have. If there were particular behaviors by the teacher to which you object, identify with as much specificity as possible the circumstances, the exact behavior (not the attitudes or motivation, just the behavior) that you observed, and precisely when it occurred. You should expect to have the principal listen to you politely, and then refuse your request for a change. In general, school administrators deplore change and are supportive of teachers in most instances of teacher-parent disagreement. Remain calm, make your case with clarity and specificity, and ask for a written notice of the principal's decision. If the decision is against your wishes, ask also for the written notice to include information on the next level of decision authority. There is no such thing as a decision that cannot be appealed, and you must pursue the matter with the district administration if necessary.

One final issue should be considered before you proceed to change teachers, schools, or systems. You must ensure that the alternative is genuinely better. That means that you have taken the time to have the same conversation with the prospective teachers in the other classrooms or alternative schools that you had with your child's current teacher. You cannot assume that simply because a school has a good reputation, is a charter school, is a private school, is exclusive, or is expensive that the individual classroom to which your child is assigned will be one of quality and challenge. There is no substitute for asking the questions listed above, starting with the simple, "What is my child expected to know and be able to do at the end of this year?"

get ready

Parents' Checklist for the Week Before School Begins

❑ **Gradually begin to move your child's bedtime back (getting up at 6 a.m. can be quite a shock after "summer hours").**

❑ **Do any last minute shopping for school supplies. Try not to leave it all until the week before school starts, as the shelves may be stripped. Instead, try to start shopping for school supplies two or three weeks before school starts.**

    ❑ **Plan ahead. Know what you need to buy before you're in the store.**

    ❑ **Try office supply stores and warehouse stores. You'll find better prices.**

    ❑ **Try to involve your child in the shopping and decision-making. After all, these are the notebooks and pencils she'll be using.**

❑ **Let your child choose something special to wear or bring on the first day of school. A new backpack or his favorite shirt may help make things less overwhelming.**

❏ If possible, visit school before it opens, and locate the places your child is likely to visit often. Once school begins, don't be surprised if your middle school student does not want you around to be helpful.

    ❏ Restrooms

    ❏ Counseling office

    ❏ Main office

    ❏ Nurse's office

    ❏ Gym

    ❏ Cafeteria

    ❏ Where to buy lunch tickets

    ❏ Locker

    ❏ Where to catch the bus

❏ Get a copy of the bell/class schedule and look it over along with a map of the school.

❏ If your child will be bringing a sack lunch to school, consult her on the menu.

❏ If your child will be walking to school or to the bus stop, make sure he is familiar with the route and with "safe places" along the way (friends' houses, stores you frequent, etc.).

❏ Be open, alert, and sympathetic to any and all questions about school, as well as to moods and behaviors that may indicate fear and anxiety on the child's part.

Parents' Checklist for the First Week of School

❏ Once again, be alert. Ask a lot of questions and make eye contact and affirming comments when your child answers. Make sure he knows you want to be involved and that you are listening to him.

❑ Some direct questions to ask:

  ❑ Where is your locker? Is it conveniently located? How often can you go to it? Do you have to carry all your books all day long?

  ❑ Where is lunch? Do you have someone to sit with? Do you know how to get through the lunch lines? Do you know where to buy lunch tickets?

  ❑ Are you having trouble with any kids?

  ❑ Are you thinking of trying out for any sports or plays, or joining any clubs? How can I help?

❑ If you happen to have one of those kids who doesn't answer direct questions, here are some indirect ones to try:

  ❑ What was your favorite part of the day?

  ❑ Was there a high part? What was it?

  ❑ Was there a low part? What was it?

❑ Pay close attention to any handouts your child brings home. The important guidelines and forms tend to be sent home in the first few weeks. If your child is not forthcoming with handouts, a "backpack search" may be in order.

❑ With your child, go over any homework, artwork, tests, or other papers she brings home. Talk openly about what was difficult and what was easy, her likes and dislikes about the assignment or project.

❑ Never be afraid to call the teacher! If something doesn't seem right or is simply unclear, a phone call at the beginning of the school year can often ward off bigger problems later.

❑ Realize that your child may be tired, overwhelmed, and even cranky the first week of school. Try to help him relax.

❑ Leaving notes of encouragement in a backpack or lunch box is a pleasant surprise that even older kids enjoy. Help them remember that you support them even if you can't be there.

The Emergency Supply Cabinet

We all remember running home from school one day saying, "Mom! I have a project due tomorrow! I have to make a replica of the Coliseum… do we have three pounds of clay and a yard of brown felt?" If it hasn't happened to you yet as a parent, it will. You can't get through even one child's school career without a school supply emergency of some sort. Here are a few things to keep on hand so that you'll be better prepared for such an occasion:

school supplies

❑ Glue and/or glue stick

❑ Construction paper

❑ Extra computer paper

❑ Extra toner or ink cartridge for the printer

❑ Blue and black ink pens

❑ Lined paper

❑ Poster board

❑ Colored pencils

❑ Markers

❑ Tape

❑ Scissors

❑ Ruler and/or yardstick

❑ Stapler and staples

❑ Paper clips

❑ Stickers

❑ Glitter

- ❑ **Dictionary**
- ❑ **Thesaurus**
- ❑ **Atlas**
- ❑ **Globe**
- ❑ **Encyclopedia**

Chapter 7

But What Do I Do Tomorrow?

The 20-Minute Learning Connection is not a quick fix. Rather, it is a commitment that will become a habit for you and for your child, leading to success in school as well as learning, discipline, intellectual development, discovery, and most importantly, the connections between parents and children that are far more important than any test or homework assignment. The path to this commitment, as with all great achievements, begins by recognizing what could go wrong and anticipating these developments. One of the first things that might go wrong is that your child might not share your enthusiasm for spending these 20 minutes together every day. This chapter suggests some practical ways for dealing with the typical differences between what children want (freedom, television, and Nintendo) and what they need: guidance, discipline, and the development of skills and knowledge that will last them a lifetime. We will consider some typical responses of children who will resist your attempts to engage them in new and challenging enterprises.

"I Can't Do This!"

Perhaps the most frequent complaints of school children and, for that matter, adults, is the allegation that because they cannot do something, it must be impossible. I am reasonably certain that the young Michael Jordan did not sink his first basket, nor did Tiger Woods ace his first golf shot. Van Cliburn probably muffed a scale or two long before achieving stardom as a concert pianist. In the abstract, we know that hard work and many mistakes, along with an occasional dose of frustration, are part of learning. When the abstract becomes our reality, however, it is much easier to succumb to the logic that the past is prologue, and that what I was unable to do yesterday I cannot do today, nor will I ever be able to do it.

Children do not invent such a negative image of their ability to learn. They are taught this pernicious lesson through the example of many adults, including teachers and parents. Every parent knows that there is a wide gulf between pride in the accomplishment of a difficult task and the anxiety that preceded the first step toward such an achievement. Whether the challenge is the first step of the baby, the first word of the toddler, the first chapter of a book, the first soccer kick, or the first sonata, there is an inevitable sequence that includes challenge, doubt, failure, perseverance, and ultimate success. The chasm from challenge to success is a wide one, but it is not filled merely with obstacles and heartache. This path also includes encouragement, small victories, glimpses of future success, and growing confidence that the goal is worth the effort. When we hear the fear-filled complaint from children, "I can't do this!" our response must be more than superficial encouragement. Rather, we must provide an immediate shift in focus away from the insurmountable goal and toward an immediately achievable objective. In other words, our focus must continually be on what children can do now and our encouragement must be focused on the immediate next step. This establishes a clear incremental process: challenge, self-doubt, encouragement, small steps, and then, the next challenge.

"I Don't Have Any Homework!
Why Should I Have to Do This?" learning

The 20-Minute Learning Connection offers parents an excellent opportunity to make learning part of life rather than mere drudgery confined to the school day. This habit can be developed as a routine, no more onerous than making one's bed or washing the dishes, and no less pleasurable than a short walk around the neighborhood or enjoying a hot cup of tea. Even though there are many other things to be done, parents and children still manage to engage in the ordinary duties and pleasures of everyday life. Learning ought to be one of those simultaneous duties and pleasures.

In order to develop the habit of learning, parents must counter the prevailing notion that the only context in which structured learning should take place is when homework is assigned by the teacher. Indeed, some parents may be skeptical about asking their children to engage in any additional activities because of what they have heard about excessive homework that today's children must endure. The myth of the sixth-grade student with five hours of homework every night should be challenged for what it is: either the result of the most grievous educational malpractice or, far more likely, the result of the fevered imagination of those who are persuaded by rumor rather than evidence. In fact, the far more common problem in many schools is the complete absence of homework, even at the secondary level. Teachers increasingly find that it takes too much time to grade, that students refuse to complete it, and that parents and even administrators fail to support the requirements that teachers place on students. When I hear complaints about excessive homework, including in my own home, I am generally inclined to examine the facts. The "five hours of homework" was, in fact, thirty minutes of homework, plus four and a half hours of phone calls, computer games, television, and other diversions. Even when there is an extensive homework assignment that might have required many hours of work, further investigation reveals that the teacher provided the requirement weeks in advance of the due date, and it was poor planning on the part of the student that caused all of the work to be required in a single sitting. The plain fact is that for the vast majority of middle school students and secondary students, the problem is not too much homework, but the habitual absence of homework that has convinced students that they ought to be liberated from anything resembling learning beyond the confines of the school day.

The skills and knowledge contained in this guide will, in fact, build confidence, speed, and efficiency in the completion of homework. Moreover, these activities offer the opportunity for parents and children to enjoy learning together, whereas the typical homework assignment is something that the teacher expects students to complete independently.

figure it out together

"It Doesn't Make Any Difference What I Do! I Just Don't Get It!"

I wish that I could offer a response to the frustration of a child that would mix the wisdom and certainty that Dr. Spock (the pediatrician and best-selling author, not the alien on *Star Trek*) offered to parents of the 1950s. Readers would recognize and challenge the superficiality of easy answers to challenging problems. In fact, children can become plagued by self-doubt, and their absolute knowledge that "I just don't get it" quickly becomes the ingrained belief that "I just *can't* get it." Here are some ideas to consider when dealing with a child who expresses feelings of inadequacy, self-doubt, and hopelessness.

First, recognize the value of these feelings. When children accurately say, "I don't get it," they are expressing the first step toward understanding. After all, it is far more difficult to convince someone to accept instruction when they think that they have the right answer and are unwilling to admit that they don't know everything. Thus, the parent's response to uncertainty and self-doubt should be clear and unequivocal affirmation. "You're right," the parent can acknowledge. "You don't know it. And you know what? You have to be *really* smart to know that you don't know something! Let's see if we can figure it out together…"

Second, determine what the child knows. For example, if the child is bewildered by the words of an authentic historical document, such as the Declaration of Independence, start with what your child knows. "So you're saying that the words of the Declaration of Independence are pretty strange, right? Well, let's start with what you already know. Why were the colonists angry at the British?" You might hear some answer about taxes or other colonial grievances that have been discussed in class. Then continue, "The Declaration of Independence includes a lot of reasons that the colonists were upset. Let's go through each one of them and put it into your own words."

Third, break the task into incremental steps. Too many textbooks, academic standards, and test requirements involve many different tasks masquerading as a single step. If the student does not recognize that there are many separate tasks, then frustration is inevitable.

For example, consider this typical item from an early middle school math test:

"Herb is a gardener who loves tomatoes. In fact, that is all he plants in his backyard garden. In his side yard he has a 12-square-foot garden with zucchinis and azaleas. In the front yard, he has a pond in the middle of his 32-square-foot flower garden. However, the backyard garden is all tomatoes. His backyard garden is 7 feet wide and 24 inches long. There are 4 tomato plants in each square foot. If each tomato plant has an average of 3 ripe tomatoes, how many tomatoes will Herb harvest?"

Some students might tackle this problem with gusto. In fact, they might do it so quickly that they will include information about the side yard and front yard gardens or forget to convert 24 inches into two feet. Other students will find the sheer quantity of information so overwhelming that they will become bogged down in some of the irrelevant details. An effective method of helping students tackle a multistep problem is the clear identification of each step. A good rule of thumb is this: If you are not sure whether you need to add an extra step, then add it. It is much less risky to have a step that you do not need than to skip a step that you did need.

Here is one approach to breaking this problem down into incremental steps.

First, circle the question—what am I supposed to know? In this case, the question is, "How many tomatoes will Herb harvest?" Whatever I do, I know that the final answer is not about feet or inches, it is about the number of tomatoes that Herb will harvest.

Second, make all the units the same. The garden is "7 feet wide and 24 inches long." To make these the same units, I need to know that there are 12 inches in one foot, and that 24 inches is the same as 2 feet. Third, draw a picture. Why? Because pictures are easier to understand than words. On some tests, students are required to draw a diagram for math problems. However, even when such a drawing is not required, it is a great idea to convert words into pictures because it makes the problem easier to understand. My picture might look like this:

24 inches (2 feet) ↕   7 feet x 2 feet = 14 square feet

7 feet

Fourth, write the problem in words. It might look something like this: "The number of tomatoes that Herb will harvest is equal to the number of tomatoes on one plant (3) times the number of tomato plants in one square foot of his garden (4) times the number of square feet in his garden (14)." Some tests require that students explain their answer in writing. However, even if it is a multiple-choice test and no one but the student will see the diagram and sentences, it is an excellent idea to write out the sentences that explain the answer. Fifth, put numbers with the words of the sentence. "The number of tomatoes that Herb will harvest is equal to 3 tomatoes per plant times 4 tomato plants per square foot times 14 square feet, or 168 tomatoes." Sixth, go back to the question in step one. Ask yourself, "Have I answered the question?"

This may seem to be a laborious process for a relatively simple math question. On the contrary, the easiest way to tackle this or any other math problem is to break it down into simple steps. Some of these steps will be the same on every single math problem, from fifth grade math through graduate school statistics. For example, the first step is always, "Circle the question—what am I supposed to know?" The last step is always, "Go back to the question in step one—have I answered the question?" This process is essential for a student to move beyond calculation into real mathematical problem solving. There are many students who know the times tables and math facts, but who cannot solve the problem of Herb's tomatoes. They do not read the problem carefully, they include irrelevant data, or they provide elaborate answers in square feet when the question is asking about the number of tomatoes that Herb will harvest.

This problem illustrates an important component of the 20-Minute Learning Connection. In this illustration, the parent was not imperiously demanding, "Don't you get it? It's 168 tomatoes!" Rather, the parent was breaking down a complex problem into steps and the child proceeded systematically through the problem.

"Everything Is Okay. Just Leave Me Alone!"

Self-reliance is a wonderful thing. A few school children still read Emerson's essay on the subject and are enjoined to revel in the independence of spirit enjoyed by that rare individual who is dependent on no other person. As a student and as a parent, I have experienced both sides of the tension that result when a parent wishes to be helpful and the child prefers to assert independence. It is at this point that the normal stress of homework can explode into a tearful confrontation. Thus, the parental response to "Just leave me alone" must be careful and measured.

Start with a positive statement. "You must be very confident to want to do this yourself without any help. I am proud of you. Please show it to me when you are done." This is not a request; it is a requirement. If the Emersonian spirit is alive and well, your self-reliant student will submit flawless work that will elicit unrestrained praise. When that daydream is interrupted, however, it is far more likely that "Just leave me alone" was a way of saying, "I don't know how to do this, but I really don't want you to think that I'm stupid. If you would just stay away, then I won't know it, but at least you won't know that I don't know it."

This is a delicate point in a conversation with any child. Whether your child is in second grade (my youngest) or twelfth grade (my oldest), the need for independence is strong. There is a world of difference between the parent who in exasperation demands, "Let me show you how to do it right," and the parent who says gently but firmly, "I'm really proud of your independence. Please show it to me when you are done." Your time is limited. Invest it wisely. If the child's confidence is appropriate, then parental support for that confidence should follow. If the child needs help but will not admit it, then no humiliation is required. The certain knowledge that a loving and supportive parent will look at the final work product will lead to a request for help. For the strong-willed, independent child, the response to a request for help is far better than imposed assistance.

a positive beginning

Daily Checklist for School Success

Whether you have one child or six, checklists are helpful ways to transform the chaos of the morning into a positive beginning to the school day. While every family has its own rituals and requirements for the start of the day, here are some items you may want to include in a visible checklist for daily review by children and parents:

❑ **Assignment notebook complete.**

If not, call a friend, call the "homework hotline" if your school has one, or call the teacher at home. If it is not written down in the assignment notebook, it will not happen.

❑ **Backpack empty and repacked.**

Archaeologists of the future will find some student backpacks and be unable, in at least a few cases, to differentiate them from time capsules. The accumulation of literature, culture, and food represent the accumulation of epochs of civilization. Let your child find a better way to be famous than in the diorama of a natural history museum of future centuries. Empty the backpack completely every night and repack it, with a place for everything and everything in its place.

❑ **Projects, tests, and other important dates on the family calendar.**

There are few more discouraging moments than finding "important" notes squashed in the residue of the bottom of a backpack that involve dates that have already passed. There should be a single large family calendar that has everything from the volunteer activities and business trips of parents to the school activities, project due dates, and tests of children. Without such a combined calendar, conflicts are inevitable.

❑ **Homework checked.**

This does not mean homework done by the parent, nor does it imply homework completed at all. It means that the parent knows what has and has not been done. The child knows that accountability begins at home and that the requirements of the parents are at least as stringent as those imposed at school.

❑ **Long-term projects reviewed.**

The myth of "five hours of homework" is frequently revealed as the month-long project that has been concealed and postponed until the night before it is due. The requirement of fifteen minutes a night for twenty nights thus became five hours in a single night, with the teacher portrayed as the architect of student misery. While it is important that parents ask about projects due "tomorrow," it is equally important that future projects and tests become the subject of daily conversation.

The "Refrigerator Curriculum"

Ray Simon and Janine Riggs are leaders in one of the most remarkable stories of educational progress in the nation. Their "Smart Start" initiative in Arkansas focused on literacy and math and created nationally recognized progress among students of every economic and ethnic group in the state. Their methods were hardly revolutionary. They set high standards and clear expectations for every child. They also had the wisdom to know that parents were essential contributors to student success. One of their most successful innovations was the "Refrigerator Curriculum," so named because it was designed to be affixed next to student work proudly displayed on the refrigerator door. This document expressed on a single page the essential knowledge and skills that students needed for each grade level. Unless you have a large refrigerator, you will not have enough space to display every state standard. Nevertheless, you can identify the most important skills that your child must acquire, and reminders of those essentials should roughly correspond to the frequency with which you open the refrigerator door.

If your child's school does not offer a refrigerator curriculum, then consider creating one. The plain fact is that every standard and academic requirement is not of equal value. Determine those that are most important and reinforce them frequently. Ask your child's teachers and school administrators this simple question: "If I can't do everything that you'd like me to do at the end of the day, what are the most important things for my child to know and be able to do in order to be successful in the next grade?" When the question is phrased in this way, the response should be brief. It will not include a laundry list full of scores of standards. Rather, the list will include some academic requirements, a focus on literacy, and an emphasis on appropriate behavior, time management, and organizational skills. These are worthy of a place on your refrigerator door.

Conclusion

Advice about how to raise the perfectly behaved and flawlessly educated child can be overwhelming, unreasonable, and silly. There is simply too much to do and not enough time to do it all. One of the central themes of this book is that even on the typical day when perfection is elusive and you cannot "do it all," there are nevertheless important and constructive things you can do in order to make a positive difference for your child. As this chapter suggests, not every conversation is easy, nor is every offer of parental support welcomed by a child. Nevertheless, in 20 minutes you can update the calendar, check the backpack, help break a complicated problem down into small steps, provide some encouragement, and maybe even share a laugh. In other words, even on the busiest day, you can make a difference.

make a positive difference

Chapter 8

Standards and Tests in Massachusetts

Putting It All Together: Standards, Tests, and Accountability

"Standards, Tests, and Accountability"—the very words have the rhythm of "Lions, Tigers, and Bears" from Dorothy's scary walk along the Yellow Brick Road. That which is unknown and mysterious is, to both students and adults, the source of fear and anxiety. This chapter will demystify the Massachusetts Comprehensive Assessment System exams, known as the MCAS. While the tests are not easy, the more students know what to expect, the less fearful they will be. It is important to note that this chapter is not a definitive guide to the content and format of the MCAS. You should expect to see periodic changes in testing policy on everything from the standards addressed to the grades tested. What this chapter does offer is sound advice for helping your student succeed on any state test. Even if the format and content change, your student will learn sound test taking principles and the importance of reading comprehension and written analysis as the keys to test success in every subject. For the latest information about the content and format of the Massachusetts middle school tests, visit the Massachusetts Department of Education website at www.doe.mass.edu/mcas.

Is Test Preparation Unethical?

There is an important difference between mindless test drills and the teaching of a curriculum that is thoughtfully linked to the assessments that students must take. Although the phrase "teaching to the test" is often used critically by those who oppose any sort of testing, consider the alternative. If teachers did not link their curriculum to state assessments, then students would be set up for failure, with every test a mystery and every question a surprise. Inevitably, anger, frustration, fear, and anxiety would stem from the failure of schools to link their instruction to the requirements placed on students during tests.

Parents are rightfully concerned when they hear rumors that a thoughtful and rigorous academic environment has been transformed into a boot camp for test preparation. I personally have investigated many such claims, including the complaint that "all students do all day is prepare for the state tests." Each time I hear such a statement, I make a point of asking for more detail. "Tell me," I inquire, "about the schedule of the most test-obsessed teacher in the entire school. How much time every day is spent on test preparation? For how many weeks does such a regimen last?" The most recent inquiry resulted in the admission that the "test-obsessed" teacher devoted one hour a day for three weeks to test preparation. That is fifteen hours out of 1,080 instructional hours (180 school days times 6 hours a day), or about 1.4 percent of the time in school. That is not, by anyone's standards, an inappropriate obsession with test preparation. My typical recommendation to educators is that they devote about twenty minutes a week to the "life skill" of test taking. We teach students many life skills, including pedestrian and bicycle safety, avoidance of alcohol, tobacco, and drugs, and a variety of skills that extend beyond the academic curriculum of school. Test taking is also a skill that students use throughout their lives. Twenty minutes a week—about 12 hours a year—is hardly transforming American schools from an academic paradise into a test preparation boot camp.

Finally, let us consider the ethical issue itself. Even at twenty minutes a week, does test preparation cross an ethical boundary? Certainly, it would be unethical if a teacher were to procure questions from the state test, copy them, and encourage students to memorize the answers. Such behavior can result in felony convictions and jail time for teachers and administrators in some states. No thoughtful person recommends such behavior. It is, however, entirely fair and reasonable for teachers and school administrators to say, "This test will require reading and, more specifically, will require students to write a summary of the stories and nonfiction passages that they read. This is not only a test requirement, but also the requirement for any well-educated student. We would do this even if there were no state test. Therefore, every day when students read a passage in their textbook or read a story, we will require students to write a brief summary of what they have read."

This is good educational practice, not unethical "teaching to the test." The same is true of requirements for students to write, know their geography, or understand mathematics. It is good education, not any sort of ethical breach. In fact, the real ethical challenge is presented by teachers who refuse to give students the information they need to be successful on tests and in the next grade. Some teachers refuse to acknowledge the value of aligning their curriculum with the skills and knowledge students need to succeed on tests. These teachers are committing an ethical violation as serious as the driver education teacher who sends students to take a driving test without an understanding of stop signs or the operation of the brake pedal.

What Students Need to Know for the Tests

The most important clarification with regard to standards and testing is this: Students do not have to be proficient on every single standard to be successful on the MCAS tests. Although the Massachusetts Curriculum Frameworks provide excellent guidelines for teachers and parents, it is impossible for any test to address every standard for each grade level. Therefore, the MCAS tests cover only a small part of the school curriculum, with a particular emphasis on reading, writing, mathematics, and science. So if someone were to ask, "What does a student need to know and be able to do to be successful on the MCAS exams?" the answer would be, "By the sixth grade, the student must be a proficient reader and writer and should master the skills of mathematical computation and problem-solving. By the seventh grade, the student must be able to read independently both fiction and nonfiction literature, and must be able to write persuasive, expository, and narrative essays. By the eighth grade, the student must have mastered the previously mentioned skills in reading, writing, and mathematics, and also must be familiar with the content knowledge—the facts—of science, technology, history, and social science."

While the labels of these subjects can sound intimidating, it is essential that middle school teachers and students focus their attention appropriately Without literacy and mathematics, the pursuit of science, technology, history, and social science is futile. Every test, regardless of its label, is essentially a test of reading. In Massachusetts, the skill of writing is absolutely essential. If a student is to succeed on the eighth-grade tests in science and social science, then the sixth- and seventh-grade curriculum must provide a mastery of reading, writing, and mathematics. Make no mistake about it: if parents and teachers must choose among these skills because the subjects of history, social science, and science and technology/engineering seem too broad, then the clear choice is to emphasize literacy skills.

There are six tests of concern to middle school students in Massachusetts: Grade 7 English Language Arts, Grade 8 English Language Arts, Grade 6 Mathematics, Grade 8 Mathematics, Grade 8 Science and Technology/Engineering, and Grade 8 History and Social Science.

On the Grade 7 English Language Arts exam, students must complete approximately thirty-six multiple-choice items, four questions requiring short written responses, and one longer written essay. The essay requires students to inform the reader, by conveying messages, instructions, and ideas. Students have the opportunity to create an outline and first draft prior to completing the final draft of the essay. It is, therefore, absolutely imperative that teachers and students practice the entire writing process, proceeding from an idea to an outline to a draft to final copy.

The Reading section of the Grade 7 English Language Arts exam requires students to encounter many different types of literature and nonfiction passages. Students are not permitted to use dictionaries, thesauruses, encyclopedias, or any other reference materials. The only exception to this rule is that some students who are learning English as a second language may use particular types of dictionaries allowed by the test administrator. The types of reading that students may encounter include the following: short stories, novel excerpts, poetry, plays, myths, legends, fables, biographies, autobiographies, essays, speeches, editorials, interviews, letters, diary entries, newspaper articles, reviews, instructions, and advertisements. Because this list is so extensive, it makes sense for teachers in the sixth and seventh grades to divide the labor, with social science teachers taking responsibility for speeches, editorials, and newspaper articles, while their counterparts in technology take responsibility for instructions and advertisements. This will allow teachers in English language arts to focus on fewer types of reading passages.

For the Grade 8 English Language Arts exam, students must complete approximately thirty-six multiple-choice items, four questions requiring short written responses, and one longer written essay. The essay requires students to write persuasively, using evidence and argument to convince the reader to accept the writer's point of view. Students have the opportunity to create an outline and first draft prior to completing the final draft of the essay. As with the Grade 7 English Language Arts exam, teachers and students should prepare by practicing the entire writing process, from idea to outline to draft to final copy

The Reading section of the Grade 8 English Language Arts exam requires students to consider much of the literature that is listed in the Massachusetts Curriculum Frameworks. When classroom time is limited, teachers should give priority to the novels, stories, poems, and other literature in the state curriculum so that students are not surprised by the content of the test. Of course, students also must be able to respond to unfamiliar literature. Therefore, it is an excellent idea for students to periodically read a story, chapter, poem, or article and then summarize it and compare it to other literature.

On the Grade 6 Mathematics exam, students must respond to multiple-choice and open-response questions, with a particular emphasis on the following areas: number sense and operations (addition, subtraction, multiplication, and division); patterns, relations, and algebra (the use of symbols and numbers together); geometry and measurement (including English and metric units of measurement); data analysis, statistics, and probability (including the use of tables, charts, and graphs). Calculator use is not allowed on the Grade 6 Mathematics exam. The state website provided in the first section of this chapter provides sample items for the sixth-grade test.

One of the most important skills students need for the Mathematics exam is the ability to represent the same idea in different ways. For example, students should be able to take a math problem that is presented in a story problem and draw an accurate picture of it. They also should be able to take a problem represented as an equation and put it into words. Because the test includes the requirement that students explain their answers, teachers and parents should encourage students to write about mathematics, including the explanations of their answers to test questions and, of equal importance, the reasons that the students have rejected wrong answers on test questions.

The Grade 8 Mathematics exam includes multiple-choice items and questions that require a written response. Students can use a calculator on part of the exam, but one section requires students to complete calculations without a calculator. Therefore, it is essential that eighth-grade students have the ability to do "mental math" and that they can multiply, divide, add, and subtract without being dependent upon a calculator. The test includes number sense and operations; patterns, relations, and algebra; geometry and measurement; and data analysis, statistics, and probability. The state website, referred to in the first section of this chapter, provides sample items for the eighth-grade test.

The Grade 8 Science and Technology/Engineering exam includes three forty-five-minute sections. Calculators are not permitted during the test. The test includes multiple-choice items and questions requiring short written responses. The most important skills that students must possess to succeed on this exam are reading and reasoning. By "reading" I do not mean that students read aloud well. Rather, students must be able to read the results of a scientific observation and draw conclusions from it. In addition, students must be able to look at a table of information, a chart, or a graph, and express in writing the conclusions that can be drawn from the data. Thus, the Science and Technology/Engineering exam is above all a test of reading, reasoning, and writing. This is good news for many science teachers, because they know that scientists must not only know the facts of science, but also must be able to encounter unfamiliar information and analyze it, interpret it, and explain it. Parents should expect their children to regularly engage in reading, writing, interpretation, and explanation in science and technology classes.

For the Grade 8 History and Social Science exam, students must respond to about forty multiple-choice items and six essay questions. The topics covered on the test include United States and world history, geography, economics, government, and civics. Two-thirds of the items on the test address U.S. history from the American Revolution through the end of the Civil War. Because the total range of knowledge involved in the History and Social Science test is so vast, teachers and school leaders must make some priority decisions. The most important skills for this examination are reading and writing. Students also should be able to create a rough timeline, placing historical events in proper sequence from ancient civilizations through the end of the nineteenth century. Students also should be familiar with the alternative forms of government, including democracy, monarchy, and dictatorship.

Writing: The Best Way to Build Thinking Skills

One of the best ways that parents can help students gain essential knowledge and prepare for the MCAS tests is to require students to read for at least 20 minutes, write a summary of what they have read, and then edit and correct their summary. The skills they gain will prepare them for the English language arts portion of the tests and for success throughout the school years ahead of them. While reading is important, the creation of a written summary, along with the editing and revision of that summary, provides one of the best ways to build the skills of thinking, comprehension, analysis, synthesis, understanding, and communication. Students may not think that they have time to create a brief outline of what they are going to write. However, they will find that the creation of a brief outline will save time and improve organization.

Student writing is required on every element of the Massachusetts examinations. Whether the subject is reading, mathematics, history and social science, or science and technology/engineering, students must write clearly and coherently. Of all the skills acquired in middle school, the one with the greatest weight on the state test is, by pleasant coincidence, the skill with the greatest impact on student success in high school and college: nonfiction writing. If parents and teachers feel overwhelmed with too much academic content and wonder where they should focus their energies, the development of writing, editing, and rewriting skills should be at the top of the list.

It is important that parents understand that the term "writing" can be applied to many different activities, and some are more helpful to students than others. While journal and story writing may be entertaining, these activities are not as useful as writing that requires students to hone summarization, analytical, descriptive, and explanatory skills.

Writing Activities to Build Thinking Skills

- **Summarization:** Listen to a parent read a story or an article. While the story is being read, make a few notes about the events, characters, and setting. Write a brief summary of that story.

- **Comparison and Analysis:** Listen to a parent read two related but different stories. Make a list of what is similar and what is different between the two stories. Then write three paragraphs. The first paragraph contains a brief introduction, followed by a statement of how the two stories are similar. The second paragraph contains statements describing how the two stories are different. The third paragraph draws conclusions about the stories and makes an evaluation about which one the student prefers.

- **Description:** Look at an object, animal, or activity for five minutes. Write down what you notice, using as many senses as you can. Then write a paragraph describing the object, animal, or activity in as much detail as possible.

- **Explanation:** Look at a process—perhaps a math problem or a scientific procedure. Explain in writing how to solve the math problem or how the scientific procedure works.

Some readers may wonder about such an emphasis on writing. Aren't the majority of questions on the test are in multiple-choice format? Student skill in writing, however, not only improves performance on the open response and short answer questions, but also helps on the multiple-choice questions. There is unambiguous proof that a greater emphasis on nonfiction writing builds the thinking, analytical, and reading skills of students. These skills, in turn, are associated with improvements on multiple-choice test scores. Finally, writing is a complex skill that improves only with consistent effort and reinforcement. Because writing takes on even greater importance in secondary school and college, middle school educators and parents are well advised to place an exceptional emphasis on writing.

Math Basics

The Mathematics skills questions on the MCAS require students to read questions (this is very important: the "math" test is, in fact, very much a test of reading ability as well), understand what the question is asking, solve simple number operations (addition, subtraction, multiplication, and division), and find the "next step" in solving mathematical problems. Make no mistake: math facts are important. Just as was the case when you were in school, students must know addition and subtraction facts from second grade on, and multiplication and division from third grade on. If your child is in a later grade and was told that, in the age of calculators and computers, math facts are not really important, then it is not too late to break out the flash cards and correct this omission in his or her education. If your child has a teacher who believes that learning the "times tables" and other drudgery is unimportant, then you need to seriously consider changing teachers. There are many areas in education about which reasonable people may differ, but this is not one of them. While the logical and analytical skills involved in mathematical problem-solving are important, they are not a replacement for understanding and knowing—and yes, that means memorizing—the facts of addition, subtraction, multiplication, and division.

Test Format and Test Preparation

The majority of test questions are multiple-choice in format. This means that students can choose an answer from among four or five possible responses provided on the test. The multiple-choice format has an important implication for students, teachers, and parents:

It is not only important to know the right answers to test questions, but also to find the wrong answers and eliminate them.

Although this may seem obvious to parents who have experience in taking multiple-choice tests, the implications for students are profound. This means that test taking need not be a game of mere memorization in which students conclude, "Either I know it or I don't, and if I don't, then I might as well give up." Rather, this focus on knowing both the right and the wrong answer gives students multiple opportunities to be successful on the test. It also gives students an incentive to persevere on a problem even if the right answer is not obvious to them. Most importantly, this insight gives teachers and parents the ability to move far beyond traditional practice tests and enhance the thinking and reasoning skills of students.

Consider this sample question:

Tamika and her family are making a round trip by car between New York and San Francisco. The distance between the cities is 2,921 miles. Her brother says that they should take the station wagon, but Tamika is concerned about the cost of gasoline and suggests the family take a smaller car instead. The station wagon consumes about one gallon of gas for each 18 miles traveled, while the smaller car consumes about one gallon of gas for each 25 miles traveled. If gas prices are $1.92 per gallon, how much money will the use of the smaller car save?

A) Cannot be determined from the information given

B) 7 miles per gallon

C) $174.48

D) $1,744.80

This could be a very time-consuming problem if each individual step is calculated. Let's use two different methods to solve this problem. First, let's solve the problem the slow way: Always start with the question: "How much money will the use of the smaller car save?" That tells us right away that the answer must be an amount of money—not miles, miles per gallon, or any of the other sorts of numbers provided in the problem. First, we need to know the total miles traveled. The total round trip distance is twice the one-way distance, or 2 x 2,921, or 5,842 miles. Next, we need to figure out the amount of gas each of the two cars would consume. With the station wagon traveling 18 miles on one gallon of gas, we can divide 5,842 total miles by 18 miles per gallon, with a result of 324.56 gallons consumed. With the smaller car traveling 25 miles on one gallon of gas, we can divide 5,842 total miles by 25 miles per gallon, with a result of 233.68 gallons of gas consumed. The difference in gasoline consumed is 233.68 subtracted from 324.56, or a difference of 90.88 gallons saved. With gasoline costing $1.92

per gallon, we then multiply $1.92 times 90.88, and determine that the smaller car would have saved a total of $174.48. That was a lot of work! There must be a faster and easier way to deal with this sort of multi-step problem.

Consider a different approach. Again, start with the question: "How much money do we save?" Let's estimate the round trip distance to be about 6,000 miles—3,000 miles each way. The smaller car gets 25 miles to the gallon, so for each 1,000 miles it travels, it uses 50 gallons of gas. Over a 6,000-mile trip, the smaller car will use about 300 gallons of gas. Gas costs about $2 per gallon, so the cost of gas for the smaller car is about $600. The larger car gets 18 miles to the gallon, or about a third less than the station wagon. Let's estimate that we'll save about $\frac{1}{3}$ of $600, or $200. Before spending any time on more calculations, let's see if the $200 estimate allows us to quickly answer this question and move on. In reviewing the choices, it's clear: the test writer is trying to catch students who read the question wrong with the choice of B: we're not looking for miles saved, but for money saved. Choice D will catch students who misplaced a decimal—something that is very easy to do when you are performing a lot of manual calculations. That leaves C as the clear choice—$200 is close enough to $174.48 so select that answer, save several minutes on the test, and move on to the next question.

The problem-solving section of math and science tests is challenging for many students, so it is a good idea to practice both ways—the slow way and the fast way—so that students build confidence both in calculation and in estimation. On the test, however, estimation can save a lot of time and avoid mistakes that frequently occur in a series of many different calculations. It is also important to know that, from an educational point of view, this sort of practice is not the "mindless test prep" that critics of standards and testing so frequently assail. In fact, this approach to the practice problem improves students' reasoning, reading, estimation, and problem solving—all skills that are essential even if state tests were eliminated tomorrow Moreover, the habit of moving from the search for the right answer to the elimination of wrong answers builds a student's power of logic and reasoning, helping to improve success on tests for many years to come.

When parents and teachers analyze multiple-choice problems in this way, they are moving far beyond the low-level test preparation that critics of standards and testing have so frequently criticized toward the thinking skills that students need. It is fair to ask this question: If all tests were eliminated tomorrow, would my student still need to think, read, write, and compute? If you answered in the affirmative, then these exercises are not merely a matter of preparation for tests, but preparation for life.

Student Writing

The MCAS exams include questions requiring short and long written responses. The long responses require students to develop skill in organization and planning to gain the maximum score. Students typically will have plenty of time to create an outline, write a rough draft, and then produce a final copy. Students who immediately start writing in response to the question frequently submit an essay that is poorly organized. One of the most important skills that you can instill in your child is the habit of rewriting. Students never should presume that their first written product is their last. Most editors would argue that this is a good rule for authors of any age. By focusing on the habit of rewriting, parents provide both an intellectual and an emotional advantage for their children. Successful writers must not only write, but also rewrite and after thought, reflection, and feedback, rewrite yet again. This intellectual attribute is directly related to the emotional trait of persistence. Students will not have the ability to rewrite unless they have the emotional strength to persist in the face of difficulty and challenge. One of the most important gifts any parent can give to a child is the habit of persistence, resilience, and rising once again to a challenge. In simple terms, rewriting is an emotional and intellectual gift to students, and it is as important as the initial gifts of reading and writing that were bestowed by parents in the earliest days of literary exploration.

Does Every Student Have to Take the Test?

Massachusetts laws and administrative regulations place a heavy emphasis on the inclusion of all students in testing. Students with Limited English Proficiency (LEP) who have been enrolled in school in the United States for more than three years, and are attending regular classes, must take the MCAS exams in English in all subject areas. LEP students enrolled in schools in the continental United States for three or fewer years must participate in the Spanish/English Mathematics, Science and Technology/Engineering, and History and Social Science exams if they can read and write near grade level in Spanish, and if they will continue to receive instruction in either a Transitional Bilingual Education Program, or English as a Second Language support, in the following school year. The vast majority of students must take the tests prescribed by the state. The clear intent of both the law and the commissioner's statements is to have maximum participation. Students with disabilities must take the assessment with appropriate accommodations and adaptations unless their Individualized Education Plan (IEP) specifies in writing that the student must be excluded from testing. Even in those cases, the IEP must provide for other means of assessing student progress.

What If Parents Object to the Tests?

Because of the clear emphasis on 100 percent participation in the state testing program, some parents may be legitimately concerned that their children are being subjected to inappropriate testing. Because of the complexity of federal laws guaranteeing the rights of individual students to appropriate testing, and the Massachusetts statutes that require 100 percent participation, parents must serve as advocates for their children in those cases where testing may not be appropriate. In general, every student, including the profoundly disabled and most students with limited English proficiency, will be assessed. The vast majority of those students will be assessed using the English Language test forms, although teachers are required to provide reasonable accommodations to students with specifically diagnosed learning disabilities. Only in the most rare cases can students be excluded from state testing, and even in those cases, it is the responsibility of the school to administer an appropriate alternative assessment.

What About the Other Tests in School?

Although the state-mandated standardized tests receive the lion's share of the publicity about testing in school, there are other tests that students routinely take that can have very significant consequences for future educational opportunities. Some of these tests include so-called I.Q. (Intelligence Quotient) Tests and Aptitude Tests. These tests frequently are used to determine the eligibility of a student for "gifted and talented" programs or for participation in special education programs. Educational assessment experts have strong differences of opinion on what these tests mean. One leading national testing company explains "aptitude" as follows:

> A combination of characteristics, whether native or acquired, that is indicative of an individual's ability to learn or to develop proficiency in some particular area if appropriate education or training is provided. Aptitude tests include those of general academic (scholastic) ability; those of special abilities such as verbal, numerical, mechanical, or musical; tests assessing 'readiness' for learning; and tests that measure both ability and previous learning, and are used to predict future performance—usually in a specific field, such as foreign language, shorthand, or nursing. (Harcourt Educational Measurement website, www.hemweb.com/library/glossary)

Some scholars question the very existence of aptitude as a consistent quality in young students, arguing that interest, environment, and early education are all variables that change rapidly in the life of a young student. Moreover, the announcement of such a quality as aptitude can become a self-fulfilling prophecy. There are large numbers of students who have been told that they lack an aptitude in math and science based on a test at an early age. This test result discouraged these students and their parents from the pursuit of the more advanced—and potentially more interesting—science and math courses. Not surprisingly, the "predictions" appeared to be accurate, as these students did not perform well in high school and college on science and math tests. Consider the case of a student who is told, "You're going to be fat, so there is no reason for you to even consider diet, exercise, or a healthy lifestyle." When that student becomes an obese and unhealthy adolescent and adult, do we blame the student or would we question the wisdom of the prediction that, not surprisingly, came to fruition?

There is a cautionary tale from comic genius Matt Groening, the creator of the television series, *The Simpsons*. In one episode of the show, Bart, the ne'er do well son of Homer and Marge, is accidentally identified as "gifted" when his test paper is switched with that of another student. As Bart exhibits the same behavior that had been routinely ridiculed and berated by teachers and school administrators, he is now applauded for his wise insights and extraordinary "gifts." The test had miraculous powers of prediction, though not in the way that its creators had intended. In this cartoon, as in real life, tests do a much better job of predicting the actions of the adults to read and believe the results than they do of predicting the success and failure of the students who take the tests.

Just as the term "aptitude" has been subject to debate among researchers, so also the term "intelligence" has been the subject of considerable controversy. Although the notion of measurable intelligence was regarded as a scientific fact in the early twentieth century, researchers in the last two decades have cast considerable doubt on the notion of general intelligence. These complex controversies have filled volumes. For the purposes of this book, suffice it to say that a few things are fairly clear. First, the younger a student is, the more variable the scores on intelligence tests tend to be. Therefore, it is wise for parents to avoid reading too much into the results. Tuesday's gifted student may, with a little more fatigue and distractions, become Wednesday's student in need of special intervention. The same student, in turn, becomes Thursday's student who is destined for a career in music because of the chance hearing of an engaging song on the radio and replicating the music and rhythm pattern on the way to the office of the school psychologist.

These observations do not indict all tests administered to all students, but only indicate the obvious: the smaller the number of measurements, the greater the opportunity for error. No adult would submit to a life-changing decision based on a single test. If the physician prescribed surgery after a single blood pressure reading, we would demand more tests. We should be no less insistent on additional measurement when someone makes life-changing decisions that affect our children.

Questions for Teachers and School Leaders

The tests in Massachusetts have consequences, both intended and otherwise, for students and parents. The most draconian consequence is the possibility of forcing a student to repeat a grade in school due to failure to pass a test. While there are many areas of educational research that yield ambiguous results, the issue of student retention is not one of them. In a tiny fraction of cases, such as those where a student started school at an inappropriately early age or where overly aggressive parents insisted on skipping the first or second grade, the requirement for a student to repeat a grade may be appropriate. In the vast majority of cases, however, the repetition of a grade is a classic example of the faulty logic demonstrated by repeating the same activity and expecting different results. It simply doesn't work. If the student has a reading deficiency, then the appropriate intervention is intensive and immediate reading instruction, not another year in which reading constitutes only sixty minutes a day of the curriculum. Because retention has such negative consequences for the students retained and, ultimately, for all students in the classroom, it is important that parents ensure that their children take the tests seriously, are well prepared, and perform well on them. Because the consequences of inadequate preparation are so serious, it is appropriate and fair for parents to ask these questions:

■ **How is the curriculum in my child's class related to the MCAS tests?**

■ **What opportunities will my child have to become familiar with the requirements of the MCAS tests?**

■ **If my child is not making adequate progress toward preparation for the MCAS tests, when and how will this be communicated to parents?**

■ **What intervention plan does the school have for students who are having difficulty so that they receive this intervention long before the MCAS tests are administered?**

■ **Do the teachers and administrators in the school believe that these tests are important?**

While most parents have observed the obnoxious behavior of the Little League Dads, and their academic counterparts who are incessantly berating teachers and students about their performance, these questions are neither inappropriate nor intrusive. The unfortunate fact is that parents cannot assume that teachers know or care about tests. There is a backlash against testing in some areas of Massachusetts, and many teachers and school administrators continue to regard the classroom curriculum to be the exclusive domain of the teacher. Thanksgiving plays, Halloween parties, and scores of hours devoted to dioramas, crafts, and coloring all have hallowed traditions and have been supported by generations of teachers, students and, indeed, parents. But none of these is more important than learning to read.

While the primacy of reading, writing, and mathematics may be obvious to some readers, a backlash to the standards movement has resulted in a growing number of places where an emphasis on academic excellence is regarded as politically incorrect. Even well-meaning parents have jumped on the bandwagon, opposing standards and testing, and decrying the increased emphasis on academics in the classroom. One wonders if the same parents would protest against the physicians who delivered the bad news that kids could benefit from cutting back on the corn chips, soda, and Twinkies. If those, too, were fixtures in classrooms for generations, a reduction in them might cause frowns and protests from students. Presumably, if the matter at hand were the health of our children, we would endure the whining about a reduction in junk food. There is no doubt about this point: Success in school, including proficiency in reading, writing, and mathematics, is a health issue. Students who are forced to repeat a grade are at substantially greater risk for dropping out of school later in life, and students who drop out of school exhibit a broad range of high-risk behaviors that threaten their very lives.

Test Preparation Without Test Anxiety: The Delicate Balance

The challenge for parents and teachers is the manner in which we convey this complex message to students. We want them to understand that the tests are important and we want them to be willing to work hard to learn in school. We also want them to have fun, enjoy school, love learning, and most importantly, deal with the inevitable stress and anxiety that occur in school without becoming paralyzed by negative emotions. While the perfect balance may be elusive, we certainly know what does not work. Telling children that "It's no big deal" or "You're wonderful and you really don't need that stuff" may be comforting in the short term, but it lays a foundation of academic quicksand for students. False reassurances now lead to failure, stress, and anxiety later. By contrast, gentle but firm challenges now are necessary for the reduction of anxiety in the months to come. Many of these gentle but firm challenges occur in school under the guiding hand of a devoted, caring, and knowledgeable teacher. The vast majority of such challenges, however, must come from home where daily routines, including the 20-Minute Learning Connection, will give students confidence, skills, perseverance, and ultimately, success.

Chapter 9

Children with Special Needs

Your Rights As a Parent

I choose my words carefully here: The rights of people with disabilities are civil rights. The last century will be marked in history not only for technological advances, world wars, and economic booms and busts, but for the battle fought and won on behalf of the disadvantaged. If you are the parent of a child with special needs, whether the child is blind, hearing-impaired, cognitively disabled, or suffers from any other disability, then school officials are not doing you a favor when they provide accommodations for your child any more than your local officials do you a favor when they allow you to vote. Meeting the needs of persons with disabilities is a civic responsibility. Having those needs met is a right, not a privilege.

If you are already confident in the accuracy of the diagnosis of your child's needs, then you may wish to proceed directly to the end of this chapter and find more detailed information on organizations that are specifically oriented to the needs of your child. If, however, you do not know if your child has a learning disability or other special need, then this chapter may offer some ideas for you to consider as you enter this very complex and challenging area of education.

In the context of standards and testing, the discussions surrounding special needs students frequently have been polarized. At one extreme are those who stereotype every special needs student as cognitively unable to meet academic standards, and thus every effort is made to exclude these students from testing. At the other extreme are those who recognize no impairment that would interfere with testing and insist on including every child in testing. In reality, the essence of the legislation at all levels regarding children with special needs is designed to protect the *individual* needs of the child. This chapter, therefore, cannot provide guidance about all children except in the most general sense. Every sentence that follows must be interpreted through the parental lens that is best able to focus on the individual needs of your child. Whether your child is included or excluded from special education, whether your child meets academic standards with or without accommodations, and whether your child participates in regular state examinations or alternative examinations that are more appropriate, is not a matter of blind bureaucratic policy, but rather an individual decision made based on the individual needs of your child.

What Are Special Needs Anyway, and How Do I Know If My Child Has Them?

Some special needs are obvious. Children with profound physical, neurological, or developmental challenges clearly need additional assistance in order to deal with the challenges of daily life, including the challenges of a school environment. Other children may be unsuccessful in school, and yet there is no clear developmental or physical disability. How then can you tell if your child needs the additional assistance that is legally guaranteed? Parents must separate the normal challenges of daily life from the challenges faced by students with developmental impairments. As the complexity of pediatric neurology grows, the field is understandably intimidating for any parent. One thing is clear: Your child will never have any advocate that is more knowledgeable and caring about the individual needs of that child than a parent. Your lack of a professional credential must not limit you from playing an active role as the primary advocate for your child. In this respect, it is important for you to advocate accuracy. You are not an advocate either on behalf of participation in special education programs nor exclusion from them, but rather you are an advocate on behalf of accurate, complete, and meaningful diagnoses of your child's needs.

independent evaluation

The Limits of "Field Diagnosis"

The field of special education includes professionals who are gifted educators and diagnosticians. When your child is entrusted to this select group of educators, psychologists, and medical professionals, their wealth of experience and personal attention to each child, as well as their expert administration of a wide battery of tests and other diagnostic assessments, will provide a high probability that the diagnosis of your child's learning disability—or the absence of any disability at all—is accurate. Unfortunately, schools across the nation are governed by resource constraints, where one school psychologist may be assigned to serve the needs of more than a thousand students. Specialists in the diagnosis of learning disabilities are overwhelmed with the immediate needs of students whose needs are obvious and profound. In some cases, this leaves the diagnosis in the hands of amateurs who have neither the experience nor technical skills to make an accurate diagnosis. Here are the most important words in this chapter:

Before you allow your child to be categorized as "special education" or "learning disabled," it is imperative that you have an independent evaluation of your child done by an independent psychologist (doctor of psychology who specializes in learning disabilities and their diagnosis—not a practitioner, regardless of degree, who gives diagnostic tests on a part-time basis).

Why is independent diagnosis so important? The literature is full of tests and questions that appear to create a link to potential learning disabilities. Among these "diagnostic questions" I have found, a parent might be alarmed to find the following:

- [ ] **Does the child have difficulty in understanding new concepts?**

- [ ] **Is the child restless in class?**

- [ ] **Does the child fidget in his seat?**

- [ ] **Does the child seem less mature than his classmates?**

By these standards, every one of my children would have sent alarm bells ringing on any given day, even though all of them have managed to perform at very high levels in school. Indeed, by these standards, I know of few children who would not send parents scurrying to a specialist in search of a diagnosis to these obvious "problems" which, in another age, we called normal childhood behavior. This does not diminish the very real presence of learning disabilities and the need for their diagnosis and treatment. Yet, when I hear of regular schools with no greater population of disabled children than the average, and more than thirty percent of the children have been labeled as "special education," then I must wonder if the problem is really with the children or in pervasive presumptions of disabilities and the need for accompanying accommodations when, in fact, the children are quite normal.

an important clue

Context: Where Does Your Child Excel?

One important clue to your child's needs is the context in which your child has difficulty and that in which your child excels. For example, a child who does not write well in class, but who at home is able to compose wonderful stories with exciting plots and characters does not have a writing disability, but rather has a disinterest in the type of writing that is presently being required in class. The child who refuses to read aloud in class may not have the suspected reading disability, particularly if the same child is able to read with enthusiasm when alone with Grandma. Some parents have been told that the requirement for multi-step mathematical problem-solving is developmentally inappropriate for their child, and yet the same child is able to engage successfully in playground games that require multi-step conditional problem-solving and to keep the score with meticulous accuracy.

Thus, the first step in your reflection on your child's learning needs is to ask the question, "Where does my child excel?" I have heard some parents and teachers insist that there is no response for such a question and that every activity involves failures. When I persist, I will sometimes get a shrug of the shoulders and the rueful observation that, "Well, at least he can excel at Nintendo!"

Curious, I persist. "Tell me more about this success in Nintendo."

"It's awful," the parent complains. "He'll sit there for two hours, hardly blinking an eye, and proudly announce that he has made the 'next level,' whatever that means. He even compares scores with seven other kids at school who seem to devote every recess period to talking about how to get better at the dumb game, and he rattles off their scores every night as if he were announcing the league standings for the NFL."

"Please let me make sure that I understand this," I respond. "This is a child who at school appears to have memory problems and a complete inability to focus and concentrate. Homework seems futile because the child cannot remember simple facts from the previous day. Just sitting and talking about schoolwork often provokes an angry and tearful confrontation and, eventually, you both give up and the child retreats to the Nintendo game, and that way at least you both get some peace and quiet. Is this a fair summary?"

"Every blessed night," the parent sighs.

"Okay, I want to make sure I understand this," I continue. "The child has memory problems, but gives a daily recitation of seven different changing Nintendo scores. The child has attention problems, yet remains engaged in a complex game with multiple levels for hours at a time. The child does not like to discuss even for a moment his areas of failure, but will revel at length in stories of his success. Let's think about where this child can excel. The child excels first when other students are similarly enthusiastic about the activity. The child also excels when there is immediate feedback— in fact, every few moments in a Nintendo game, the child knows if there is success or failure, and every session reveals whether a 'next level' has been achieved. And, it is fair to say that this child, like most humans, enjoys talking with those he loves and respects— his parents—about his successes much more than he enjoys dwelling on his failures. And when he talks with his friends, he talks about how to get better, not about how terrible his failures make him feel."

"So what?" the parents counter. "Playing Nintendo won't get him into college. In fact, it won't get him into the seventh grade, and that's what we're worried about right now."

"That's true, and as someone who (I trust my children will never make it to this chapter) has hidden the family Nintendo machine for several months now, I share your frustration with what seems like a mindless game that robs time from homework and other more appropriate pursuits. But let me share what I have learned from Nintendo and my good friend, Dr. Jeff Howard. Dr. Howard is the founder of the Efficacy Institute. He's a Harvard-trained psychologist who has devoted a good deal of his life to helping students on whom many other people have given up. Jeff doesn't like Nintendo games any more than I do, but he made me pay attention to what they offer that kids need. He asked me one day, 'How long would those kids be playing Nintendo if their scores were put in a package and given to them at the end of the week?' After I thought about it, I knew that the answer would be, 'Not very long.' Then Dr. Howard persisted, 'They stay focused on Nintendo because the feedback is immediate and relevant. They know when they succeed and, even if they fail, they have an immediate chance for redemption. When was the last time a homework assignment did that? In fact, it gets shoved into the parent packet and the child sees it at the end of the week, if ever, and the feedback inevitably focuses on their failure to do something that was required many days (an eternity for a sixth grader) earlier. Trust me—the kid can focus, memorize, and excel, but only if there is feedback that is timely and relevant, and only if the conversations about the activity focus on success rather than failure.'"

"So," the exasperated parent demands, "You and Dr. Howard want kids to play Nintendo?"

"Not at all," I offer reassuringly. "We just want students to apply the Nintendo Effect to the classroom and to family discussions of schoolwork. What would happen if we applied these rules to learning at school? First, feedback doesn't happen at the end of the week amidst a sea of red ink in the parent packet, but it happens right away. That means that you ask the teacher for immediate feedback, so that whenever there is an error, your child has the opportunity to correct it immediately. Teachers almost always have some free time built into the day, and this could be devoted to allowing your child to leave the school day with success rather than with ambiguity or failure. At the very least, your child could take the work home and deal with it Monday night rather than over the weekend—typically Sunday night after an exhausting weekend. Second, your child might be encouraged to talk with friends and parents about strategies to get better, and even an incremental gain—each time he reaches the 'next level'—is the cause of some celebratory phone calls. That might be a new chapter, a new reading level, or a new performance level in writing. Each gain may be, like Nintendo, only a few points, but it is at least as worthy of celebration as is game success."

The point of this extended dialogue is not to suggest that Nintendo will solve the development challenges of children. Rather, the central question must always be, "Where does my child excel?" Whether or not your child has a learning disability, the context, conversation, and process of those areas where your child excels will provide clues for application to other areas where your child needs help. This is one of many areas in which the lessons of special education can be broadly applied to every other area of education for learners of any age.

Adaptations, Accommodations, and Truth

Children with special needs are entitled to the "least restrictive environment" for learning. They are also entitled to adaptations and accommodations that allow them to participate in regular classrooms to the maximum extent possible. The greatest entitlement, however, for students with special needs and their parents is the truth, including the truth about what the student has and has not yet accomplished. Too frequently, the discussions surrounding adaptations have as the underlying theme that an adaptation is equivalent to a loss of rigor. This is summed up in statements such as, "She was in special education, so I had to give her a B," or, "Sure, he passed the test, but only because he received special accommodations, so it really doesn't mean very much." There is a more appropriate way to discuss student achievement, and that is with an unwavering focus on truth.

If a child were blind, few people would presume that the Braille version of the test had less rigor than the printed version used by children with no visual impairments. In fact, some might argue that success on these tests by students who are blind requires more memory and better analytical skills than are required by other students. After all, the student reading Braille has to solve the Pythagorean theorem on a middle school math test, whether the problem about right triangles is posed in print or the problem is presented in the form of raised symbols. Now let's consider a child who has a different disability that is less obvious. The child has no guide dog, cane, or other external indicator of a disability, but nevertheless this student has an impairment that prevents the processing of printed text. The accommodation in such a case might include the presence of an adult to read the test. For another child with an attention deficit, the accommodation might include testing in a different room. For another child, there might be a scribe who writes the answers as dictated by the child. But all of these children must solve the problem with the Pythagorean theorem. In other words, the presence of an accommodation does not necessarily indicate a reduction of rigor. If these students can solve that equation, then it would be prejudicial in the extreme to conclude that they didn't "really" know that the square of the hypotenuse is equal to the sum of the square of the two sides.

Let's consider the case of a student who, perhaps due to a cognitive delay, does not correctly solve the problem. Rather than conclude that, "This child cannot do the Pythagorean theorem," or more broadly, that the child has a mathematics disability, we should focus our attention on truth and accuracy. We know what the child has not done yet, so what *can* this student do? Special educators are masterful at breaking standards and other academic requirements down into incremental tasks. In this example, the special educator might say that the real problem is text processing, not an inability to manipulate numbers. When the problem is presented as a story problem, the child "can't" do the Pythagorean theorem, but when the problem is presented with symbols and numbers, the child quickly calculates that $c^2 = a^2 + b^2$ or otherwise solves the problem without relying on text. Perhaps the student does not understand exponents, but does understand multiplication, or in this example, $c \times c = (a \times a) + (b \times b)$. Or perhaps the child does not yet grasp multiplication, but does understand the nature of addition as the total represented by groups of other numbers or objects. And so the task of incremental analysis continues. It is not done until we have more than the obvious information, such as the test item that the child missed. Our task as educators and parents remains incomplete until we have identified what the child can do, and the small incremental steps that are ahead of us, separating the present moment from the ultimate solution of the problem. A well-drafted Individualized Education Plan (IEP) will contain a series of such small increments, including a clear identification of what the student has already accomplished and the next steps to be accomplished.

The Individualized Education Plan (IEP)

The IEP is an important document that governs everything from classroom expectations to curriculum to assessment. This plan, as the name implies, must be focused on the individual needs of each student. While accommodations may be similar for several different students, the plan itself must be distinct, unique, and individual. The IEP is an evolving document, and the needs of your child may change. As a student gains skills, improves development, modifies behavior, or otherwise changes over the course of time, the IEP should also change.

The IEP is the result of the careful collaboration of a group of teachers, frequently labeled the IEP Team. This includes the classroom teacher, special education specialists, other specialists (such as speech pathologists), and school administrators. Parents should be personally involved in the IEP Team and should plan to attend meetings of the team. Your observations about the successes and challenges in the daily life of your child will provide valuable information that is more detailed and timely than may be obtained from classroom records.

Reporting Student Achievement of Standards— Beyond the Report Card

A frequent source of miscommunication between educators and parents has to do with the student report card. Many parents have contributed to this confusion by insisting that teachers must use a regular report card because parents perceive that this document is part of the "inclusion" to which their child is entitled. Although it is true that "regular" students routinely receive a traditional report card, this is among the many practices applied to regular education students that are of questionable value. For students who need very specific feedback on what they can do and have not yet done, the traditional report card provides inadequate information. Rather than focus on the report card, parents should focus on the imperatives of accuracy and fairness. What they really need to know is what standards their child has met and what specific incremental steps remain to be achieved in those areas where the student has not yet met a standard. When teachers and parents pretend that a standard has been met, or otherwise indicate achievement on a report card that is at variance with the facts, then the child does not benefit. In fact, when the adults in the system focus on factors other than objective indicators of real achievement, the child is left wondering what the meaning of success and failure really is. One of the best ways to resolve this dilemma is to make better use of the IEP and other documents that teachers and IEP members have collected. In fact, one of the best ways to individualize curriculum and instruction for a student with special needs is to start with an individualized report card that includes narrative descriptions, the IEP itself, evidence of student achievement in a portfolio, and narrative descriptions of what the child has achieved. This is far superior to the traditional set of letters and numbers that represent judgments which are typically inconsistent and poorly related to the individual needs of your child.

assistance and support

For Further Information

There are a number of national organizations devoted to helping parents of children with special needs advocate for their children. Because the needs of your child are likely to be complex and significantly different from the needs of other children, it might be helpful to find a group of parents across the nation who face similar challenges. You may feel that your circumstances are unique in your school, and thus you and your child can be made to feel very isolated. In fact, there are many parents who share the same challenges and successes, frustrations and triumphs. Here is a partial list of such organizations that you may wish to contact:

Children and Adults with Attention Deficit/Hyperactivity Disorder
(800) 233-4050
www.chadd.org

Council for Exceptional Children
(888) CEC-SPED
www.cec.sped.org

Learning Disabilities Association

(412) 341-1515

www.ldaamerica.org

National Center for Learning Disabilities

(888) 575-7373

www.ncld.org

National Information Center for Children and Youth with Disabilities

(800) 695-0285

www.nichcy.org

International Dyslexia Association (formerly, the Orton Dyslexia Society)

(800) 222-3123

www.interdys.org

Access America

www.disAbility.gov

Federation for Children with Special Needs

(617) 236-7210

www.fcsn.org

Alexander Graham Bell Association for the Deaf and Hard of Hearing

(202) 337-5220

www.agbell.org

American Foundation for the Blind

(800) 232-5463

www.afb.org

Autism Society of America

(800) 3AUTISM

www.autism-society.org

Brain Injury Association

(800) 444-6443

www.biausa.org

Tourette Syndrome Association, Inc.

(718) 224-2999

www.tsa-usa.org

20-Minute
Learning
Connection

Contact Numbers and Websites for the Massachusetts Department of Education and National Resources

If you are interested in staying abreast of the latest educational policy as well as finding various ways to support and supplement your child's education, the numbers and sites below should prove helpful.

Massachusetts Department of Education

http://www.doe.mass.edu

National Resources

U.S. Department of Education's Main Site
www.ed.gov
(800) USA-LEARN

Individuals with Disabilities Education Act (IDEA)
www.ed.gov/offices/OSERS/IDEA

National Assessment of Educational Progress (NAEP)
nces.ed.gov/nationsreportcard/site/home.asp
(202) 502-7458

National Center for Educational Statistics (NCES)
nces.ed.gov
(202) 502-7420

No Child Left Behind (President Bush's Statement on Education)
www.ed.gov/inits/nclb/index/html

Safe and Drug-free Schools
www.ed.gov/offices/OESE/SDFS
(800) 624-0100

PART II

MASSACHUSETTS

CURRICULUM

FRAMEWORKS

with Home Learning Activities

Massachusetts Curriculum Frameworks* with Home Learning Activities

• English Language Arts • Mathematics
• Science and Technology/Engineering • History and Social Science

Annotated with Home Learning Activities by Abby Remer

Reviewing practice questions isn't the only—or even the best—way to help your child succeed on the MCAS. If you and your child spend 20 minutes every day on activities that are interesting, challenging, and directly related to Massachusetts's academic requirements, your child's test performance and grades will improve. Relax, have fun, enjoy your child's company, and help your child become a confident, capable learner.

The activities in this section are designed to help your child master the knowledge and skills required by the state of Massachusetts for students in grades 5 through 8. Although there are many ways to approach the standards and activities, here are some suggestions:

- Read through the standards for all grades. This will help you understand how the "power standards" (see Chapter 5) apply to the Massachusetts Curriculum Frameworks. Although not every standard is of equal value, reading the complete set of standards will give you a general overview of the knowledge and skills the state expects your child's school to cover.

- Browse through all the activities. Many of the activities are appropriate for several grades, so it's best to choose those that will be most appealing to your child, rather than limiting your choice to activities aligned to standards for your child's grade. If your child especially enjoys writing, drawing, music, drama, or athletics, the icons will help you identify these types of activities.

- Look for activities that will build skills in an area where your child needs help in school. Ask your child's teacher to identify the standards your child needs to work on, and select corresponding activities for your 20-Minute Learning Connection.

- If you are concerned that the arts or physical education have been reduced at your child's school, this guide offers many opportunities to reinforce their importance at home. Icons for fine arts, performing arts, and physical education will help you identify activities in these categories.

Materials needed for each activity are identified by the following icons:

writing materials   drawing materials   Internet access   newspapers

magazines   TV or VCR   reference books   money

The following subject icons are used to indicate that more than one subject is covered by an activity:

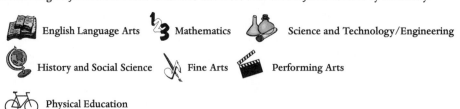

English Language Arts   Mathematics   Science and Technology/Engineering

History and Social Science   Fine Arts   Performing Arts

Physical Education

The Massachusetts Curriculum Frameworks are reprinted in this guide with the permission of the Massachusetts Department of Education. Permission to use them does not signify or imply that the Department approves or endorses this product. The Learning Activities in this guide and their alignment to the Curriculum Frameworks are the creation of the author and not the Massachusetts Department of Education. Up-to-date information about the Massachusetts Curriculum Frameworks is available at http://www.doe.mass.edu/frameworks/.

English Language Arts

Grades 5-8

Language

PREK-12

Standard 1: Discussion*

Students will use agreed-upon rules for informal and formal discussions in small and large groups.

Group discussion is more effective when students listen actively, stay on topic, consider the ideas of others, avoid sarcasm and personal remarks, take turns, and gain the floor in appropriate ways. Following agreed-upon rules promotes self-discipline and reflects respect for others.

(Continue to address earlier standards as needed and as they apply to more difficult texts.)

1.3   **Apply understanding of agreed-upon rules and individual roles in order to make decisions.**

For example, a group chooses which scene from a play to enact and decides who will play each character, using agreed-upon rules for eliciting and considering suggestions from each group member, and for coming to consensus.

(Continue to address earlier standards as needed and as they apply to more difficult texts.)

1.4   **Know and apply rules for formal discussions (class-room, parliamentary debate, town meeting rules).**

Standard 2: Questioning, Listening, and Contributing*

Students will pose questions, listen to the ideas of others, and contribute their own information or ideas in group discussions and interviews in order to acquire new knowledge.

Group discussions may lead students to greater complexity of thought as they expand on the ideas of others, refine initial ideas, pose hypotheses, and work toward solutions of intellectual problems. Group work helps students gain a deeper understanding of themselves as they reflect upon their own thinking in relation to that of others.

(Continue to address earlier standards as needed and as they apply to more difficult texts.)

2.3 Gather relevant information for a research project or composition through interviews.

For example, students generate questions about their family history, interview family members, and present their information to the class.

Hiring help

Tell your child to imagine that she runs a zoo, and you are coming to interview for a job. Have your child interview you as the prospective employee, asking about your talents, interests, and experience as it relates to working in the zoo. Before the interview, discuss with your child some of the different types of jobs available at zoos, including the individuals who feed and care for the animals, the ticket takers at the gates, the veterinarians who care for the animals' health, the architects who design the habitats for the animals, and so on. Then discuss some of the characteristics of good zoo employees: individuals who love animals, individuals who are knowledgeable about each of the animals' preferred diets and habitats, individuals who are observant (to notice when animals are sick or need things), individuals who are strong (for moving feed bags and equipment), and so forth. Explain to your child that, during the interview, she should paraphrase your answers to each question to make sure she understands your response. At the end of the interview, ask your child which job she might place you in and why. Ask your child to cite the specific interview responses that led to her decision.

(Continue to address earlier standards as needed and as they apply to more difficult texts.)

2.4 Integrate relevant information gathered from group discussions and interviews for reports.

For example, as part of a unit on Irish immigration to this country in the 19th century, students generate questions to ask neighbors, family members, or local experts about the topic. They also develop discussion questions to guide their reading of chapters from books treating the topic. Finally they integrate the information into a group report on the immigrants' reasons for migrating to America, the social and economic conditions they faced on arrival, the socioeconomic status of Irish Americans in the 20th century, and the reasons for the extraordinary differences.

Roots historian

Help your child generate questions to ask older relatives about why and how the family first came to the United States. Even if the original relatives who arrived are not available, your child can pose them to you or another knowledgeable adult. When interviewing, your child should take careful notes and then use them to develop an outline for an oral presentation that she will give at the next family gathering. Also, have your child create an illustrated "roots" poster, depicting the relatives who first came, where they began, how they traveled, and what it was like when they first arrived. Your child should use this poster as a visual aid during her presentation. Have her make smaller versions of the poster to give to family members as gifts.

PREK-12

Standard 3: Oral Presentation*

Students will make oral presentations that demonstrate appropriate consideration of audience, purpose, and the information to be conveyed.

Planning an effective presentation requires students to make an appropriate match between their intended audience and the choice of presentation style, level of formality, and format. Frequent opportunities to plan presentations for various purposes and to speak before different groups helps students learn how to gain and keep an audience's attention, interest, and respect.

(Continue to address earlier standards as needed.)

3.8 Give oral presentations for various purposes, showing appropriate changes in delivery (gestures, vocabulary, pace, visuals) and using language for dramatic effect.

> ### "Ain't I a woman?"
>
> **WWW** 📖 *Together, learn about Sojourner Truth using library resources or by typing in her name into any major Internet search engine (such as Yahooligans at http://search.yahooligans.com). Explore the many sites dedicated to this formerly enslaved woman who fought against slavery in the United States. Afterward, have your child study and then read aloud Truth's famous "Ain't I a woman?" speech given during the Akron, Ohio women's rights convention of 1851. (The text of the speech is available at http://www.hartford-hwp.com/archives/45a/170. html.) Before performing the speech in a clear and passionate voice, your child should determine what Truth meant to convey—how she wanted to affect the audience. Have your child present the speech to others playing the audience at the nineteenth century convention. After, have your child ask people how they felt after hearing Truth's words and discuss her impact on American history.* 🌐 🎬

3.9 Use teacher-developed assessment criteria to prepare their presentations.

(Continue to address earlier standards as needed and as they apply to more difficult texts.)

3.10 Present an organized interpretation of a literary work, film, or dramatic production.

Have your child organize and run a book club for household members and friends. Before the first meeting, your child should create a list of recommended readings, with a brief, well-organized summary (without giving away the ending) and the reasons for the recommendation next to each title. Have your child organize his list of recommended readings by theme (stories set in the present, past, or future, for example), and then reproduce the list and give it to all book club members. At the first book club meeting, have your child orally elaborate on his summaries and the reasons for his recommendations, and then conduct a democratic vote to determine the order in which the books will be read and discussed at future book club meetings.

3.11   Use appropriate techniques for oral persuasion.

Here's why

Ask your child to develop an oral presentation designed to change your mind about a topic, such as his bedtime (why later would be better), his allowance (why larger would be better), plans for the weekend (why a baseball game would be better than cleaning his room), and so forth. Have him begin with a written outline that presents his main point at the beginning, followed by well-organized facts and reasons to support his argument, and a closing statement that summarizes his key points. As he is creating his outline, ask him to consider the topic from your point of view, to make sure that his persuasive points address all of your concerns. When he has completed his outline, each of you should silently rate each of his supporting facts and reasons on a scale of 1 to 5 (1 representing weak arguments, 5 representing strong arguments), and then compare your ratings. Discuss the cases where your ratings are far apart. Why did you find an argument ineffective? Why did your child think a particular point would change your mind? Have your child revise his outline and make his oral presentation in favor of his cause. Afterward, provide feedback on the presentation and discuss how it influenced your decision one way or another.

3.12　Give oral presentations to different audiences for various purposes, showing appropriate changes in delivery (gestures, vocabulary, pace, visuals) and using language for dramatic effect.

For example, students modify their original science project, designed to be presented to parents, when they explain it to a third-grade class.

Switching hats

✍ **FIVE HATS OR CAPS, TAPE, BIG BAG** Write the words "informal conversation," "debate," "project" (e.g., making a model airplane, cleaning out a closet), "informational presentation," and "imaginative presentation" on separate cards. Tape every card to the back of a hat or cap. Place the all the hats/caps in a big bag. Have your child take one of the hats out of the bag and look at the word, without letting you see what is written. Your child should then start speaking in a way appropriate to what is written as soon as she places the hat on her head (with the writing facing the back so you can't read it). It's up to you to guess which hat your child has selected. Replace the hat and repeat until you've eventually covered all five scenarios.

3.13　Create a scoring guide based on categories supplied by the teacher (content and presentation style) to prepare and assess their presentations.

PREK-12

Standard 4: Vocabulary and Concept Development

Students will understand and acquire new vocabulary, and use it correctly in reading and writing.

Our ability to think clearly and communicate with precision orally or in writing depends on our individual store of words. A rich vocabulary enables students to understand what they read, and to speak and write with flexibility and control. As students use a variety of strategies for acquiring new vocabulary, the delight in finding and using that perfect word can heighten interest in vocabulary itself.

(Continue to address earlier standards as needed and as they apply to more difficult texts.)

4.17 Determine the meaning of unfamiliar words using context clues (*definition, example*).

For example, students choose vocabulary words and write them in sentences that use definition or example context clues, such as "Residents were aghast—shocked—at the destruction."

You've stumped me!

Explain to your child that she is going to try to stump you with words you don't know. Tell your child to select a word from the dictionary that is new to her and read the definition silently. Your child then should read the definition aloud and ask you to guess the correct word. For instance, your child might read, "the basic monetary unit of Estonia from 1928 to 1940." You then would try to guess the corresponding word (Kroon), and if you don't know the word say, "You've stumped me!" You get the point if you guess the correct word, and you child gets the point if she "stumped" you. (If there are any words within the definition your child doesn't know, such as Estonia, have her look these up in the dictionary.) Play seven rounds, listing the word and who got the points. The person with the most points wins.

4.18 Determine the meaning of unfamiliar words using knowledge of common Greek and Latin roots, suffixes, and prefixes.

4.19 Determine pronunciations, meanings, alternate word choices, and parts of speech of words using dictionaries and thesauruses.

(Continue to address earlier standards as needed and as they apply to more difficult texts.)

4.20 Determine the meaning of unfamiliar words using context clues (*contrast, cause* and *effect*).

For example, students collect examples of sentences that contain contrast or cause-and-effect clues, such as "Most organisms need oxygen to survive, <u>but</u> many types of bacteria are anaerobic." (contrast) or "<u>Because</u> so much of the town was destroyed, rebuilding it will be an arduous task (cause and effect)." Students compile a list of words and phrases that cue contrast clues, such as but, however, on the other hand, except, and cause-and-effect clues, such as because, since, as a result, therefore.

Switch-aroo

CHILDREN'S BOOK *Have your child read aloud from a favorite book or magazine. When he comes across an unfamiliar word, look together at the surrounding word clues. Repeat the sentence aloud, saying "blank" in place of the unknown word, and then continue on. Ask your child what other word(s) might be substituted for the unknown word in the sentence so that it still makes sense. For instance, "José's mother is proud of him because he is <u>responsible</u>. He always completes his chores on Saturday before he goes to the park." Ask your child to look for clues in the sentence that suggest a meaning for the unknown word. For example, José's mother is proud, so being responsible must be a good thing. Also, José does his work before he goes off to have fun. Then, ask your child to think of words that can be switched for the word* responsible *in the sentence; for instance, other words that might be used to describe José in this passage are* dutiful, reliable, dependable, *and* trustworthy. *Based on the surrounding word clues and the switched words, your child can conclude that a person who is described as responsible is "someone who does what he is supposed to do." Help your child understand whether the word(s) or definition he selected is close to the meaning of the original unknown word, asking him to use the dictionary as a resource. Ask your child to use the newly understood word in another sentence to enhance comprehension.*

4.21   Determine the meaning of unfamiliar words by using knowledge of common Greek and Latin roots, suffixes, and prefixes.

For example, while reading about men and women who pioneered in space and under the sea, students come across such words as astronaut and nautical and use their knowledge of Greek and Latin roots and the context to work out the meaning of these words. They then compile a list of words they find in their science materials that are based on other common Greek and Latin roots.

It's Latin to me

 Together, use a dictionary that includes etymologies (word histories) to explore words with Greek and Latin roots, suffixes, and prefixes. Begin by looking up the origins of common prefixes such as bio- *(from the Greek* bios, *meaning "life"),* trans- *(from the Latin* trans, *meaning "beyond"),* tele- *(from the Greek* tele, *meaning "at a distance"),* super- *(from the Latin* super, *meaning "over" or "above"),* pro *(from the Latin* pro *, meaning "in favor of," and the Greek* pro *, meaning "before" or "in front of"),* psych- *(from the Greek* psukhe, *meaning "soul"), and so forth. As you look up these prefixes, show your child how dictionaries provide readers with information about the history of words. Use the word* biathlon *as an example:* bi- *comes from the Latin word* bis, *which means "twice;"* athlon *is a Greek word, meaning "contest." Browse through the dictionary together and look for interesting words with Greek and Latin prefixes, suffixes, and roots, keeping a list of the words and their origins as you go. Review your list together and ask your child to think of other words that include these Greek and Roman elements. For example,* marathon, triathlon, *also contain the root* athlon.

Defeat the book

 Explain to your child that he is going to play a game against the thesaurus. First, have your child select a word that is new to him in a glossary. (Try looking in textbooks, cookbooks, and how-to books for a glossary.) Have your child read the definition of the new word in the dictionary, and then write the definition in his own words on a piece of paper. Now, have your child list as many synonyms for the word as possible. Feel free to help your child by giving him hints when he runs out of ideas. When your child's list is complete, have him compare the synonyms he came up with to those listed in the thesaurus, to see which list had more synonyms—and to discover ones he might have missed. Finally, your child should be able to use the new word in a sentence that clearly demonstrates an understanding of its definition.

Standard 5: Structure and Origins of Modern English

Students will analyze standard English grammar and usage, and recognize how its vocabulary has developed and been influenced by other languages.

The English language has changed through time and through contact with other languages. Knowledge of its history helps students appreciate the extraordinary richness of its vocabulary, which continues to grow. The study of its grammar and usage gives students more control over the meaning they intend in their writing and speaking.

GRADES 5-6

(Continue to address earlier standards as needed and as they apply to more difficult texts.)

5.9   Identify all eight parts of speech (noun, pronoun, verb, adverb, adjective, conjunction, preposition, interjection).

Hunt and change

 Have your child use a dictionary to look up the definitions for the eight parts of speech listed in the Standard. After reading each definition, ask your child to paraphrase the dictionary definition and define each term in his own words. Give your child eight sheets of paper and have him write one term with his definition at the top of separate pages. Next, give your child a short newspaper or magazine article on a topic of interest to him—an article about his hobby, a recent sports event, or a movie he'd like to see. Ask your child to sort each word in the article into one of the eight categories. (If the word doesn't fit into one of the categories—an article, for instance—have him circle it.) Once a word has been entered on its category page (for example, the word "and" on the conjunction page), additional uses can be recorded with checkmarks. If your child finds this activity challenging, show him how dictionaries provide readers with information about parts of speech, and encourage him

to look up words he cannot categorize. When your child has completed this task, review his list and use a dictionary to clarify the parts of speech for any words placed in the wrong category.

5.10   Expand or reduce sentences (*adding or deleting modifiers, combining or decombining sentences*).

5.11   Identify verb phrases and verb tenses.

5.12   Recognize that a word performs different functions according to its position in the sentence.

For example, students identify light *as a verb in the sentence,* The children light the candles. *Then they write using the word* light *in other places in sentences and discuss the meaning and function of* light *in each.*

5.13   Identify simple and compound sentences.

5.14   Identify correct mechanics (*apostrophes, quotation marks, comma use in compound sentences, paragraph indentations*) and correct sentence structure (*elimination of sentence fragments and run-ons*).

GRADES 7-8

(Continue to address earlier standards as needed and as they apply to more difficult texts.)

5.15   Recognize the basic patterns of English sentences (noun-verb; noun-verb-noun; noun-verb-noun noun; noun-linking verb-noun).

5.16   Distinguish phrases from clauses.

5.17   Recognize the makeup and function of prepositional phrases.

5.18   Identify simple, compound, and complex sentences.

5.19   Recognize appropriate use of pronoun reference.

"For"-noun hunt

Ask your child whether she is "pro" or "con" extra servings of ice cream upon request (or any other question likely to get a "pro" answer). Have your child define the term "pro," in this case meaning "for." Using this knowledge, what definition can your child devise for "pronoun"? A <u>pronoun</u> is a word that stands "for" the noun without naming it (e.g., I, we, you, he, it, they, my, yours, ours). Give your child a short newspaper or magazine article on a topic of interest—preferably an article about an individual or a group of individuals, since these types of articles are likely to include lots of pronouns. Have your child read the first few paragraphs aloud, substituting an appropriate pronoun whenever a noun is used and substituting the correct noun whenever a pronoun is used. Discuss some of the advantages of using pronouns (you don't have to keep repeating people's names, and you can refer to a whole group of people as 'they") and some of the disadvantages (if not used properly, pronouns can cause confusion).

5.20 Identify correct mechanics (*comma after introductory structures*) correct usage (*pronoun reference*) and correct sentence structure (*complete sentences, properly placed modifiers*).

5.21 Employ grammar and usage rhetorically by combining, including, reordering, and reducing sentences.

5.22 Describe the origins and meanings of common words, as well as of foreign words or phrases used frequently in written English.

For example, students research the origins of common nouns (popcorn, denim, bus), as well as the meanings and origin of erudite foreign phrases (sub rosa, caveat emptor, carte blanche), and popularly used foreign phrases (bon appetit, au revoir, numero uno), for the purpose of creating their own etymological dictionary.

Scientific origin game

NOTE CARDS, TIMER Have your child select an article on a scientific topic of interest. Read the article together and have your child highlight (or underline) any scientific terms. When you are done, have your child transfer the terms to individual note cards. Next, ask your child use a dictionary to find the origin of each word, writing its origin and definition on the back of the respective note card. Every night for three evenings, shuffle the "deck" with the terms facing up.

Time your child as he goes through each term, defining it correctly in his own words, identifying its origin, and using it in a sentence. Each time your child gives the correct information, take the respective card out of the pile. Place any missed answer cards back into the deck. The game is over when your child has eliminated all the cards. Write down the time, and then compare this day's results to the next two games played on successive nights to see if your child can beat his own score!

Foreign language adventure

 Give your child a dictionary with etymologies (histories of words) and show your child how to find this information with each word's definition. Point out the section of the dictionary that explains the abbreviations used for etymologies: this list will show her all of the different languages that have influenced our own. Challenge her to find words with as many different origins as possible. Get her started by looking up the words pretzel *(German),* bolero *(Spanish),* chit *(Hindi) and* amen *(Hebrew). This activity is even more fun when conducted as a timed competition between household members, so invite others to participate, give everyone a dictionary, and set a timer for fifteen minutes. (For this activity, each origin can only be counted once.) Whoever has found the longest list of word origins after fifteen minutes is the winner!*

PREK-12

Standard 6: Formal and Informal English

Students will describe, analyze, and use appropriately formal and informal English.

Study of different forms of the English language helps students to understand that people use different levels of formality in their writing and speaking as well as a variety of regional and social dialects in their conversational language.

(Continue to address earlier standards as needed and as they apply to more difficult texts.)

6.4   Demonstrate through role-playing appropriate use of formal and informal language.

6.5   Write stories using a mix of formal and informal language.

6.6   Identify differences between oral and written language patterns.

Extinct is forever!

WWW **TAPE RECORDER** *Have your child imagine that he is a speech writer for an environmental or animal rights organization, and that he has been asked to give a persuasive speech on a topic he cares deeply about. Have him choose an environmental or animal rights topic to research for this purpose, and help him conduct research using library or online resources. Have him take notes while conducting his research, keeping track of the sources for all facts and data he plans to use in his speech. Have your child organize his notes into an outline, and then have him give his speech using his notes as a guide and speaking into the tape recorder. Next, have him use the same outline to write a persuasive article on the same topic. After he has created a draft and edited his work for organization, grammar, spelling, and punctuation, have him create a final written version and read it aloud into the tape recorder. Have him listen to the recording of the speech and the article, and ask him to compare the two. In which version did he express his ideas most effectively? Ask him to identify one advantage and one disadvantage for each type of presentation (oral and written).*

(Continue to address earlier standards as needed and as they apply to more difficult texts.)

6.7   Analyze the language styles of different characters in literary works.

For example, students compare selections of dialogue by various characters in Mark Twain's The Adventures of Tom Sawyer in order to identify and analyze differences in language style.

Dialect lingo

✎ 📺 **BOOK PORTRAITS** Explain to your child that <u>dialect</u> is a regional pattern of speech. Authors use dialect to give readers information about where characters are from and how their speech sounds. Have your child read a book that includes character(s) who speak in dialect. (If you need help, ask your librarian to recommend a book.) Ask your child to find sections that include examples of dialect and read them aloud. What does the dialect convey about that character? What is it that the author is trying to communicate? Now, have your child be a "dialect detective." When watching television, ask your child to identify any character who speaks with a dialect and describe how this helps build a sense of the person. Help your child detect various types of dialects and compare them and the information they convey. Finally, examine painted or photographed portraits and have your child invent a dialect for the person that helps convey something about his or her character based on the visual clues your child sees in the image.

Reading and Literature

PREK-12

Standard 7: Beginning Reading

Students will understand the nature of written English and the relationship of letters and spelling patterns to the sounds of speech.

Phonemic awareness, knowledge of the relationships between sounds and letters, and an understanding of the features of written English texts are essential to beginning reading, and should be taught, continually practiced, and carefully monitored in the early grades. Students who gain a strong grounding in these skills are ready to take on the concurrent tasks of comprehension and communication. (See Standards 4, 8, 9, 19, and 22.)

The majority of students will have met these standards by the end of Grade 4, although teachers may need to continue addressing earlier standards.

PREK-12

Standard 8: Understanding a Text

Students will identify the basic facts and main ideas in a text and use them as the basis for interpretation.

When we read a text closely, we work carefully to discern the author's main ideas and the particular facts and details that support them. Good readers read thoughtfully and purposefully, constantly checking their understanding of the author's intent and meaning so that their interpretations will be sound.

GRADES 5-6

(Continue to address earlier standards as needed and as they apply to more difficult texts.)

For imaginative/literary texts:

8.19   Identify and analyze sensory details and figurative language.

You are there

Ask your child to close her eyes for a moment and think of a favorite place. Then without saying the name of the location, have your child describe as much as possible about it and her experience there. Can you guess the location from the description? Reverse roles and then discuss which aspects of the descriptions were most helpful in imagining each place. Afterward, both of you should draw your location and discuss how visual representations capture things that words might not, and vice versa. (For example, art might convey the exact color of the ocean or lake at a location, but not the sounds of the waves.)

8.20 Identify and analyze the author's use of dialogue and description.

For informational/expository texts:

8.21 Recognize organizational structures (chronological order, logical order, cause and effect, classification schemes).

Sports editor

✍ 📖 📺 *Ask your child to read an article or watch a television show about a favorite sport, team, or player (or attend a sporting event). Then ask her to choose one of the organizational structures mentioned in the Standard and write an article about the event as the local newspaper sports editor. Before handing in the draft, have your young sports editor (your child) revise its organization for clarity.*

8.22 Identify and analyze main ideas, supporting ideas, and supporting details.

GRADES 7-8

(Continue to address earlier standards as needed and as they apply to more difficult texts.)

For imaginative/literary texts:

8.23 Use knowledge of genre characteristics to analyze a text.

Charting genres

✍ *EXAMPLES OF DIFFERENT LITERARY GENRES At home or in a library, have your child examine samples of different genres (poetry, drama, science fiction, fantasy, nonfiction, etc.) and take notes on each genre's distinguishing characteristics. Have him create a chart that identifies the features of each. Explanations on the chart should be in cursive and legible, with proper spelling, punctuation, and grammar. Using the information in the chart, have your child answer, if he was to become a writer, which genre would he pursue and why?*

8.24 Interpret mood and tone, and detail supporting evidence in a text.

For example, students read excerpts from A Gathering of Days *by Joan W. Blos, a novel written in diary form of the last year a fourteen-year-old girl lived on the family farm in New Hampshire. Students write in their own journals and then discuss in groups how the difficulties of the year – her best friend's death, for instance – are reflected in the writing's tone, and the extent to which detail in the writing helps the reader to understand and relate to the text.*

8.25 Interpret a character's traits, emotions, or motivation and give supporting evidence from a text.

For informational/expository texts:

8.26 Recognize organizational structures and use of arguments for and against an issue.

Put it in writing!

The next time your child asks for a permanent or temporary change involving your house rules (a later bedtime, permission to stay out late to attend a special event, an advance on her allowance to make a special purchase) ask her to put her request in writing. Encourage your child to use all of her powers of persuasion! Explain that, in order to be effective, your child's written request should include a clearly stated position supported with relevant evidence, presented in an organized fashion. It is also important for your child's written request to demonstrate that she has taken the reader's (your) point of view into consideration. After your child has created a first draft, have her revise it to correct spelling, punctuation, and grammar. Read your child's revised request and respond in writing. Your written response should explain how her written powers of persuasion influenced your answer.

8.27 Identify evidence used to support an argument.

Put it in writing II!

After receiving your feedback in part one of this activity, have your child revise her writing, citing specific evidence that will further strengthen the argument.

8.28 Distinguish between the concepts of theme in a literary work and author's purpose in an expository text.

Standard 9: Making Connections

Students will deepen their understanding of a literary or non-literary work by relating it to its contemporary context or historical background.

By including supplementary reading selections that provide relevant historical and artistic background, teachers deepen students' understanding of individual literary works and broaden their capacity to connect literature to other manifestations of the creative impulse.

GRADES 5-6

(Continue to address earlier standards as needed and as they apply to more difficult texts.)

9.4 Relate a literary work to information about its setting.

For example, students read The Remarkable Journey of Prince Jen *by Lloyd Alexander. In order to understand its historical background, they read information about the T'ang dynasty of China and excerpts from the* Analects of Confucius *and relate what they learn to events and characters in the book.*

GRADES 7-8

(Continue to address earlier standards as needed and as they apply to more difficult texts.)

9.5 Relate a literary work to artifacts, artistic creations, or historical sites of the period of its setting.

For example, students read Irene Hunt's Across Five Aprils *or Stephen Crane's* Red Badge of Courage. *In order to understand the historical background of the work, they examine Matthew Brady's photographs from the Civil War, read excerpts from various soldiers' diaries and letters, and study Julia Ward Howe's "Battle Hymn of the Republic" and other Civil War songs. Then they relate what they learn to events, settings, and characters from the book.*

Bronte, Dickens, Twain...

Choose a literary classic from an earlier era to read together. (Consider books by Charlotte and Emily Bronte, Charles Dickens, or Mark Twain.) Read a chapter aloud together each evening, or read the book independently, but simultaneously. You and your child should both take notes regarding the details that establish the story as being part of another era (language, customs, etc.). When you both have completed the book, research the author and his or her era, using online or library resources. Look for more information about the book's historical details that you noted. For example, Charles Dickens lived in a time when child labor was prevalent and this became a prominent theme in his books.

PREK-12

Standard 10: Genre

Students will identify, analyze, and apply knowledge of the characteristics of different genres.

We become better readers by understanding both the structure and the conventions of different genres. A student who knows the formal qualities of a genre is able to anticipate how the text will evolve, appreciate the nuances that make a given text unique, and rely on this knowledge to make a deeper and subtler interpretation of the meaning of the text.

Massachusetts Curriculum Frameworks with Home Learning Activities

(Continue to address earlier standards as needed and as they apply to more difficult texts.)

10.3 Identify and analyze the characteristics of various genres (poetry, fiction, nonfiction, short story, drama) as forms with distinct characteristics and purposes.

For example, students read a variety of materials and write a short anthology of works, including several genres of literature, on an event or person in American history, or on an animal they have studied.

(Continue to address earlier standards as needed and as they apply to more difficult texts.)

10.4 Identify and analyze the characteristics of various genres (poetry, fiction, nonfiction, short story, drama) as forms chosen by an author to accomplish a purpose.

For example, students read Anne Frank's Diary of a Young Girl *and the play based on it. After analyzing the differences between them, students take excerpts from the diary not used in the play, create a scene, and perform it.*

Genre game show

*✏ **LITERARY SELECTIONS OF NONFICTION, FICTION, DRAMA, AND POETRY** Recruit another player for a game in which two contestants (one of which is your child) will compete to see who can correctly identify the genre for the greatest number of writing examples. Together, review the genres listed in the Standard and discuss the characteristics of the various genres. (Which genre is most likely to use quotation marks? rhymes? similes? dialogue? persuasive arguments?) In your role as game show host, select three to five different examples of each genre, without letting the contestants see your selections. Have the two contestants sit on separate chairs facing you. For each round, read a short selection from one of the examples and ask one contestant if it is A. nonfiction, B. fic-*

tion, C. drama, or D. poetry. The player gets a point if his or her answer is correct; if the answer is incorrect, the other contestant gets a chance to answer the same question and earns a point for a correct answer. If both players answer incorrectly, add the sample back into your selection for a later round. Have your child keep score. Alternate players for each round until all of your writing samples have been identified correctly. The first player to score ten points wins! 123

Standard 11: Theme

Students will identify, analyze, and apply knowledge of theme in a literary work and provide evidence from the text to support their understanding.

Understanding and articulating theme is at the heart of the act of reading literature. Identification of theme clarifies the student's interpretation of the text. Providing evidence from the text to support an understanding of theme is, like a proof in algebra or geometry, the most essential and elegant demonstration of that understanding.

GRADES 5-6

(Continue to address earlier standards as needed and as they apply to more difficult texts.)

11.3   Apply knowledge of the concept that theme refers to the main idea and meaning of a selection, whether it is implied or stated.

For example, students explore the theme, "Heroism demands courage and taking risks" in King Arthur and the Knights of the Round Table *and* The Adventures of Robin Hood *and write paragraphs explaining how each author illustrates this theme in different ways.*

(Continue to address earlier standards as needed and as they apply to more difficult texts.)

11.4   Analyze and evaluate similar themes across a variety of selections, distinguishing theme from topic.

For example, students explore the theme, "Understanding involves putting yourself in someone else's shoes," in interviews with adults, in fiction and in biographies to identify what real and fictional people have experienced, and report their findings to the class

Standard 12: Fiction

Students will identify, analyze, and apply knowledge of the theme, structure, and elements of a work of fiction and provide evidence from the text to support their understanding.

We learn from stories. They are vehicles for a student's development of empathy, of moral sensibility, and of understanding. The identification and analysis of elements of fiction—such as plot, conflict, setting, character development, and foreshadowing—make it possible for students to think more critically about stories, to respond to them in more complex ways, to reflect on their meanings, and to compare them to each other.

(Continue to address earlier standards as needed and as they apply to more difficult texts.)

12.3   Identify and analyze the elements of setting, characterization, and plot (including conflict).

For example, students read selections of their own choice stressing survival, such as Julie of the Wolves *by Jean George,* Island of the Blue Dolphins *by Scott O'Dell and* The Big Wave *by Pearl Buck. They explore conflict and characterization by posing and answering questions such as, "What qualities of the central characters enable them to survive?"*

GRADES 7-8

(Continue to address earlier standards as needed and as they apply to more difficult texts.)

12.4   Locate and analyze elements of plot and characterization and then use an understanding of these elements to determine how qualities of the central characters influence the resolution of the conflict.

For example students read stories by Edgar Allan Poe such as "The Tell-Tale Heart" and "The Black Cat," identify characters' traits and states of mind, and analyze how these characteristics establish the conflict and progression of the plot.

Alternative screen writers

Together, watch a rented movie that is new to both you and your child. Stop it two-thirds of the way through. Have your child summarize the story line, setting, and main conflict or problem. Both of you will now be "screenwriters," devising a fascinating resolution to the main conflict using correct grammar, punctuation, and spelling as well as clarity of ideas. Afterward, watch the end of the film to see how your screenplays differ from the original. Then, vote on which of the three versions was the best and why.

Standard 13: Nonfiction

Students will identify, analyze, and apply knowledge of the purpose, structure, and elements of nonfiction or informational material and provide evidence from the text to support their understanding.

Most students regularly read newspapers, magazines, journals, or textbooks. The identification and understanding of common expository organizational structures help students to read challenging nonfiction material. Knowledge of its textual and graphic features extends a student's control in reading and writing informational texts.

GRADES 5-6

(Continue to address earlier standards as needed and as they apply to more difficult texts.)

13.13 Identify and use common textual features (*paragraphs, topic sentences, glossary, index*).

A bug's tale

 Have your child select a bug to research—a ladybug, grasshopper, beetle, ant, butterfly, praying mantis, ant, or any other insect that catches his fancy. Help your child research the insect, using online resources and library reference materials. As your child conducts his research, show him how to use an index, a table of contents, an alphabetical listing, and online search engines such as Yahoo and Alta Vista. If possible, obtain a live specimen and use what you have learned from the research to create a safe, comfortable habitat for the insect so your child can observe its behavior. Based on his research, ask your child to write a "day-in-the-life" poem from the bug's point of view, and then set the poem to music. Your child can use an existing melody or invent an entirely new one, but his song should include several facts about the insect obtained from his research and observation.

13.14 identify and use knowledge of common graphic features (*charts, maps, diagrams, captions, illustrations*).

Zanzibar or Timbuktu

 WORLD MAP, WORD PROCESSING SOFTWARE Ask your child to pick a faraway place he might like to visit and have him research the destination using the tools listed in the Standard. Tell your child to take careful notes about the locale, people, environment, social customs, and so forth. Next, have your child locate his destination on a map and determine the best way to travel there, starting from your hometown. (Use websites such as www.travelocity.com to find the best route.) Finally, ask your child to imagine that he works for the tourist bureau at his chosen destination, and ask him to write a promotional jingle to encourage tourism. Have him incorporate details from his research, and make sure the lyrics convey the special qualities of the place. He should draft and revise his song using word processing software, and save it on the computer to share with a friend later.

13.15 identify and use knowledge of organizational structures (*chronological order, logical order, cause and effect, classification schemes*).

Short vs. long

 Have your child read a summary (either online or in a newspaper or magazine) of a book she has read. Ask your child to grade the summary, from A+ to F according to how accurately it captured the main idea, critical details, and primary underlying meaning of the book. Then, have your child write an A+ summary, editing the work for organization, meaning, and correct spelling, grammar, and punctuation.

13.17 identify and analyze main ideas, supporting ideas, and supporting details.

For example, students write logical, one-paragraph summary reports after a visit by an author and arrange and identify the most important points made by the author.

(Continue to address earlier standards as needed and as they apply to more difficult texts.)

13.18 Identify and use common textual features (*paragraphs, topic sentences, concluding sentences, introduction, conclusion, footnotes, index, bibliography*).

13.19 Identify and use knowledge of common graphic features (*charts, maps, diagrams*);

13.20 Identify and use knowledge of common organizational structures (*logical order, comparison and contrast, cause and effect relationships*).

For example, students read a variety of informational materials (biography, diary, textbook, encyclopedia, magazine article) on a Civil War figure and write a report using an appropriate organizational structure.

13.21 Recognize use of arguments for and against an issue.

13.22 Identify evidence used to support an argument.

13.23 Distinguish between the concepts of theme in a literary work and author's purpose in an expository text.

Reading and Literature

Students will identify, analyze, and apply knowledge of the theme, structure, and elements of poetry and provide evidence from the text to support their understanding. (See also Standard 15.)

From poetry we learn the language of heart and soul with particular attention to rhythm and sound, compression and precision, the power of images, and the appropriate use of figures of speech. And yet it is also the genre that is most playful in its attention to language, where rhyme, pun, and hidden meanings are constant surprises. The identification and analysis of the elements generally associated with poetry—metaphor, simile, personification, and alliteration—have an enormous impact on student reading and writing not only in poetry, but in other genres as well.

GRADES 5-6

(Continue to address earlier standards as needed and as they apply to more difficult texts.)

14.3   Respond to and analyze the effects of sound, figurative language, and graphics in order to uncover meaning in poetry.

■   sound (*alliteration, onomatopoeia, rhyme scheme*);

■   figurative language (*personification, metaphor, simile, hyperbole*);

Words that sell

If necessary, have your child use a dictionary to define the terms simile, metaphor, hyperbole, *and* personification. *Next, together explore advertisements in magazines and newspapers and identify examples of each term, seeing how they are used to sell a product. For example, what kind of hyperbole (exaggeration) is used in toy or food ads? Make sure to examine both words and images. Next, use examples from the Standard to create your own advertising jingle that will sell others on a personal idea, product, or activity. Make sure all of the words in your child's jingle are spelled correctly and written legibly.*

■   graphics (*capital letters, line length*).

Literary poem

For this activity, you and your child will write a poem together, including assonance, alliteration, and similes. To prepare, look up the definitions for the terms in a dictionary or find the definitions online by typing each term into any major Internet search engine. Next, together think of as many silly examples of <u>assonance</u>, (the repetition of vowel sounds, i.e., feet dare to meet), <u>alliteration</u> (the repetition of initial consonant sounds in neighboring words, i.e., jumping jars, pickled pixies), and <u>similes</u> (the comparison of two unlike things using "like" or *"as," i.e., "Her eyes were shining like stars in the midnight sky") as you can. (If you need help getting started, you'll find many entertaining examples in Lewis Carroll's poem, "The Walrus and the Carpenter" in Through the Looking Glass.) Then create a poem together, using your favorite examples from your practice session. Add assonance, alliteration, and similes to your everyday conversation for fun, and point out examples when you read together.*

GRADES 7-8

(Continue to address earlier standards as needed and as they apply to more difficult texts.)

14.4   Respond to and analyze the effects of sound, form, figurative language, and graphics in order to uncover meaning in poetry form:

■   sound (*alliteration, onomatopoeia, internal rhyme, rhyme scheme*);

■   figurative language (*personification, metaphor, simile, hyperbole*);

■   graphics (*capital letters, line length, word position*).

For example, students explore ways in which poets use sound effects (as accompaniment) in humorous poems. They read authors such as Laura Richards, Lewis Carroll, Ogden Nash, or Shel Silverstein; or (as reinforcement of meaning) in serious poems by such writers as Robert Louis Stevenson, Edna St. Vincent Millay, Marianne Moore, or Alfred Noyes. They incorporate these effects in their own poems.

Analyze this!

POEM Have your child select a favorite poem, or share one that you particularly like. Ask your child to imagine being an English professor teaching a class (household members) about the poem. Ask him to prepare the "lecture" by analyzing the poem as outlined in the Standard, paying particular attention to how tone or meaning is conveyed, and then taking "students" through the process of understanding the piece more deeply from his own findings. You, as one of the students, should pose questions or make observations about punctuation, rhythm, repetition, or rhyme to make the class more interesting and interactive.

> **Snap, crackle, pop**
>
> *✍ Describe <u>onomatopoeia</u>—the use of words whose sounds suggest their meaning. Think of some examples together (sizzle, snap, pop, crackle, and the like), having your child create movements that enhance the sound as he says it aloud.*

PREK-12

Standard 15: Style and Language

Students will identify and analyze how an author's words appeal to the senses, create imagery, suggest mood, and set tone and provide evidence from the text to support their understanding. (See also Standard 14.)

Above all, authors are wordsmiths, playing their craft at the level of word and sentence—adding, subtracting, and substituting, changing word order, even using punctuation to shift the rhythm and flow of language. Much of a student's delight in reading can come from identifying and analyzing how an author shapes a text.

GRADES 5-6

(Continue to address earlier standards as needed and as they apply to more difficult texts.)

15.3   Identify imagery, figurative language, rhythm, or flow when responding to literature.

For example, after reading and discussing Cynthia Rylant's poems in Soda Jerk, students write their own poems choosing words that evoke a sense of the soda jerk's drug store.

15.4   Identify and analyze the importance of shades of meaning in determining word choice in a piece of literature.

CHILD'S FAVORITE BOOK Have your child select his favorite book, one that he believes is particularly well written. Go through the book and write down selected sentences, underlining the most evocative words or phrases. Then have your child read the sentences and write down suggestions for replacing the underlined word or phrase with related words. What slightly different tone, image, or connotation is conveyed by each choice? Have your child expand the list with a thesaurus, and consider some of these other possible choices. Ask him to write down and carefully consider many word choices before selecting the one that he feels is the best replacement for the original word or phrase. After your child writes his final selected words into the sentences you wrote, compare them to the author's original text. Discuss the differences and similarities in results and why the author might have made those particular word selections.

GRADES 7-8

(Continue to address earlier standards as needed and as they apply to more difficult texts.)

15.5 Identify and analyze imagery and figurative language.

Visual symbols

 Both you and your child should each list something you really love (possibly chocolate chip cookies), some place you like being (a warm beach in wintertime), and an event that is exciting (a sports event or music concert). Then, on drawing paper, both of you should create evocative collages or drawn images, and write metaphors that describe these three things. (For example, you might write that chocolate chip cookies have "as many delicious chocolate chips as there are stars in the sky" to accompany pictures of gold speckled stars in the night sky.) You can mix your three selections together into one "poetic" composition, if you wish. Discuss how your words and images are both metaphors for the real things.

For example, students listen to three poems from Stephen Dunning's anthology,
Reflections On a Gift of Watermelon Pickle, that employ extended metaphor.
They discuss the effect of extended metaphor on the reader or listener and then write
their own extended metaphor poems.

15.6 **Identify and analyze how an author's use of words creates tone and mood.**

Standard 16: Myth, Traditional Narrative, and Classical Literature

Students will identify, analyze, and apply knowledge of the themes, structure, and elements of myths, traditional narratives, and classical literature and provide evidence from the text to support their understanding.

Young students enjoy the predictable patterns, excitement, and moral lessons of traditional stories. In the middle grades, knowledge of the character types, themes, and structures of these stories enables students to perceive similarities and differences when they compare traditional narratives from different cultures. In the upper grades, students can describe how authors through the centuries have drawn on traditional patterns and themes as archetypes in their writing, deepening their interpretations of these authors' works.

GRADES 5-6

(Continue to address earlier standards as needed and as they apply to more difficult texts.)

16.7 **Compare traditional literature from different cultures.**

For example, students read stories about constellations from several cultures, and show how each culture configured and explained a group of stars.

Like and unlike me

BOOK ABOUT YOUNG PEOPLE FROM ANOTHER CULTURE *All people share some characteristics and also have unique traits. Have your child select a book at the local library about a young person from a different culture. After reading it, ask your child to draw two portraits, one of himself and another of the child in the book. Ask your child to use one color marker to sketch the elements they share in common (such as similar hobbies, schoolwork, family structure) and then use a different color marker to draw elements that are different (cuisine, social customs, holiday observances). Use the opportunity to explore what is unique and special about your own family's culture, as well as to learn about others.*

16.8   Identify common structures *(magic helper, rule of three, transformation)* and stylistic elements *(hyperbole, refrain, simile)* in traditional literature.

GRADES 7-8

(Continue to address earlier standards as needed and as they apply to more difficult texts.)

16.9   Identify conventions in epic tales *(extended simile, the quest, the hero's tasks, special weapons or clothing, helpers).*

For example, after reading stories about Perseus, Theseus, or Herakles, students create their own hero tale employing conventions such as interventions of the gods, mythical monsters, or a series of required tasks.

16.10   Identify and analyze similarities and differences in mythologies from different cultures *(ideas of the afterlife, roles and characteristics of deities, types and purposes of myths).*

Ancient constellation myths

WWW 📖 *Ask your child, "How can we prove that constellations have been around for centuries?" Together, read about the same star patterns we see today in the ancient constellation-related myths from different cultures (Greek and Roman, Native American, Chinese, and Indian) using library resources or any major Internet search engine. (Examples of Greek and Roman mythology of the constellations can be found online at http://www.emufarm.org/~cmbell/myth/myth.html.) Have your child chart the similarities and differences across cultures about the stars, their meaning, and the stories behind them.*

PREK-12

Standard 17: Dramatic Literature

Students will identify, analyze, and apply knowledge of the theme, structure, and elements of drama and provide evidence from the text to support their understanding.

Since ancient times, drama has entertained, informed, entranced, and transformed us as we willingly enter into the other worlds created on stage and screen. In reading dramatic literature, students learn to analyze the techniques playwrights use to achieve their magic. By studying plays as well as film, television shows, and radio scripts, students learn to be more critical and selective readers, listeners, and viewers of drama.

GRADES 5-6

(Continue to address earlier standards as needed and as they apply to more difficult texts.)

17.3   Identify and analyze structural elements particular to dramatic literature (*scenes, acts, cast of characters, stage directions*) in the plays they read, view, write, and perform.

Watch out Broadway!

WWW **COPIES OF A SHORT PLAY** *Help your child select (or ask a librarian for assistance) a short play or scene from a longer play that he will direct. Before heading for the Broadway stage, however, your young director first must be able to define the theater terms in the Standard. (He can find most of the terms in a dictionary or online using an Internet search engine.) Your child should easily incorporate this new vocabulary into his communication with actors as he proceeds with the casting (of household members and friends), rehearsals, and staging. Ask your young director to come out before the final performance and explain to the audience what they are about to see, incorporating as many of the the-atrical terms as possible in his description.*

17.4   Identify and analyze the similarities and differences between a narra-tive text and its film or play version.

For example, after reading Norton Juster's novel, The Phantom Tollbooth, *and watching the filmed version, students adapt passages of the novel as they write their own scripts, present them, and justify their specific choices in adapting the narrative to a script edition.*

GRADES 7-8

(Continue to address earlier standards as needed and as they apply to more dif-ficult texts.)

17.5   Identify and analyze elements of setting, plot, and characterization in the plays that are read, viewed, written, and/or performed:

■   setting *(place, historical period, time of day);*

■   plot *(exposition, conflict, rising action, falling action); and*

■   characterization *(character motivations, actions, thoughts, development).*

17.6   Identify and analyze the similarities and differences in the presenta-tion of setting, character, and plot in texts, plays, and films.

Standard 18: Dramatic Reading and Performance *

Students will plan and present dramatic readings, recitations, and performances that demonstrate appropriate consideration of audience and purpose.

Rehearsal and performance involve memorization, and the use of expressive speech and gestures. Because of their repetitive nature, they demand of student actors a level of active engagement that surpasses that of reading. The excitement and satisfaction of performing in front of an audience should be part of every student's school experience.

GRADES 5-6

(Continue to address earlier standards as needed and as they apply to more difficult texts.)

18.3   Develop characters through the use of basic acting skills (*memorization, sensory recall, concentration, diction, body alignment, expressive detail*) and self-assess using teacher-developed criteria before performing.

Director's call

POEM, SPEECH, OR PLAY Ask your child to imagine that you are a film director, and that you would like to "audition" her for a part in your upcoming movie. For the tryout, you would like your child to recite a single poem, excerpt from a speech, or dramatic soliloquy. Help direct your child to make the proper volume and gesture adjustments as she tries out for the newest blockbuster.

GRADES 7-8

(Continue to address earlier standards as needed and as they apply to more difficult texts.)

18.4 Develop and present characters through the use of basic acting skills *(memorization, sensory recall, concentration, diction, body alignment, expressive detail)*, explain the artistic choices made, and use a scoring guide with teacher-developed categories *(content, presentation style)* to create scoring criteria for assessment.

For example, pairs of students create biographies for the characters in an open script (with no stage directions or character descriptions), and improvise appropriate vocal qualities and movement for them. The class analyzes the dramatic interpretations of each pair.

Composition

Standard 19: Writing

Students will write with a clear focus, coherent organization, and sufficient detail.

We write to tell stories, to record actual and imagined sights, sounds, and experiences, to provide information and opinion, to make connections, and to synthesize ideas. From their earliest years in school, students learn to provide a clear purpose and sequence for their ideas in order to make their writing coherent, logical, and expressive.

Little pictorial odyssey

Together explore the mesmerizing optical illusions in the art of Maurits Cornelis Escher (1898–1972) using library art books or online (type "Escher" into any major Internet search engine). Have your child take notes about the works and his reactions to them. Ask your child to share his thoughts and feelings with you verbally, and ask questions to help him clarify his response. Next ask your child to use his notes to create an outline for a letter that will explain the Escher experience to a friend or relative who has never seen the artist's work. Using the outline,

have him draft a letter with a clear focus and organization, along with supporting details about the mind-shifting compositions. Encourage him to use a dictionary and a thesaurus to find the right words to evoke the fascinating images. As your child reviews the first draft of his letter, ask him to make sure that his main idea is stated clearly at the beginning, and that the final paragraph includes a summary of his reaction to Escher's work. Have him revise the draft, and mail the polished letter!

GRADES 5-6

(Continue to address earlier standards as needed.)

For imaginative/literary writing:*

19.14 Write stories or scripts containing the basic elements of fiction *(characters, dialogue, setting, plot with a clear resolution).*

Now what?

 MISCELLANEOUS HOUSEHOLD ITEMS Explain to your child that you are going to give her a "set up" for a story, which she will then develop into a written narrative. For props, find two unrelated household objects, such as an eggbeater, toothbrush, or Halloween mask. For the "set up," hold the items in your hands and then walk into the room, stop short, and ask, "Now what?" It's up to your child to take it from there, using the elements in the Standard to write a gripping tale, edited for correct spelling, grammar, punctuation, and tone.

19.15 Write poems using poetic techniques *(alliteration, onomatopoeia),* figurative language *(simile, metaphor),* and graphic elements *(capital letters, line length).*

For example, students use a postcard of their favorite painting or sculpture from an art museum they have visited as the inspiration for their own paintings. They write a poem or short story to go with their artwork, revise, edit, and critique it, and share their work at a school art exhibit or local senior center. (Connects with Arts Standards 1, 3, and 4.)

For informational/expository writing:

19.16 Write brief research reports with clear focus and supporting detail.

If I had a pet giraffe

 Have your child select a very unlikely animal for a household pet, such as a giraffe, crocodile, porpoise, or aardvark. Have him answer the question, "What would I have to do if I had a pet _____?" Have your child investigate online or at the library what he would have to do, learn, get, and change in your home to accommodate this new pet. After gathering all the information, have your child organize it into a persuasive essay that describes why getting such an animal would be a good idea. Then, have your child argue the opposite, stating in an opposing essay why it might not be such a wise idea for your household or the animal!

19.17 Write a short explanation of a process that includes a topic statement, supporting details, and a conclusion.

19.18 Write formal letters to correspondents such as authors, newspapers, businesses, or government officials.

Dear author

 Ask your child if all readers share the same opinions about books, or if readers have personal preferences. Have your child read several (if possible, contrasting) reviews of a book he has read recently. (Online bookselling sites often feature a variety of reviews for individual titles.) Ask your child to compare and contrast the reviews. Does each reviewer support his or her position with details from the book? Do some of the reviewers express personal preferences that are consistent or inconsistent with your child's reading tastes? Then, have your child write a letter to the book's author sharing his interpretation. Your child's letter should demonstrate a careful reading and analysis of the work, and should be organized around a clearly stated main idea, supported with details from the story. After drafting, editing, and revising the correspondence (checking for correct spelling, punctuation, and grammar), mail the letter to the author in care of the book's publisher.

(Continue to address earlier standards as needed.)

For imaginative/literary writing:*

19.19 Write stories or scripts with well-developed characters, setting, dialogue, clear conflict and resolution, and sufficient descriptive detail.

19.20 Write poems using poetic techniques (*alliteration, onomatopoeia, rhyme scheme*), figurative language (*simile, metaphor, personification*), and graphic elements (*capital letters, line length, word position*).

For informational/expository writing:

19.21 Write reports based on research that include quotations, footnotes or endnotes, and a bibliography.

19.22 Write and justify a personal interpretation of literary, informational, or expository reading that includes a topic statement, supporting details from the literature, and a conclusion.

19.23 Write multi-paragraph compositions that have clear topic development, logical organization, effective use of detail, and variety in sentence structure.

Random funny story

TWO PAPER BAGS On individual pieces of paper, write down ten miscellaneous nouns (e.g., trampoline, avocado, penguin, robot, spotlight) and place them in a bag; do the same for ten miscellaneous verbs (e.g., hiccup, snooze, scramble, freeze, twist, bellow). Then, have your child randomly select five words from each of the two bags and ask your child to use all ten words in an expository essay. Have him begin the essay writing process by creating an outline with the guidelines of the Standard in mind; then, have him create a first draft and revise it. He must incorporate the ten words into his essay, so encourage him to use, similes, metaphors, and humor to work them all in! Review your child's finished essay together and discuss its topic development, organization, use of detail, and varied sentence structure. Help him correct any mistakes in capitalization, punctuation, or spelling, and have your child read his entertaining essay aloud at the next family meal.

Composition

Standard 20: Consideration of Audience and Purpose

Students will write for different audiences and purposes. (See also Standards 3, 6, and 19.)

When students adapt their writing for a variety of purposes, they learn that different organizational strategies, word choices, and tones are needed. They learn that this is also true when considering audience. Through this process students gain a deeper understanding of the world around them and grow in their ability to influence it.

GRADES 5-6

(Continue to address earlier standards as needed.)

20.3 **Make distinctions among fiction, nonfiction, dramatic literature, and poetry, and use these genres selectively when writing for different purposes.**

For example, fifth graders visit the Revolutionary battlegrounds in Lexington and Concord and write a press release about their trip for the local newspaper and a script about the Revolution to be performed for younger students.

GRADES 7-8

(Continue to address earlier standards as needed.)

20.4 **Select and use appropriate rhetorical techniques for a variety of purposes, such as to convince or entertain the reader.**

For example, in preparation for an upcoming election, student candidates and their supporters discuss the most appropriate and appealing methods of presenting their messages. They then write speeches, make posters, design campaign buttons, or compose jingles for targeted audiences, As a group, students discuss how genre and audience work together to support arguments being advanced.

WWW Have your child study, interpret, and present a moving speech, such as Martin Luther King Jr.'s 1963 "I Have a Dream" speech at http://web66.coled.umn.edu/new/MLK/MLK.html or at http://www.7cs.com/king.html, or perhaps President Lincoln's 1863 "Gettysburg Address" at http://lcweb.loc.gov/exhibits/gadd/. How will your child's understanding of the speech impact the way he presents it to others? Afterward, discuss how it felt to speak passionate words spoken by a real person in history.

PREK-12

Standard 21: Revising

Students will demonstrate improvement in organization, content, paragraph development, level of detail, style, tone, and word choice (diction) in their compositions after revising them.

A flawless first draft is a rarity, even for the most gifted writer. Writing well requires two processes that sometimes appear to be in opposition: creating and criticizing. As they expand their imaginative thinking on paper, students must at the same time learn the patience and discipline required to edit, reshape, and polish their final work. Revising to get thoughts and words just right can be the most difficult part of writing, but also the most satisfying.

What's good?

CHILD'S FAVORITE BOOK, EXAMPLES OF CHILD'S WRITING Have your child select a book that she thinks is excellent. Help her identify the reasons why she likes the book (an exciting plot, an imaginative setting, snappy dialogue, and so forth), and have her make a list of the criteria that contributed to the book's success. Then, have your child review examples of her own written work. Do they meet the standards of her favorite book? Have your child select one of her writing samples and revise it to try to more closely meet her own standards, checking them off her list when successful.

GRADES 5-6

(Continue to address earlier standards as needed.)

21.4 Revise writing to improve level of detail and precision of language after determining where to add images and sensory detail, combine sentences, vary sentences, and rearrange text.

For example, students write autobiographies entitled "The Worst and Best of Me." In pairs they read each other's work and suggest places where more descriptive detail is needed and where sentences could be combined for variety in length and structure.

Fine tuning

Have both you and your child create separate campaign leaflets, imagining you are both running for president of your neighborhood association. What will you write to convince others that you should be elected? What personal characteristics, experiences, and ideas will you try to get across? Swap leaflets and critique one another's writing. What is clear, unclear, strong, weak, confusing, and so forth? Then each edit your own work as indicated in the Standard, and rewrite the final leaflet on plain paper, adding illustrations that will attract voters to your words.

21.5 Improve word choice by using dictionaries or thesauruses.

GRADES 7-8

(Continue to address earlier standards as needed.)

21.6 Revise writing to improve organization and diction after checking the logic underlying the order of ideas, the precision of vocabulary used, and the economy of writing.

21.7 Improve word choice by using a variety of references.

Composition

PREK-12

Standard 22: Standard English Conventions

Students will use knowledge of standard English conventions in their writing, revising, and editing.

We write to make connections to the larger world. Writers' ideas are more likely to be taken seriously when the words are spelled accurately and the sentences are grammatically correct. Use of standard English conventions helps readers understand and follow the writer's meaning, while errors can be distracting and confusing. Standard English conventions are the "good manners" of writing and speaking that make communication fluid.

Cap it off

 Look through the arts & entertainment section of the newspaper with your child and circle the instances where capitalization is used. Note all the different cases, including titles of books and musical compositions, names of individuals and organizations, and so forth. Also find the use of capitalization in quotations.

Right mark

 Read all about punctuation marks by clicking on each term at http://grammargirl.9ug.com/toc.html or by researching the topic at the library. Then have your child circle an example of each type of punctuation in the daily newspaper, explaining why the particular punctuation mark is used in each situation. Refer back to the website or reference books if necessary.

GRADES 5-6

(Continue to address earlier standards as needed.)

22.7 Use additional knowledge of correct mechanics (*apostrophes, quotation marks, comma use in compound sentences, paragraph indentations*), correct sentence structure (*elimination of fragments and run-ons*), and correct standard English spelling (*commonly used homophones*) when writing, revising, and editing.

I start . . . you finish

 Write the beginning of a silly sentence that your child will complete in writing (e.g., "Maria stood on her head because . . ."). Reverse the process and ask your child to begin sentences that you will complete. After you have completed each sentence, ask your child how she had imagined finishing it. Look at each finished sentence together and have your child check for punctuation, spelling, and so forth. To extend the game, write a whole story using silly sentences. You can begin the game by creating one silly sentence (for example, "The jellyfish wished they had legs and feet so they could walk up on the beach and join the noisy party hosted by the flock of seagulls"). Then invite your child to write the next sentence to continue the story ("Then the jellyfish spied the sea turtles and asked for a ride across the sand to the party") and so forth, alternating until a complete story is told.

GRADES 7-8

(Continue to address earlier standards as needed and as they apply to more difficult texts.)

22.8 Use knowledge of types of sentences (*simple, compound, complex*), correct mechanics (*comma after introductory structures*), correct usage (*pronoun reference*), sentence structure (*complete sentences, properly placed modifiers*), and standard English spelling when writing and editing.

Chief editor game

 THREE WRITING SAMPLES Ask your child to imagine that she is the editor-in-chief of a magazine, and that she has been asked to consider three articles for publication. Use three samples of your child's writing

(created for the activities in this book or for classroom assignments) as submissions. Ask your young editor-in-chief to consider each submission in relation to the Standard. Are sentences constructed properly? Is the punctuation correct? Are words spelled and used correctly? Ask your child to revise the three writing samples according to the guidelines in the Standard, as if she was editing the work for publication. As a first step in the revision process, have her re-read each piece and circle errors (misspelled words, incorrect grammar and punctuation, misplaced modifiers) on the original document. For the next step, ask her to review each writing sample sentence by sentence. Can any of the sentences be made more effective by simplifying them, or by combining them with another sentence to make one compound or complex sentence? Have your child write her editorial suggestions for stronger sentences on each original piece. Then, ask your child to play the role of the writer receiving these editorial suggestions, and have her rewrite each piece so it is fully polished for publication. Encourage your child to use this editorial process when preparing homework assignments.

PREK-12

Standard 23: Organizing Ideas in Writing

Students will organize ideas in writing in a way that makes sense for their purpose.

When ideas are purposefully organized to advance the writer's intentions, they have the greatest impact on the writer's audience. Writers who understand how to arrange their ideas in ways that suit their purposes for writing will achieve coherence and clarity.

GRADES 5-6

(Continue to address earlier standards as needed.)

23.6   Decide on the placement of descriptive details about setting, charac-
        ters, and events in stories.

For example, when writing their own mystery stories, students plan in advance where clues will be located, what red herrings will complicate the search, and what special talents the detective will employ to solve the mystery.

Around about words

Help your child hone his descriptive skills. Ask your child to describe his favorite snack without identifying it by name. Encourage your child to use details relating to the senses—the way the food smells, tastes, looks, feels, sounds, and so forth—being as descriptive as possible. For example, "It's got two round, dark brown disks, which are crisp and crunchy. Between these two disks is a white, soft, creamy circle that holds the two sides together." (An Oreo cookie.) After your child has had some practice using descriptive words, play a game called "Person, Place, or Thing." One player begins by saying, "I'm thinking of a person (or a place, or a thing)" and then gives the other player a one-word descriptive clue. (For example, if the first person is thinking of the beach, he or she might offer clues such as "sandy," "wet," and "sunny.") The other player should try to guess the person, place, or thing the first player is describing. If he or she guesses incorrectly, the first player should offer another clue, and the second player should guess again, continuing until the second player guesses the answer correctly. The goal of the game is for the first player to help the second player guess the answer with the least number of clues, by choosing the most descriptive words. If the person, place, or thing has not been guessed after ten clues, the first player should reveal it, and the second player should suggest some descriptive words that might have helped him or her guess correctly.

23.7   Group related ideas together and place them in logical order when
        writing summaries or reports.

For example, students write a summary of a biography of George Washington, group-ing their ideas in categories that make sense for the biography (early life, education, battle strategies, actions as president) and place the categories in a logical order as they compose a multi-paragraph report.

23.8   Organize information about a topic into a coherent paragraph with a topic sentence, sufficient supporting detail, and a concluding sentence.

(Continue to address earlier standards as needed.)

23.9   Integrate use of organizing techniques that break up strict chronological order in a story (*starting in the middle of the action, then filling in background information, using flashbacks*).

For example, after reading the short story, "The Bet" by Anton Chekov, students use a flashback in their own stories and discuss the effect of this technique.

23.10   Organize information into a coherent essay or report with a thesis statement in the introduction, transition sentences to link paragraphs, and a conclusion.

23.11   Organize ideas for writing comparison-and-contrast essays.

*For example, in writing a comparison between two characters, students consider two forms for organizing their ideas. In the opposing form they describe all the similarities together, write a transition, and then describe all the differences. In the alternating form, they create categories for their information (*appearance, character traits, and relationships with other characters*), and describe both similarities and differences within each category.*

Standard 24: Research★

Students will gather information from a variety of sources, analyze and evaluate the quality of the information they obtain, and use it to answer their own questions.

As the amount and complexity of knowledge increases, students need to understand the features of the many resources available to them and know how to conduct an efficient and successful search for accurate information.

GRADES 5-6

(Continue to address earlier standards as needed and as they apply to more difficult texts.)

24.3 **Apply steps for obtaining information from a variety of sources, organizing information, documenting sources, and presenting research in individual and group projects:**

■ use an expanded range of print and non-print sources *(atlases, databases, electronic, on-line resources)*

Young consumer report

ACCESS TO CARD CATALOG, READER'S GUIDE TO PERIODICAL LITERATURE, A COMPUTER CATALOG Have your child research the very best sneakers (or backpack or sports equipment) on the market using the elements listed in the materials list above. Next, ask your young analyst to write a "consumer report" (with appropriate graphs and charts), supporting his findings with specific references and citations.

■ follow established criteria for evaluating information;

■ locate specific information within resources by using indexes, tables of contents, electronic search key words;

■ organize and present research using the grades 5-6 Learning Standards in the Composition Strand as a guide for writing; and

■ provide appropriate documentation in a consistent format.

GRADES 7-8

(Continue to address earlier standards as needed and as they apply to more difficult texts.)

24.4 **Apply steps for obtaining information from a variety of sources, organizing information, documenting sources, and presenting research in individual projects:**

- differentiate between primary and secondary source materials;

First-hand history

***PRIMARY SOURCE MATERIALS SUCH AS FAMILY MEMORA-BILIA, LETTERS, GOVERNMENT RECORDS, PHOTOGRAPHS, NEWSPAPER CLIPPINGS, CERTIFICATES, AND SO FORTH** Have your child study the history of a relative (perhaps yourself, a grandparent, aunt, or uncle) up close by examining <u>primary</u> <u>sources</u> (those created during the time period being studied, including photographs, letters, and personal memorabilia). Help your child assemble a variety of primary sources and piece together a "history" of the person's life, creating a mini-exhibition on a table, counter, shelf, or other open flat space. Have your child create labels that explain each item and what it reveals about the person's history. Afterward, discuss the difference between studying history with these primary sources, and <u>secondary</u> <u>sources</u>, which are materials prepared later by people who studied the primary sources, such as textbooks, biographies, or documentaries. Have your child create her own secondary source by writing an introductory essay to the exhibition. Make sure your child's essay is legibly written and correctly spelled and punctuated.*

- differentiate between paraphrasing and using direct quotes in a report;

- organize and present research using the grade 7-8 Learning Standards in the Composition Strand as a guide for writing;

- document information and quotes and use a consistent format for footnotes or endnotes; and

- use standard bibliographic format to document sources.

For example, students read Dickens' A Christmas Carol. Grouped into "families" from various strata of Victorian society, they use electronic, Internet, and print resources to gather information about daily life in Victorian England before hosting a period tea party for parents and administrators, imitating the social graces of the period. During the tea, the adults ask students questions about the roles they are playing. Then students organize and write a report presenting and documenting their research.

Standard 25: Evaluating Writing and Presentations*

Students will develop and use appropriate rhetorical, logical, and stylistic criteria for assessing final versions of their compositions or research projects before presenting them to varied audiences.

Achieving a high standard of excellence in writing is a goal for all schools. It is important for students to recognize the hallmarks of superior work so that they know what they need to do in order to improve and polish their writing and speaking. Classrooms and schools that make standards of quality explicit help students learn to become thoughtful critics of their own work.

GRADES 5-6

(Continue to address earlier standards as needed and as they apply to more difficult texts.)

25.3 Use prescribed criteria from a scoring rubric to evaluate compositions, recitations, or performances before presenting them to an audience.

For example, as they rehearse a program of original poetry for residents of a nursing home, students apply criteria for poetry writing and presentation skills.

Sports organizational review

 Have your child read a sports article about a game that she played in or watched. Ask your child to reflect upon her personal experience of the game to offer insight into how and why the journalist chose to organize the account of the game in a particular manner. Additionally, have your child "review the review," by grading the effectiveness of the article's content, purpose, and organization. Afterward, have your child use her personal experience of the game to devise a different organizational structure for the article, and then draft and revise this new version.

Critique the critic

WWW *Have your child read a critic's review of a movie, television show, or album in which she is interested. Ask your child to "grade" the critic in terms of how well he or she supported any claims (e.g., "It was the best show ever..." "The singer's first album was far superior...") and where the critic might have been biased—perhaps toward or against the show, movie, or particular performer—and any evidence of stereotyping. Have your child write her own "A+" review on the same topic, correcting the inadequacies or inaccuracies she noted in the critic's original piece.*

GRADES 7-8

(Continue to address earlier standards as needed and as they apply to more difficult texts.)

25.4   As a group, develop and use scoring guides or rubrics to improve organization and presentation of written and oral projects.

Media

PREK-12

Standard 26: Analysis of Media★

Students will identify, analyze, and apply knowledge of the conventions, elements, and techniques of film, radio, video, television, multimedia productions, the Internet, and other technologies, and provide evidence to support their understanding. (See also Standards 17, 18, 24, 27, and the Theatre Standards of the *Arts Curriculum Framework*.)

The electronic mass media developed during the twentieth century—radio, film, video, multimedia and the Internet—have the capacity to convey information, entertain, and persuade in ways that are distinctly different from print media. In English language arts classes students have traditionally learned to analyze how an author chooses words and manipulates language. Given the prevalence of media in their lives, students also need to be able to analyze how images, sound, and text are used together effectively in the hands of a skillful director or website designer.

Four-way news

 Together, watch the local news and have your child select a story that interests her. It can be a story about an event, a movie review, or a weather or sports report. Afterward, have your child use newspapers, magazines, and online information to research and write additional information about the topic. Have your child note next to each bit of information which type of media was used and its particular structural features. Then, have your child discuss the differences and similarities in the information each resource provided on her topic.

GRADES 5-6

(Continue to address earlier standards as needed and as they apply to more difficult texts.)

26.3 Identify techniques used in educational reference software and websites and describe how these techniques are the same or different from the techniques used by authors and illustrators of print materials.

For example, students research the lives of authors and illustrators on the Internet and compare the kind of information they receive through this technology to the kind of information they can find in printed reference books.

GRADES 7-8

(Continue to address earlier standards as needed and as they apply to more difficult texts.)

26.4 Analyze the effect on the reader's or viewer's emotions of text and image in print journalism, and images, sound, and text in electronic journalism, distinguishing techniques used in each to achieve these effects.

For example, students compare how newspapers, radio, television, and Internet news outlets cover the same story, such as the Boston Marathon or a day in a political campaign, analyzing how words, sounds, and still or moving images are used in each medium. For their final project they write about how the medium of communication affects the story conveyed.

Word power I

At the breakfast table, have your child examine a box of cereal and identify all the words the company has used to make the product enticing. Examine all of the word choices as well as the ways the words are presented. (Some words are large and brightly colored, others just appear in small type on the side of the box.) What does the cereal box seem to "promise" if you eat the product? Have your child write and design her own persuasive advertisement for a favorite television show, movie, toy, dessert, or drink. Make sure your child writes legibly, and uses correct spelling, punctuation, and capitalization for her advertisement.

Fad diets

With your child, watch television advertisements or listen to radio ads for diet products and weight-loss foods (or any "miracle" cure). Discuss which claims seem likely and which do not (such as losing ten pounds in two days). How does the fact that the advertiser's claims are broadcast publicly affect what you might believe about them? Would you be more or less likely to believe the claims if they were printed in a scientific or medical journal? How about if they were confirmed by a "real person" (as opposed to a paid actor) on TV? What if you heard the claims from a friend? Based on your conclusions, discuss the methods advertisers use to persuade customers to buy other categories of products (toys, clothes, sneakers, etc.).

Standard 27: Media Production*

Students will design and create coherent media productions (audio, video, television, multimedia, Internet, emerging technologies) with a clear controlling idea, adequate detail, and appropriate consideration of audience, purpose, and medium. (See also Standards 18, 24, 26, and the Theatre Standards of the *Arts Curriculum Framework*.)

Students grow up surrounded by television, movies, and the Internet. The availability in schools of recording and editing equipment and computers offers students opportunities to combine text, images, and sounds in their reports and creative works. Putting together an effective media production—whether a relatively simple radio play or a complex film documentary entails as much discipline and satisfaction as writing a good essay. Both require clarity of purpose, selectivity in editing, and knowledge of the expressive possibilities of the medium used.

GRADES 5-6

(Continue to address earlier standards as needed and as they apply to more difficult texts or media productions.)

27.3   Create a media production using effective images, text, music, sound effects, or graphics.

For example, students create a storyboard for an animated or live filmed version of Shiloh, *by Phyllis Reynolds Naylor. As they work, they consider places in the script in which close-up and distance shots, voice-over narration, or captions would enhance viewers' understanding.*

(Continue to address earlier standards as needed and as they apply to more difficult texts and media productions.)

27.4 **Create media presentations and written reports on the same subject and compare the differences in effects of each.**

For example, two groups of students create reports on the United States Supreme Court: one a written report and the other a multimedia presentation. When both groups have presented their reports to the class, classmates evaluate the information they learned from each presentation.

Ad agency

COMPUTER, SOFTWARE *Have your child imagine that she works at an advertising agency that has just been hired to create a marketing campaign for a hot new sneaker. Have your young employee combine computer-generated text and art, hand-drawn illustrations, handwritten copy, and music to create a persuasive ad. Before finalizing her ad campaign, have your child review campaigns for other sneaker brands, including print ads in magazines and newspapers, online ads, and TV commercials. Have her compare and contrast her campaign with existing campaigns. Does her campaign provide consumers with the same amount of inspiration and information? Are the visual and text elements of her campaign as effective as those for other sneakers? After she has revised her work based on this analysis, ask her to present the proposed campaign to the client (you), describing in a well-supported, specific manner, how and why it will sell millions of sneakers to eager consumers around the world.*

27.5 **Use criteria to assess the effectiveness of media presentations.**

Mathematics

Grades 5-8

Number Sense and Operations

GRADES 5–6

Students engage in problem solving, communicating, reasoning, connecting, and representing as they:

6.N.1 Demonstrate an understanding of positive integer exponents, in particular, when used in powers of ten, e.g., 10^2, 10^5.

Power-walk race

✐ **WWW** 📄 **SIXTEEN NOTE CARDS, TWO BAGS** Together, begin by reviewing the definition for <u>exponent</u>—*the raised number to the right of the base number that indicates how many times the base number is multiplied by itself; it is also referred to as a "power." (If necessary, review further with library materials or click on "exponents" at http://www.*

mathleague.com/help/decwholeexp/decwholeexp.htm.) Write a simple example, such as 2^3, on a note card and have your child write out and solve for 2 to the third power on the back of the card (2 x 2 x 2 = 8). Continue with more examples on separate note cards until you have written one on each of the sixteen note cards, particularly using the power of 10, as described in the Standard. (Help your child note that in the power of 10, the exponent indicates the number of zeros that will follow the integer 1. For instance, 10^5 = 10,0000.) Check to make sure that all the answers on the backs of the cards are correct. Then, have your child shuffle the note cards and place eight in each bag. Move outside to an area where you can walk a long distance. Together, start from the same place and then each of you randomly pick "power cards" from your bags, looking at the side with the number written with an exponent. Each player computes the power and gets to move forward the resulting number of steps, if after turning over the card the answer is correct. (If the number of steps is greater than space allows, ask your child to keep count of the total number of steps each of you has earned.) Whoever gets the farthest from the starting point at the end of eight cards wins! For an extra workout, substitute hops or jumping jacks for the correct number of steps forward.

6.N.2 Demonstrate an understanding of place value to billions and thousandths.

Millions and billions

Share with your child that in an average life span, a human heart beats 2.5 billion times, pumping about 100,000 million gallons of blood. Have your child represent this numerically (2,500,000,000 and 100,000,000,000 respectively), placing the commas properly (after every third zero starting at the right).

6.N.3 Represent and compare very large (billions) and very small (thousandths) positive numbers in various forms such as expanded notation without exponents, e.g., 9724 = 9 x 1000 + 7 x 100 + 2 x 10 + 4.

6.N. 4 Demonstrate an understanding of fractions as a ratio of whole numbers, as parts of unit wholes, as parts of a collection, and as locations on the number line.

WWW *Ratio* means relationship. It is a comparison between two numbers. (For instance, if there are two adults and three children watching television, this would be written as $^2/_3$, 2:3, or 2 to 3.) Explain that when written as 2:3, the colon is an abbreviation for the division sign. Batting averages can also be expressed as ratios. Together, watch a little league or professional baseball game and have your child keep score for each player, writing down the number of base hits and times at bat. At the end of the game, have your child express each player's batting average as a ratio. Batting averages are calculated by taking the number of hits out of a 100 times at bat, and multiplying the result by 10. A batting average of .300, means that the batter gets 30 hits out of every 100 times at bat; this can be expressed in a ratio from as 30:100. Learn more about ratios at http://www.mathleague.com/help/ratio/ratio.htm.

6.N.5 Identify and determine common equivalent fractions, mixed numbers, decimals, and percents.

Point out that your child works with decimals every day! Money is typically written with decimals. For instance, a dime is $.10, which can also be expressed as $^{10}/_{100}$ or $^1/_{10}$. Play a game in which you place a number of bills in a pile on the right and a pile of coins on the left. Sweep some of the bills and some of the coins toward your child for each step in the game. (The coins should always equal less than the amount of dollar bills.) Your child is to write out the relationship of the coins to the bills as percents, fractions, and decimals. Each time he gets the equation correct, your child sweeps the money onto his side. When all the money is gone, the first round of the game is complete. Now switch roles. Write out various ratios, percents, fractions, and decimals and ask your child to use the money to represent each of them in at least two variations. For example, if you wrote 1.25, your child could create the monetary equation of a quarter in the left-hand pile and a dollar in the right-hand pile, as well as five quarters in the left-hand pile. Again, each time your child gets an answer correct, he gets to sweep the money off to the side until there is none left from the initial pile.

Product numbers hunt I

✍ *HOUSEHOLD PRODUCTS Together with your child, search the kitchen cabinets, refrigerator, and the bathroom cabinet for an array of products with weights and/or sizes listed in various forms (whole or mixed numbers, fractions, decimals, and so forth). Place them all on a table. Ask your child to divide the items into groups with similar expressions (all the products listed in ounces together, all those in pounds together, and so forth). Then, have your child line up the items in each group from the smallest to largest quantity. Hence, a .5-ounce bottle of perfume would go before a 2.5-ounce jar of hand cream. For further practice, play this game while waiting on line at the supermarket, having your child "size order" the goods in your shopping cart. Move on to the next step.*

6.N.6 Find and position integers, fractions, mixed numbers, and decimals (both positive and negative) on the number line.

6.N.7 Compare and order integers (including negative integers), and positive fractions, mixed numbers, decimals, and percents.

Product numbers hunt II

✍ *HOUSEHOLD PRODUCTS, TIMER Have your child review his groups from the first step of this activity. Then ask your child to write the amount of each product in a different form, changing decimals to fractions, fractions to mixed numbers, and so forth. For example, a 2.5-ounce jar of hand cream could be written as 2 $\frac{1}{2}$ ounces or $\frac{25}{10}$ ounces, and so forth. Every time your child gets one of his equivalent format answers correct, he can take the product off the table, until none are left. Play a second round with other household products that display different number formats and try to have your child "beat the clock," setting a timer that allows forty-five seconds for writing an answer for each product.*

6.N.8 Apply number theory concepts–including prime and composite numbers, prime factorization, greatest common factor, least common multiple, and divisibility rules for 2, 3, 4, 5, 6, 9, and 10–to the solution of problems.

6.N.9 Select and use appropriate operations to solve problems involving addition, subtraction, multiplication, division, and positive integer exponents with whole numbers, and with positive fractions, mixed numbers, decimals, and percents.

Special fractions

 Explain that <u>decimals</u> are fractions with denominators (the bottom number of a fraction) of 10, 100, 1,000, etc., increasing by one zero each place to the right of the decimal point. Help your child understand this by placing a decimal on a page and then four short lines to the right (._ _ _ _). Have your child write the name for each decimal place (tenths, hundredths, thousandths, ten thousandths) above the appropriate line. Then, ask your child to fill in the corresponding representation of the fraction for each below the lines ($\frac{1}{10}$, $\frac{1}{100}$, $\frac{1}{1000}$, $\frac{1}{10,000}$). Give a hint, if necessary, providing the first fraction ($\frac{1}{10}$). Show how decimals play an important role in everyday transactions by examining the way prices are represented in advertising. Together, find advertisements in newspapers, magazines, or catalogs. The decimal point separates the dollars from the cents. In $10.95, the cents could be expressed as the fraction $\frac{95}{100}$. Have your child practice translating the cents from various listed prices into fractions. In addition, have your child express the cents as a percent of a dollar. For instance, .25 is 25% of a dollar ($1.00).

6.N.10 Use the number line to model addition and subtraction of integers, with the exception of subtracting negative integers.

6.N.11 Apply the Order of Operations for expressions involving addition, subtraction, multiplication, and division with grouping symbols (+, −, x, ÷).

Operating order

 COTTON BALLS, BAND AIDS, Q-TIPS, SMALL BOX Create a visual demonstration to clarify for your child the concept of order of operations in an algebraic expression. Explain that you are going to write an algebraic expression that will represent the first aid items your child will then assemble into a first aid kit. Write the following equation with

plenty of space between each symbol on a large piece of paper: x + 3y + z + 2x + x(2 + 6) = First Aid Kit. Now write out a key: x = cotton balls, y = Band Aids, z = Q-tips. Have your child place the corresponding number of first aid items on the paper under their respective symbols (e.g., 3 Band Aids under 3y). Your child should notice that cotton balls (x) appear in the equation three times. First, perform any operations with parentheses (i.e., 2 + 6 = 8). The equation now looks like this: 1 cotton ball + 3 Band Aids + 1 Q-tip + 2 cotton balls + 1 cotton ball x 8. Next multiply and divide, whichever comes first, from the left to right of the equation (1 cotton ball x 8 = 8 cotton balls.) The equation is now: 1 cotton ball + 3 Band Aids + 1 Q-tip + 2 cotton balls + 8 cotton balls. Finally, add or subtract, whichever comes first, from left to right. Have your child rearrange the cotton balls to represent this last function (11 cotton balls + 3 Band Aids + 1 Q-tip) and then place them in their individual groups into a first aid box. To further reinforce the concept, together review information about order of operations at http://www.math.com/school/subject2/lessons/S2U1L2GL.html or research the term using library resources.

6.N.12   Demonstrate an understanding of the inverse relationship of addition and subtraction, and use that understanding to simplify computation and solve problems.

6.N.13   Accurately and efficiently add, subtract, multiply, and divide (with double-digit divisors) whole numbers and positive decimals.

Home banking

 SPARE BANK BOOK FOR RECORDING BANK ACCOUNT TRANSACTIONS OR NOTEBOOK, CALCULATOR Obtain a spare bank account transaction book for your child (or have her recreate the format on a page of notebook paper, using an empty page from your own bank book as a model). Have your child begin by listing the amount of money she has in savings. Each day for a week your child should add in any deposits, such as earnings from chores, gifts, or allowance, and subtract any money used for expenses, including gifts, food, entertainment, and

hobbies. (For this activity you can also have your child select an amount to have in her pretend savings, and then make imaginary transactions each day.) Every night have your child calculate how much additional money she will earn through interest, using the rate of 4% per day (multiplying the evening's savings total by .04). Have your child check her answers for the entire day's transactions, including the interest earned, with a calculator. You can "donate" the money to your child's bank each night that all the calculations are made correctly.

6.N.14 Accurately and efficiently add, subtract, multiply, and divide positive fractions and mixed numbers. Simplify fractions.

Nutty mixed fractions

✐ ⟨WWW⟩ NUTS Use visual aids to help your child understand how to write <u>mixed numbers</u> (consisting of whole numbers and fractions). First, write the improper fraction 9/5 on a piece of paper. In <u>improper fractions</u>, the numerator (top number) is equal to or greater than the denominator (bottom number). Have your child lay a pencil horizontally on the table and then place nine nuts above this "fraction line" and five nuts below it. Explain that this fraction equals more than a whole and there is another way to write it: as a mixed number. Have your child "divide" the number 5, (the amount of the denominator of the 5 nuts below) into the numerator of 9 nuts on top. Your child should remove 5 of the top nuts (leaving 4 on top). Have your child move these 5 just to the left of the pencil fraction line, assembling them to create the number 1. Then, looking at the nuts, ask your child to articulate the entire equation, which is the mixed fraction 1 4/5. Give your child more written improper fractions to translate, seeing how quickly she can transform them into nutty mixed fractions. Finally, if possible, explore fractions further at the "All About Fractions" website at http://www.aaamath.com/fra.html.

6.N.15 Add and subtract integers, with the exception of subtracting negative integers.

6.N.16 Estimate results of computations with whole numbers, and with positive fractions, mixed numbers, decimals, and percents. Describe reasonableness of estimates.

Raisins in a box

CEREAL WITH RAISINS, MEASURING CUP, BOWL Have your child determine a mathematical method for estimating how many raisins there are in an entire box of cereal. Have him pour a single serving (listed on the box) into a measuring cup, and then into a bowl. Then ask him to count the raisins in this single serving and multiply the number of raisins by the total number of servings in the box. For more cereal math, have your child devise a formula for estimating how many raisins there are in every spoonful of cereal. (Count the number of spoonfuls it takes to eat a single serving and then divide into the number of raisins per serving.) After your child is familiar with the number of raisins in the cereal, have him look at the image on the box. Is the representation of raisins in the picture accurate according to his experiments? If your child's estimates are lower, have him write an edited and carefully revised letter (with correct grammar, spelling, and punctuation) to the company explaining his experiment and suggesting more "truth in advertising."

Patterns, Relations, and Algebra

GRADES 5-6

Students engage in problem solving, communicating, reasoning, connecting, and representing as they:

6.P.1   Analyze and determine the rules for extending symbolic, arithmetic, and geometric patterns and progressions, e.g., ABBCCC; 1, 5, 9, 13 ...; 3, 9, 27, ...

Fibo' patterns

PINE CONES Have your child try his hand at a special type of pattern—Fibonacci patterns. Show your child the following sequence: 1, 1, 2, 3, 5, 8, 13, and have him extend it (21, 34, 55, etc.). Share that this pattern was first described in 1202 by the Italian mathematician Leonardo Fibonacci. Together, explore how these patterns are found in nature (flower petals, tree branches, mating patterns of bees,

and so forth) at http://www.mcs.surrey.ac.uk/Personal/R.Knott /Fibonacci/fibnat.html. View examples of Fibonacci patterns in a pine cone by clicking on "Pine cones" on the site. Have your child use online or library resources to learn more about Leonardo Fibonacci, and have him create an illustrated biography of this medieval mathematician, with correct spelling, grammar, punctuation, and details to support his main idea.

6.P.2   Replace variables with given values and evaluate/simplify, e.g., $2(\bullet)$ + 3 when $\bullet$ = 4.

6.P.3   Use the properties of equality to solve problems, e.g., if $\blacksquare$ + 7 = 13, then $\blacksquare$ = 13 – 7, therefore $\blacksquare$ = 6; if 3 x $\blacksquare$ = 15, then $^{1}/_{3}$ x 3 x $\blacksquare$ = $^{1}/_{3}$ x 15, therefore $\blacksquare$ = 5.

6.P.4   Represent real situations and mathematical relationships with concrete models, tables, graphs, and rules in words and with symbols, e.g., input-output tables.

Home archaeology

TWO BLANKETS, TWO TAPE MEASURES, BALL OF STRING, SCISSORS, FIVE TO TEN SMALL OBJECTS Before asking your child to participate in this activity, set up the "dig" on the floor. First, spread a large blanket flat on the floor. Open both tape measures as far as possible and place them on the blankets from edge to edge so they cross at the center. The horizontal tape measure is the x axis and the vertical tape measure is the y axis. Now place five to ten items from your home in the different quadrants. Cover the "dig" with another blanket, serving as the top layer of "dirt." Bring your child in and ask her to imagine that she is an archaeologist of the future, who is uncovering this "find" from an ordinary twenty-first-century home. Like all archaeologists, your child must carefully record any finds on paper, which she will do on graph paper, before removing them for further study. Your child should draw an x and y axis in the center of a piece of graph paper and then carefully dig (pull away the blanket) to see what she will uncover. Eureka! Your child has found many items in this small plot! Ask your child to carefully mark the items on the graph paper as they appear in the dig. Have your child use taut string to draw straight lines from the x and y axes to each object to help determine the correct points on which the objects sit. When transferring the information to the graph, your child should use the inch marks on the tape measure as the coordinates on the graph. Hence, if your child discovers a coin 5 inches to the left of the central point and 7 inches down, its coordinates on the graph would be (x,y) = –5, –7. Have your child carefully chart all the objects before removing them. Then, have your young archaeologist examine all the objects, and from the point of view of a future scientist, discuss what the materials reveal about this era of human civilization.

Cell equations

 Together, learn about cell division using an encyclopedia, science reference book, or online at http://www.icnet.uk/kids/cellsrus/cellsrus.html. Then, have your child create both sketches and algebraic equations (using letter variables) to tell the story of cell division. Afterward, have your child narrate—in a clear, engaging, and articulate manner—his drawing of the cell's adventure as it multiplies, using specific references to the researched material.

6.P.5 Solve linear equations using concrete models, tables, graphs, and paper-pencil methods.

Popped equations

WWW *LARGE BOWL OF UNBUTTERED POPCORN, SMALL CUP, NOTE CARDS LABELED INDIVIDUALLY WITH SIGNS FOR =, +, –, ×, AND ÷ Begin by asking your child what clue exists within the word "equation" that provides a hint about this type of mathematical expression. The idea of "equal" is the key here. In a <u>linear equation</u>, the expression on the left side of the equal sign has the same value as the expression on the right side. Start simply. Place 3 popped corn kernels on the table. Place the + sign after them, and then put down 8 popped corn kernels and the = sign. Place the empty cup on the right side of the equal sign, explaining that this represents the unknown variable. Ask your child to solve the equation, putting the correct amount of popped corn kernels into the cup (11). Together, eat the correct "variable" while you create a harder* *popped-corn equation (3x – 2 = 7). Remind your child that to keep both sides of the equation equal, you must do exactly the same thing to each side. Here, add 2 popped corn kernels to each side (3x – 2 + 2 = 7 + 2). Have your child simplify the expression, giving you 3x = 9. Finally, have your child divide each side by 3 (i.e., $\frac{3x}{3} = \frac{9}{3}$) and then simplify for the final value of the variable (x = 3). Continue snacking on the found "variables" while your child works on increasingly difficult equations. Find further explanations and expressions to solve at http://www.aaamath. com/equ725-equation6.html.*

6.P.6   Produce and interpret graphs that represent the relationship between two variables in everyday situations.

Cookie data entry

 GRAPH PAPER Together, examine three different ways to organize data—line graphs, pie charts and bar graphs—using math reference books or online at http://www.mathleague.com/help /data/data.htm. Then, ask your child to keep track of how many cookies are eaten in the household every day for one week. Once the week is over, have her create a line graph, pie chart, and bar graph to represent the results. Finally, have your child discuss how different ways of presenting this data can lead to different interpretations.

6.P.7   Identify and describe relationships between two variables with a constant rate of change. Contrast these with relationships where the rate of change is not constant.

Geometry

GRADES 5–6

Students engage in problem solving, communicating, reasoning, connecting, and representing as they:

6.G.1 Identify polygons based on their properties, including types of interior angles, perpendicular or parallel sides, and congruence of sides, e.g., squares, rectangles, rhombuses, parallelograms, trapezoids, and isosceles, equilateral, and right triangles.

Architectural geometry

 WWW *Explain to your child that an innovative technology company has come to her architectural firm for a design proposal for its new headquarters. The company is open to any idea, as long as the building is not shaped like a standard cube. Before starting any sketches, your young architect needs to become familiar with existing buildings that have different geometric forms. For each example, your young architect should identify the geometric properties (planes, angles, area, and so forth) of the shape of the building. Use library resources or the Internet to view I.M. Pei's famous pyramid-shaped entrance to the Louvre Museum in Paris. See the sharp points of the East Wing in the National Gallery of Art in Washington D.C., and also examine the tilt of Pisa's famed leaning cylindrical tower. Finally, study the ancient Egyptian pyramids. Then have her develop a proposal for a building composed of unique geometric shapes and present it to the "firm" (you).*

6.G.2 Identify three-dimensional shapes (e.g., cubes, prisms, spheres, cones, and pyramids) based on their properties, such as edges and faces.

6.G.3 Identify relationships among points, lines, and planes, e.g., intersecting, parallel, perpendicular.

6.G.4 *Graph points and identify coordinates of points on the Cartesian coordinate plane (all four quadrants).

* Although this standard is important and appropriate for this grade span, it will not be included in the state assessment program at the 5–6 grade span at the present time.

WWW *GRAPH PAPER, TWO TAPE MEASURES, SMALL OBJECTS Have your child create a "graph" on the floor. Cross two tape measures over one another so they make a plus (+) sign. Make sure they meet at an inch mark. This will serve as 0, with successive inch marks in all directions corresponding to positive integers (up the vertical y axis and to the right on the horizontal x axis) and negative integers (to the left on the horizontal x axis and down the vertical y axis). If Internet access is available, you can view an example online at http://www.funbrain.com/co/ index.html, and also have your child play the related interactive game before using the floor graph. Then, play a game in which you have ten rounds to try and get your child into a physical "knot" that she can not maintain. Call out coordinates for a point on the graph (e.g., x = −4, y = 9). Have your child place her right hand at the correct point. Continue calling out to your child the coordinates for points and indicating which appendage to place on each point (left hand, right foot, and so on), and repeating for ten rounds, or until your child falls over. Reverse roles, so your child can try to tie you in knots. Also, have your child check to make sure that you place your hands and feet on the correct points for the coordinates she calls out.*

6.G.5 Find the distance between two points on horizontal or vertical number lines.

6.G.6 Predict, describe, and perform transformations on two-dimensional shapes, e.g., translations, rotations, and reflections.

WWW *Ask your child to imagine that a world famous clothing store has just hired him to design a tee shirt for kids. But the client has a specific request. The store wants a tee shirt with one image on the front that is transformed on the back using a concept mentioned in the Standard. Have your child sketch a fairly simple design with basic geometric shapes on graph paper. Then view illustrations of translation, rotation, and reflection online at http://www.harcourtschool.com/glossary/math/glossary6.html. Have your young designer make a final*

sketch for the front of the tee shirt, and then apply one of the transformation concepts from the Standard for the back of the tee shirt. Ask your child to present the design to the client (you and other household members), explaining specifically, using mathematical terms, how the image has been manipulated for an intriguing result.

6.G.7 Identify types of symmetry, including line and rotational.

6.G.8 Determine if two shapes are congruent by measuring sides or a combination of sides and angles, as necessary; or by motions or series of motions, e.g., translations, rotations, and reflections.

Congruent detective race

PROTRACTORS, RULERS, STRING OR YARN, TIMER Explain that players will search for ten minutes through household cabinets, closets, shelves, and so forth, seeking pairs of geometric-shaped objects that are congruent—have exactly the same shape and size (e.g., soup can and canned peas, plate and Frisbee, box and book). Players must not only find object pairs, but prove they are congruent, measuring and noting each item's angles and side length, or height and circumference on their answer sheet. (For circumference, wrap a string around the cylinder-shaped object, unfold, and then measure its length with a ruler.) Remind contestants to think big (same-sized window frames or window panes) and small (buttons). After ten minutes, ask all players to return and share their findings and measurements. The one with the most correctly measured congruent examples wins. Play successive rounds to increase your child's and other players' ability to find congruency around the home. Finally, ask your child to consider what he has learned about the word congruent *in terms of objects, and apply the concept to another context. What does the word indicate in the sentence, "The mother and father were congruent in their belief that José could go to the party."? (The parents agreed.) Have your child compose his own sentence using the word* congruent *to reinforce comprehension.*

6.G.9 Match three-dimensional objects and their two-dimensional representations, e.g., nets, projections, and perspective drawings.

Measurement

GRADES 5-6

Students engage in problem solving, communicating, reasoning, connecting, and representing as they:

6.M.1 Apply the concepts of perimeter and area to the solution of problems. Apply formulas where appropriate.

Interior designer

TAPE MEASURE, CARDBOARD, SCISSORS Ask your child to imagine that he is your newly hired interior designer. You will pretend to want to rearrange the furniture in each room at home, but first need to see a floor plan of what it will look like. Have your child/young interior designer use a tape measure to measure the dimensions of each room and then calculate the area for each (width × height). Your child also should note the dimensions and the perimeter for the main pieces of furniture (beds, tables, chairs), measuring the approximate amount of space each piece occupies on the floor. (If necessary, review the formula for perimeter, which is 2 (l +w), with your child.) Have your young designer draw a floor plan to scale on plain paper, draw each piece of furniture to scale on cardboard or thick paper, and then cut out the furniture shapes out and label them "bed," "couch," etc. Have him arrange the cardboard shapes on the floor plan to devise inventive ways of reorganizing your furniture without really having to move it!

6.M.2 Identify, measure, describe, classify, and construct various angles, triangles, and quadrilaterals.

Missing-angle stomach strength

RULER, PROTRACTOR Together, review the definition of complementary angles (two angles whose sum is 90°) and supplementary angles (two angles whose sum is 180°). Definitions and visual representations also appear at http://www.mathleague.com/help/geometry/angles.htm. Then, have your child practice mental addition and subtraction. Draw an acute angle within a right angle, writing the angle's

measurement (say 52°). How fast can your child find the complementary angle (38°)? Conduct the same activity for supplementary angles, and then continue to help your child increase his speed and recognition of the two types of angles. Now, turn the game into a physical exercise. Say the degree measurement of an angle aloud. Your child will look at the pro-tractor and then, sitting on the floor with legs stretched out ahead, use his legs to imitate the base of the protractor. Your child will now lean backward or forward to create a correct visual representation of the angle you stated. If you say 40°, your child will lean back just a bit more than halfway between upright (90°) and flat on the floor (0°). You then will call out either "supplementary" or "complementary" and your child will cal-culate the degree measurement of the new angle necessary to make the equation complete. (If you call out "complementary at 40°," your child will say "50°." If his calculation is correct, he gets to sit to the comple-mentary (upright) or supplementary (prone) position to rest his abdomi-nal muscles.

6.M.3 Solve problems involving proportional relationships and units of measurement, e.g., same system unit conversions, scale models, maps, and speed.

Recipe switch-aroo

WWW 📖 *RECIPE AND INGREDIENTS, MEASURING TOOLS, U.S. VOL-UME UNIT CHART Together, review the breakdown of U.S. volume units for teaspoons, tablespoons, ounces, pints, quarts, etc. using a chart from a basic recipe book or one found online at http://www.aaamath.com/ mea69-us-volume.html. (If you use the website, scroll down to the "Play" section for fun interactive games that test your volume memory.) Next, find a recipe to cook together. When measuring the ingredients, have your child put her knowledge of units of measure to work. Tell her that she needs to measure the ingredients accurately, but she cannot use the unit of measure called for in the recipe. So, for example, if the recipe calls for a tablespoon of an ingredient, she must use an equivalent measure (three teaspoons) instead. Tell your child that this is an "open book test," so she can consult the measurement chart as often as necessary. Enjoy the completed recipe together!*

How far/how long

✍ **ROAD MAP WITH DISTANCE NOTATIONS, CALCULATOR** *Together, find your home's location on a road map. Then, have your child select a destination on the map for an imaginary trip. Ask your child to figure out how long it will take to drive there. Your child should use the legend on the map to figure out the distance to the location. Then, have your child determine how long the trip will take, using an average of fifty-five miles an hour in his calculations. Help your child check the mathematics with a calculator. Have him consider his final answer and, if the distance appears to be too long for a single car trip, have him add in time for rest stops, meals, and overnight stays. Have your child conduct this activity before you leave on your next actual car trip, so you won't have to answer the inevitable question, "How long until we get there?"* 📖

6.M.4 Find areas of triangles and parallelograms. Recognize that shapes with the same number of sides but different appearances can have the same area. Develop strategies to find the area of more complex shapes.

Geo-jigsaw puzzle race

✍ 🖌 www 📖 *First, both you and your child will create abstract pieces for jigsaw puzzles. Draw lines on construction paper to create straight-edged geometric shapes—squares, triangles, and rectangles of different dimensions so that no space remains. (Your respective pieces of paper should resemble a geometric jigsaw puzzle.) Then cut out the shapes to create your puzzle pieces. Now review the formulas for finding the <u>perimeter</u> (the sum of the lengths of the sides) and <u>area</u> (area = length x width) for these forms using an encyclopedia or math reference book, or by going online at http://pittsford.monroe.edu/jefferson/calfieri/geometry/geoframe.html or http://www.math.com/tables/index.html. With pencil and scrap paper for calculations in hand, start the game. Each player must find the perimeter and area for every piece in his or her puzzle. After doing so, the player can put the piece in its correct place to eventually reform the original rectangular puzzle composition. The player whose entire set of calculations is correct and whose puzzle is complete first, wins! Play successive rounds with new pieces of cut construction paper to hone your skills.*

6.M.5 Identify, measure, and describe circles and the relationships of the radius, diameter, circumference, and area (e.g., d = 2r, p = C/d), and use the concepts to solve problems.

Orange mathematics

✎ WWW 📖 *ORANGE, STRING, RULER, KNIFE, CARDBOARD Challenge your child to find the approximate circumference (the distance around a circle) of an orange using just string and a ruler. (Wrap the string around the circle once, mark its length, unfold, and then measure it against the ruler.) Now help your child find the orange's circumference using the formula circumference = π x diameter, to prove whether his estimated string measurement is correct. (If necessary, review that the <u>diameter</u> is a straight line passing through the center of the circle and meeting the circumference at each end.) Have your child find the diameter of the orange either by cutting the orange in half and measuring its diameter, or placing the cardboard flat across the top of the orange and measuring the distance from the table top to the cardboard. Then ask your child to plug the diameter's number into the formula. Your child should now solve the formula, using 3.14 for π to test whether his string estimate is correct. As you share the orange, point out to your child that the circumference is always just a bit more than three times the size of the diameter. Together review information about circumference and test yourselves with a few online examples at http://www.ncsa.uiuc.edu/edu /RSE/RSEorange/application.html.*

6.M.6 Find volumes and surface areas of rectangular prisms.

6.M.7 Find the sum of the angles in simple polygons (up to eight sides) with and without measuring the angles.

Data Analysis, Statistics, and Probability

GRADES 5–6

Students engage in problem solving, communicating, reasoning, connecting, and representing as they:

6.D.1 Describe and compare data sets using the concepts of median, mean, mode, maximum and minimum, and range.

In the middle

 Have your child write the ages of everyone (including pets) in your household along a horizontal line on a piece of paper. Explain that to find the mean of these numbers, your child should divide their sum by the number of people. The resulting number is the mean. For example, add everyone's ages: 1 year (cat) + 6 years (sibling) + 12 years (self) + 35 years (dad) + 36 years (mom) = 90. Now divide 90 (total ages) by 5 (beings in household) = 18 (the mean age in the household). Have your child find the median, the middle value of a group of numbers arranged in order. (The median in the above example is 12.) Now, if the mom and dad were both 35 years of age, then 35 would be the mode, which in a list of numbers is the one that occurs most often. For further reinforcement, together use the online glossary, clicking on "mean," "median," "mode," and "central tendency" at http://www.harcourtschool. com/glossary/math/glossary7.html. (Alternatively, research these terms using library resources.) Finally, have your child practice finding the mean, median, and mode by adding the ages of friends and relatives.

6.D.2 Construct and interpret stem-and-leaf plots, line plots, and circle graphs.

Graphic perspective

 Have your child look through the newspaper for graphs that illuminate information related to social issues such as school performance, voting rates, and so forth. Together, determine what infor-

mation the graph provides and then read the accompanying article to see what important information may not be represented in the graph. To view many examples of different types of graphs and charts in this category, ask for a copy of American Demographics magazine at your local library, or visit the magazine's website at www.demographics.com. Have your child try designing his own graph that will provide all pertinent information about an issue of personal importance.

6.D.3   Use tree diagrams and other models (e.g., lists and tables) to represent possible or actual outcomes of trials. Analyze the outcomes.

Vanilla or chocolate statistics

Ask your child to imagine that he has just been hired by an ice cream manufacturer to research ice cream preferences. Specifically, the manufacturer wants to know if consumers prefer vanilla-based ice creams, or chocolate-based ice creams. (For example, if Cookies 'n Cream has a vanilla base, it would be considered vanilla. If Rocky Road has a chocolate base, it would be considered chocolate.) Before gathering information, have your junior analyst (child) hypothesize about the flavor he thinks will be the most popular, and have him explain some of the reasons for his hypothesis. Then, have your child conduct some field research. Have him station himself in front of an ice cream store or in the ice cream aisle of a grocery store and keep track of the ice cream flavor purchased by each consumer during a fifteen-minute period. At home, have your junior analyst create a table, graph, or chart to present his findings, and have him share his conclusions with the ice cream manufacturer (household members).

6.D.4   Predict the probability of outcomes of simple experiments (e.g., tossing a coin, rolling a die) and test the predictions. Use appropriate ratios between 0 and 1 to represent the probability of the outcome and associate the probability with the likelihood of the event.

Batter up II

🖉 *Have your child review her work with ratios and batting averages for players in "Batter up I" (Standard 6.N.4). Before the next game, have your child estimate the probability of each player's hits for the upcoming game, expressing them as ratios, proportions, and decimals. After the game, have your child compare her numbers to the actual results. Have your child continue throughout the season, practicing and honing her ratio, average, and probability skills.*

Number Sense and Operations

Understand numbers, ways of representing numbers, relationships among numbers, and number systems

Understand meanings of operations and how they relate to one another

Compute fluently and make reasonable estimates

GRADES 7–8

Students engage in problem solving, communicating, reasoning, connecting, and representing as they:

8.N.1 Compare, order, estimate, and translate among integers, fractions and mixed numbers (i.e., rational numbers), decimals, and percents.

8.N.2 Define, compare, order, and apply frequently used irrational numbers, such as $\sqrt{2}$ and π.

Constant π

🖉 *FOUR DIFFERENT SIZE LIDS, STRING, MEASURING TAPE Share that the circumference of any circle is slightly more than 3 times that of its diameter. π, which is the relationship between the circumference and the diameter, remains constant (approximately 3.14) no matter how large or small the circle! Help your child prove that this is true. Ask him to create*

a chart with three vertical columns labeled "Circumference," "Diameter," and "Circumference Divided by Diameter." Have your child use string and a measuring tape to measure the circumference and diameter of four different size lids. (To find the circumference, wrap a piece of string around the outside of the lid, lay the string down in a straight line, and then use the measuring tape to see how long the string is.) Ask your child to divide the diameter into the circumference for each example and place the number, written as a decimal, in the column labeled "Circumference Divided by Diameter." What whole number appears in each answer? (3.) All the answers will be close to 3.14, either slightly more or less. Have your child continue the experiment by measuring a very large circle, such as the bottom of a trash pail, and a tiny one, such as dime, to see that π still remains constant. Your child has just proved that circumference = π x diameter.

8.N.3 Use ratios and proportions in the solution of problems, in particular, problems involving unit rates, scale factors, and rate of change.

3 for $1.00

✏️ WWW 📋 Visit the supermarket together and find sales where an item costs less if you buy it in bulk (e.g., 3 peaches for $1.00 or one peach for $.39) Have your child create a two-column chart listing "sale price per unit/item" and "regular price per unit/item." For each example you discover in the store, have your child use division to discover the unit price for the items if bought in bulk, and then compare this to how much each unit would cost if bought at the regular price. While on line or at home, have your child do the math for all the items you bought on sale to tell you exactly how much money you saved today!

8.N.4 Represent numbers in scientific notation, and use them in calculations and problem situations.

Mathematical shorthand

✏️ WWW 📋 Ask your child to write the number one thousand (1 followed by 3 zeros), one million (1 followed by 6 zeros), and, one billion (1 and 9 zeros). Tired of writing zeros? Explain that <u>scientific notation</u> is an

efficient way to express extremely large or small numbers. Scientific notation states a number as a product of a number from 1 to 10, and a power of 10. Thus, 1,000 would be 10 to the 3rd power or 10^3. The 3 here is the exponent, used in an expression to indicate that the same number is multiplied repeatedly. The exponent is written as a small number above and to the right of a symbol or quantity. An exponent of 3 tells us that the equation is $10 \times 10 \times 10 = 1,000$ (or 10^3). Scientists developed this shorthand because some numbers are immensely large (distances between stars or planets, for instance). Other numbers are tiny, such as a virus whose diameter measures 10^{-6} (or 10 to the negative 6th power). Have your child write the scientific notation for the expression of the diameter of our galaxy (the Milky Way), which is about 100,000 light years (10^5). To get a sense of the distance of a light year itself, research the topic online or using library resources, or visit http://school.discovery.com/schooladventures/universe/itsawesome/lightyears/index.html to understand why we use scientific notation when dealing with such overwhelmingly large numbers.

8.N.5 Apply number theory concepts, including prime factorization and relatively prime numbers, to the solution of problems.

Prime it out game

Share that prime factorization is a fairly easy concept to understand, if you think of it as getting to the "bottom of a number." The key to grasping the idea is being able to define <u>factor</u> (a number multiplied within a multiplication expression), and <u>prime</u> <u>number</u> (a whole number greater than 1 that has exactly two factors: itself and 1). Check to make sure your child can describe both factor and prime number in his own words. For more information, use the online math glossary at http://www.harcourtschool.com/glossary/math/glossary7.html for an explanation of prime factorizations or research the terms using library resources. Now, try your hands at writing the prime factors for a number: begin dividing by the smallest possible prime and continue until the quotient is a prime number. Then use exponents (the number that indicates how many times the base is multiplied) where possible. For example, find the prime factors of 12: 12 = 2 x 6; 12 = 2 x 2 x 3; 12 = 2^2 x 3. Now play a

game in which you each prime factor different numbers. The player with the higher number of exponents in the prime factorization (or the higher numbered base, if both of your exponents are equal) wins the round. Play five rounds to see who wins the game.

8.N.6 Demonstrate an understanding of absolute value, e.g., $|-3| = |3| = 3$.

8.N.7 Apply the rules of powers and roots to the solution of problems. Extend the Order of Operations to include positive integer exponents and square roots.

Root it out

WWW *CARROTS, KNIFE Explain that, whereas exponents indicate the number of times that the base number is multiplied by itself, square roots are the number which, when multiplied by itself, produces the base. For instance, the square root of 4 is 2 (2 x 2 = 4). Have your child demonstrate this square "root" by breaking a carrot (a "root" vegetable) into four equal pieces in length, and placing them in a pile. Next, ask your child to "write" a multiplication equation with the carrot pieces in which the same factor is multiplied by itself to give you the original number (e.g., 2 carrot bits x 2 carrot bits = 4 carrot bits). While you each snack on a "root" (2 carrot pieces), have your child find the roots for 9 (3), 16 (4), 25 (5), and 36 (6). For further explanation and practice use library materials or go to http://www.math.com/school/sub ject1/lessons/S1U1L9 GL.html. Finally, together review the order of operations for equations that include numbers in exponent form. They should be tackled right after computing any operations inside parentheses or above and below a fraction bar. See this demonstrated by clicking on "order of operations" at http://www.harcourtschool.com/glossary/math/glossary8.html, or use library resources as an alternative. Finally, ask your child to express, in her own words, a succinct definition for square roots.*

8.N.8 Demonstrate an understanding of the properties of arithmetic operations on rational numbers. Use the associative, commutative, and distributive properties; properties of the identity and inverse elements (e.g., $-7 + 7 = 0$; $\frac{3}{4} \times \frac{4}{3} = 1$); and the notion of closure of a subset of the rational numbers under an operation (e.g., the set of odd integers is closed under multiplication but not under addition).

8.N.9 Use the inverse relationships of addition and subtraction, multiplication and division, and squaring and finding square roots to simplify computations and solve problems, e.g. multiplying by $^1/_2$ or 0.5 is the same as dividing by 2.

8.N.10 Estimate and compute with fractions (including simplification of fractions), integers, decimals, and percents (including those greater than 100 and less than 1).

Catalog delight

 ✍ **WWW** *GIFT CATALOG, CALCULATOR Have your child imagine that she has just received a $1,000 check from a mysterious benefactor. The note with the check says your child can buy whatever she wants with the money, as long as she also buys gifts for others in the household. Also, she is required to make all of her purchases from one catalog. Have your child select her purchases (keeping a running estimate of her total) and then fill out the catalog order form. To complete the form, she should total the order and calculate the sales tax and shipping costs as indicated in the instructions. If her total after sales tax and shipping exceeds her $1,000 budget, ask her to revise her order. She should do all of her calculations first, and then use the calculator to check her work. For additional fun, together play the "Estimated Total Price with Sales Tax and Tip" game at http://www.aaamath.com/rat68-tip-estimate.html, which requires similar calculations.*

8.N.11 Determine when an estimate rather than an exact answer is appropriate and apply in problem situations.

8.N.12 Select and use appropriate operations—addition, subtraction, multiplication, division, and positive integer exponents—to solve problems with rational numbers (including negatives).

Patterns, Relations, and Algebra

Understand patterns, relations, and functions

Represent and analyze mathematical situations and structures using algebraic symbols

Use mathematical models to represent and understand quantitative relationships

Analyze change in various contexts

GRADES 7-8

Students engage in problem solving, communicating, reasoning, connecting, and representing as they:

8.P.1   Extend, represent, analyze, and generalize a variety of patterns with tables, graphs, words, and, when possible, symbolic expressions. Include arithmetic and geometric progressions, e.g., compounding.

Five more days of Christmas

First, have your child discern the pattern of the song "The Twelve Days of Christmas" (the addition of one item for each day). Use a library copy or the visual and auditory version online at http://www.12days.com/library/carols/12daysofxmas.htm). Next, have your child add another five days of gifts to the popular tune. Ask your child to draw a pyramid diagram for the full seventeen days, with simple images representing the gifts for each day, including his new ones. Afterward, ask your child to represent the graph in mathematical equations. First, how would your child write the equation to discover the sum of the gifts (1 + 2 + 3 + 4...through 17)? Next, have your child describe the relationship of one set of gifts to another, writing them as ratios (for example the number of "turtle doves" to "geese a laying"). Finally as reinforcement, ask your child to create additional lyrics for the song to extend the pattern and include his five new gifts.

8.P.2   Evaluate simple algebraic expressions for given variable values, e.g., $3a^2 - b$ for $a = 3$ and $b = 7$.

✏️ **WWW** 📖 *WASHED GRAPES, LARGE SERVING PLATE, CUTTING BOARD, OR CLEAN COUNTERTOP, INDIVIDUAL NOTE CARDS MARKED WITH PLUS, MINUS, AND MULTIPLICATION SIGNS AND PARENTHESES Explain to your child that you are going to compute edible algebraic expressions. First on plain paper, write the example: $3a^2 - b$. Then write: a = 3 and b = 7. Now, ask your child to translate the written expression, using grapes and the note cards, on a large serving plate, cutting board, or clean countertop. (3 grapes [3 grapes x 3 grapes] – 7 grapes). Now, have your child solve the expression, if necessary reviewing the "order of operations" with library materials or online at http://www.harcourtschool.com/glossary/math/glossary8.html. ([3 x 9] – 7 = 27 – 7 = 20 grapes) Repeat the activity, substituting other equations and have your child solve with grapes, eating the final answers after each round! For more information and reinforcement on algebraic equations, click on each "equations" section at http://pittsford.monroe.edu/jefferson/calfieri/algebra/AlgebraMain.html, or type the word "algebra" into any major Internet search engine.*

8.P.3 Demonstrate an understanding of the identity $(-x)(-y) = xy$. Use this identity to simplify algebraic expressions, e.g., $(-2)(-x+2) = 2x - 4$.

8.P.4 Create and use symbolic expressions and relate them to verbal, tabular, and graphical representations.

8.P.5 Identify the slope of a line as a measure of its steepness and as a constant rate of change from its table of values, equation, or graph. Apply the concept of slope to the solution of problems.

8.P.6 Identify the roles of variables within an equation, e.g., $y = mx + b$, expressing y as a function of x with parameters m and b.

8.P.7 Set up and solve linear equations and inequalities with one or two variables, using algebraic methods, models, and/or graphs.

 ✏️ *SALAD INGREDIENTS, BOWLS FOR INDIVIDUAL SERVINGS Ask your child to be your salad chef. For this activity, you want her to create and write down her own special salad recipe as if it were an algebraic equa-*

tion. Wash, dry, and slice all the ingredients first. Then place the individual bowls in a row on a counter. Have your child place a handful of lettuce in each bowl and then note this on paper as x. (x = 1 handful of lettuce.) Have your child place the desired number of tomato slices in each bowl, marking this down, too, with a different expression. (For three slices per bowl, your child would write 3y, for instance.) Continue on, having your child add new ingredients and marking their number and assigned algebraic symbol. Before serving, have your child write out the complete algebraic expression for the salad. It would look something like x + 3y + 5m (mushrooms) + n (1 onion slice) + $\frac{1}{2}$d ($\frac{1}{2}$ teaspoon of dressing) = 1 mixed salad. Have your child save her recipe to recreate at another dinner.

8.P.8 Explain and analyze—both quantitatively and qualitatively, using pictures, graphs, charts, or equations—how a change in one variable results in a change in another variable in functional relationships, e.g., $C = \pi d$, $A = \pi r^2$ (A as a function of r), $A_{rectangle} = lw$ ($A_{rectangle}$ as a function of l and w).

8.P.9 Use linear equations to model and analyze problems involving proportional relationships. Use technology as appropriate.

8.P.10 Use tables and graphs to represent and compare linear growth patterns. In particular, compare rates of change and x- and y-intercepts of different linear patterns.

Geometry

Analyze characteristics and properties of two- and three-dimensional geometric shapes and develop mathematical arguments about geometric relationships

Specify locations and describe spatial relationships using coordinate geometry and other representational systems

Apply transformations and use symmetry to analyze mathematical situations

Use visualization, spatial reasoning, and geometric modeling to solve problems

Students engage in problem solving, communicating, reasoning, connecting, and representing as they:

8.G.1 Analyze, apply, and explain the relationship between the number of sides and the sums of the interior and exterior angle measures of polygons.

8.G.2 Classify figures in terms of congruence and similarity, and apply these relationships to the solution of problems.

Congruent and similar menu

 Begin by reviewing the definitions of <u>congruent</u> figures—having exactly the same size and shape (e.g., two dimes), and <u>similar</u> figures—those that have the same shape, but may not have the same size (a dime and a nickel). Then, explain that your child is going to design a menu for a new restaurant. This eating establishment will not list items according to appetizers, entrées, and dessert, but instead will organize all the food into just two categories—congruent and similar. Have your child fold a large piece of drawing paper in half, writing "congruent" on the left and "similar" on the right side. Now, ask your to child list various items for the menu, thinking about different types of foods. A congruent example would be a stack of pancakes. Similar examples would be spaghetti and licorice. See how many congruent and similar food matches your child can come up with to help this new restaurant devise a wide and varied menu. Your child should make quick sketches on the menu for each paired item. Finally, have your child invent a fun but descriptive name for the dining establishment. Later, at dinner, have everyone cut their food into congruent and similar shapes before eating, with your child making sure everyone understands which ones are congruent and which are similar.

8.G.3 Demonstrate an understanding of the relationships of angles formed by intersecting lines, including parallel lines cut by a transversal.

CHOPSTICKS, PENCILS OR STRAWS, PROTRACTOR
Together, learn about angles created by a <u>transversal</u> (a line that intersects two or more lines), using library materials or by clicking on the term at http://www.harcourtschool.com/glossary/math/glossary8.html. Then, for real-life practice, place a transversal chopstick across two parallel chopsticks. (You can substitute pencils or straws for chopsticks throughout this activity.) The transversal chopstick will have created two sets of supplementary angle. (Use reference materials to review the definition, if necessary.) Have your child use a protractor to measure one of the angles in one of the pairs of supplementary angles. Have your child measure the other supplementary angle in the stick set-up. Now, place a large handful of chopsticks in a pile so that the lines overlap. Starting on the top-most surface, your child should use the protractor to measure one of the angles and then calculate the angle of the other in the pair. (Some of these angles will be supplementary, others will be complimentary, and so forth.) After writing down the calculation, have your child measure the angle in question. If your child's initial calculation is right, she gets to keep the stick, removing it from the stack. If the calculation is wrong, the "house" gets it. Whoever has the most sticks at the end wins!

8.G.4 Demonstrate an understanding of the Pythagorean theorem. Apply the theorem to the solution of problems.

 LONG RULER, TAPE MEASURE *The Pythagorean theorem relates to triangles that contain a right angle. Together, learn about the theorem (triangle leg a^2 + triangle leg b^2 = hypotenuse^2, or $a^2 + b^2 = c^2$) using math reference books or an encyclopedia, or online at http://www.harcourtschool.com/glossary/math/glossary8.html. Then get online interactive practice at http://www.gomath.com/algebra/pythagorean.asp. Finally, create right angles with different length legs against your own walls. Kneel by a wall and place a ruler diagonally from a spot on the floor to a spot on the wall. The wall and floor are the legs and the ruler is the hypotenuse. Have your child use the tape measure to measure two of the variables (either both legs or one leg and the*

hypotenuse) and then complete the equation for the unknown quantity. Follow up by having your child research Pythagoras himself (using an Internet search engine or library materials). Afterward, ask your child to write a letter to Pythagoras, describing what it is like to learn and use his theorem today, more than two thousand years later. Your child should edit and revise his letter for correct spelling, punctuation, and grammar, and clearly communicate his understanding of the theorem.

8.G.5 Use a straightedge, compass, or other tools to formulate and test conjectures, and to draw geometric figures.

8.G.6 Predict the results of transformations on unmarked or coordinate planes and draw the transformed figure, e.g., predict how tessellations transform under translations, reflections, and rotations.

Fill 'er up!

HONEYCOMB OR PICTURE OF ONE Together, look at a cross-section of a honeycomb and ask your child to identify how its pattern repeats and fills up the entire surface. These characteristics define tessellation patterns. (Learn about tessellation using library materials or online at http://forum.swarthmore.edu/geometry/rugs/symmetry/ and http://www.harcourtschool.com/glossary/math/glossary8.html.) Traditional Islamic mosaics and carpets incorporate tessellation patterns because of the Islamic religion's prohibition against depicting figures. Have your child identify tessellation patterns in the online exhibition of the Metropolitan Museum of Art's Islamic department at http://www.met museum.org/collections/department.asp?dep=14 or use art books about Oriental carpets from the library. Then, ask your child to sketch models for a carpet, using geometric shapes to create a tessellation pattern. Have your child predict how the tessellation pattern will transform under translation, reflection, or rotation; ask her to sketch a "companion" textile, using these transformations.

8.G.7 Identify three-dimensional figures (e.g., prisms, pyramids) by their physical appearance, distinguishing attributes, and spatial relationships such as parallel faces.

8.G.8 Recognize and draw two-dimensional representations of three-dimensional objects, e.g., nets, projections, and perspective drawings.

Measurement

Understand measurable attributes of objects and the units, systems, and processes of measurement

Apply appropriate techniques, tools, and formulas to determine measurements

GRADES 7-8

Students engage in problem solving, communicating, reasoning, connecting, and representing as they:

8.M.1 Select, convert (within the same system of measurement), and use appropriate units of measurement or scale.

8.M.2 Given the formulas, convert from one system of measurement to another. Use technology as appropriate.

Mayan math

Together, explore the symbols the ancient Mayans developed to represent numbers by researching the topic using an Internet search engine or library resources, or exploring "Maya Mathematics" online at http://www.michielb.nl/maya/astro.html. Have your child use the symbols to express the individual ages of everyone in your household. Then play a game that requires scorekeeping, and have your child keep score using Mayan mathematic symbols.

8.M.3 Demonstrate an understanding of the concepts and apply formulas and procedures for determining measures, including those of area and perimeter/circumference of parallelograms, trapezoids, and circles. Given the formulas, determine the surface area and volume of rectangular prisms, cylinders, and spheres. Use technology as appropriate.

NOTE CARDS Together, review the math formulas for volume at http://www.math.com/tables/index.html or find them in a math reference book or textbook. Have your child take notes, transferring the formula for each solid onto an individual note card. (Write the name of the corresponding solid on the back of the card.) Also, have your child sketch an image of each solid on a separate card. When complete, play a game by placing all the image cards on the left and all the volume formulas face-up on the right. Time your child as she tries to match up the correct visual image with the right formula card. After making the matches, give your child numbers to plug into the formulas for the length, height, and so forth for each image. Your child gets to keep the card for every correctly calculated volume until all the cards are removed from the table. Play successive rounds to see if your child can beat her time.

8.M.4 Use ratio and proportion (including scale factors) in the solution of problems, including problems involving similar plane figures and indirect measurement.

8.M.5 Use models, graphs, and formulas to solve simple problems involving rates, e.g., velocity and density.

Velocity races

STOPWATCH, MEASURING TAPE, PING-PONG BALL Before heading to the "races" (recruit contestants from friends and the household), discuss a major concept of motion with your child. <u>Velocity</u> is the rate at which a body moves in space in a given direction. Velocity is expressed in distance and time, such as miles per hour or meters per second. Why aren't speed and velocity the same thing? Speed indicates the rate of motion, but not the direction. Look at the formula for computing uniform velocity (where the distance and direction traveled in each unit remains the same): velocity = distance ÷ time. Now, have your child prepare for a race, creating a score chart with a column for each contestant's name, distance traveled, time elapsed, and velocity. Then, measure the race course, say, the length of a room at home. (Make the distance an even number so it's easily divisible by each person's time.) Next, hold a timed

competition in which every player (household members and friends) pushes a ping pong ball the length of the "course" with his or her nose (or crawls backward across the room, whatever challenge you wish). Have your child fill in the chart after each person's turn, and then use the formula d/t = v to find out the velocity for each player.

Data Analysis, Statistics, and Probability

Formulate questions that can be addressed with data and collect, organize, and display relevant data to answer them

Select and use appropriate statistical methods to analyze data

Develop and evaluate inferences and predictions that are based on data

Understand and apply basic concepts of probability

GRADES 7-8

Students engage in problem solving, communicating, reasoning, connecting, and representing as they:

8.D.1 Describe the characteristics and limitations of a data sample. Identify different ways of selecting a sample, e.g., convenience sampling, responses to a survey, random sampling.

8.D.2 Select, create, interpret, and utilize various tabular and graphical representations of data, e.g., circle graphs, Venn diagrams, scatterplots, stem-and-leaf plots, box-and-whisker plots, histograms, tables, and charts. Differentiate between continuous and discrete data and ways to represent them.

GRAPH PAPER Review with your child the definition of a <u>scatterplot</u>—a graph made by plotting points on a coordinate plane to illustrate the relationship between two variables in a data set. Reinforce the concept with the online example and definition at http:// www.harcourtschool.com/glossary/math/glossary8.html. Then, have your child use the sports pages or watch a live game to plot the relationship between two variables in the sport, such as hits per inning. After plotting for a few units (say, innings of a baseball game), have your child draw conclusions and make predictions based on the information, testing them against the eventual actual results.

8.D.3 Find, describe, and interpret appropriate measures of central tendency (mean, median, and mode) and spread (range) that represent a set of data. Use these notions to compare different sets of data.

m & ms (OPTIONAL HANDFUL OF MIXED NUTS), GRAPH PAPER Have your child review of the terms mode, mean, and median, online at http://www.mathleague.com/help/data/data.htm, or in library books. Repeat for central tendency using library resources, or online at http://www.mste.uiuc.edu/hill/dstat/dstat.html (which offers fun games that will put mode, mean, median into a real-life context). Finally, have your child graph the number of each color in a bag of m & ms (or each type of nut in a handful of mixed nuts), and then find the mode, mean, and median for this group of data.

8.D.4 Use tree diagrams, tables, organized lists, basic combinatorics ("fundamental counting principle"), and area models to compute probabilities for simple compound events, e.g., multiple coin tosses or rolls of dice.

Cheeseburger dependent

INGREDIENTS FOR HAMBURGERS OR TURKEY BURGERS, CHEDDAR CHEESE, MOZZARELLA CHEESE, OLIVE Together, first review information about dependent compound events using library resources, or online at http://www.mathgoodies.com/lessons/vol6/ dependent_events.html. Then, have your child help you prepare hamburgers or turkey burgers. This is an excellent opportunity for him to practice measuring skills with the necessary ingredients. When forming the patties, insert a small piece of cheddar cheese, a small piece of mozzarella cheese, and half an olive in each (the items should be separated from one another). After cooking, cut the burgers into bit-sized pieces and serve on a plate with the rest of the meal. Have your child randomly select the first "unit" to eat. Before actually biting into the piece, have your child mark the probability as a ratio of this first bite containing the cheddar cheese. (If the burger is cut into sixteen pieces, then it would be a $\frac{1}{16}$ chance.) After eating, have your child mark the probability as a ratio of getting a piece of mozzarella (or any other item he hasn't eaten yet) in the next randomly selected bite. (This would be $\frac{1}{15}$.) Repeat with the olive ($\frac{1}{14}$), having your child write statistics with each diminishing bit of the burger.

Science & Technology / Engineering

Grades 6-8

Earth and Space Science

GRADES 6 - 8

MAPPING THE EARTH

1. Recognize, interpret, and be able to create models of the earth's common physical features in various mapping representations, including contour maps.

Homemade earth

 WWW LARGE ORANGE OR GRAPEFRUIT, CLOVES, VEGETABLE PEELER *Together, examine maps and globes—using the Internet or library materials—that indicate Earth's physical features. Help your child roughly sketch the major continents on a large orange or round grapefruit "Earth" with a pen. Then use the maps as reference to add Earth's three-dimensional features, such as cloves to build mountain*

ranges, a vegetable peeler to cut out the valleys, blue marker to indicate oceans, rivers, and lakes, and so forth. Everyone in the household can create his own "Earth" model, and your child can check for accurate details, using your research as reference.

EARTH'S STRUCTURE

2. Describe the layers of the solid earth including the lithosphere, the hot convecting mantle, and the dense metallic core.

Baked Earth

COOKING INGREDIENTS AS MENTIONED IN THE ACTIVITY Together, create a yummy cross-section of Earth, with a different tasty treat for each layer. Begin by having your child toss together 1 $\frac{1}{2}$ cups crushed graham crackers, one well-beaten egg, $\frac{1}{4}$ stick butter, and $\frac{1}{4}$ cup brown sugar. Blend well and spread the mixture, which will be Earth's "core," in a 9-inch pie pan. Bake in a 350 degree oven until the sugar and butter melt. Remove to let the "core" harden. On top, pour sixteen ounces semisweet chocolate, softened and melted in a microwave, or carefully and slowly on the top of the stove. (Help your child with this step as the chocolate is hot.) This is Earth's movable "mantle." Let cool and then, finally, sprinkle completely with lightly toasted nuts of your choice, making the brittle lithosphere or Earth's outer shell. Before chowing down, have your child explain each of Earth's layers to anyone sharing the dessert. Keep leftovers covered in the refrigerator.

HEAT TRANSFER IN THE EARTH'S SYSTEM

3. Differentiate among radiation, conduction, and convection, the three mechanisms by which heat is transferred through the earth's system.

Cool off!

SILVER SPOON, CUP OF HOT CHOCOLATE Make a cup of hot chocolate that's too steamy to drink right away. Show your child that one way to cool it down more quickly is to put in a metal (preferably silver) spoon. Have your child place the spoon in the mug and very carefully put his fingers on the part of the stem nearest the hot liquid. Ask your child to note as the heat transfers into the cool metal spoon, rising upward. Then, have your child describe what this experiment illustrates. (Heat always moves from hotter to cooler objects.) But there's more to it. This is an example of <u>conduction</u>*—the movement of heat through a material without the flow of matter. What is it that moves to create the heat? Ask your child to rub his hands together very fast for thirty seconds. What happens to his palms? They heat up! The rubbing hands create warmth. When heat travels by conduction, the atoms likewise vibrate quickly, producing heat. As they jostle ever faster, they strike cold, slow-moving atoms next to them, thereby making these neighboring atoms vibrate and thus heat up as well. The vibrating atoms transfer—ping-pong style—the heat/vibrations up through the cooler material. Now your child should be able to explain to a friend or household member not only how to cool off a hot drink more quickly, but why it works!*

Warm air rising

SPACE HEATER OR RADIATOR Have your child stand in a small, cool room, such as a bathroom. Turn on the radiator or a space heater and ask your child to stand nearby with hands raised about shoulder height. Have your child note when the heat reaches her hands. Ask your child to explain what this reveals about the direction in which hot air moves. (Hot air is lighter than cold, so it rises, while cool air sinks.) Eventually, the whole room will become warm because as the hot air rises, the cold air sinks toward the heater, becomes warm, and rises, pushing down cold air, and so forth. This up and down movement of air is called convection currents. Have your child create a physical movement or short dance piece titled "Convection Currents" that physically and visually embodies this type of movement. 🎬 🚲

4. Explain the relationship among the energy provided by the sun; the global patterns of atmospheric movement; and the temperature differences among water, land, and atmosphere.

EARTH'S HISTORY

5. Describe how the movement of the earth's crystal plates causes both slow changes in the earth's surface (e.g., formation of mountains and ocean basins) and rapid ones (e.g., volcanic eruptions and earthquakes).

Shake, rattle, and explode

INGREDIENTS FOR EXPLODING VOLCANO, MUSIC Using reference books or the Internet, together explore earthquakes and plate tectonics (online at http://wwwneic.cr.usgs.gov/neis/plate_tectonics/rift_man.html). Then read about volcanoes in reference books or online at http://library.thinkquest.org/17457/english.html. Ask your child to define the difference between volcanoes and earthquakes in his own words. Then build your own exploding volcano with simple kitchen ingredients as described at http://www. spartechsoftware.com/reeko/Experiments/volcano.htm. While working on the experiment, listen to music that parallels the energy of Earth's transformation, such as Russian composer Modest Moussorgsky's "A Night on Bald Mountain" (best known from the Disney movie Fantasia).

Colliding, sliding plate

For an overview of plate tectonics, together visit http://www.pbs.org/wgbh/aso/tryit/tectonics/intro.html. Then explore the "Plate Tectonics and People" section at http://pubs.usgs.gov/publications/text/dynamic.html to see how Earth's constant movement underfoot affects humankind. (If you prefer, research plate tectonics using library resources.) Have your child use the research to write and illustrate a dramatic story, with correct grammar, spelling, and punctuation, that conveys an imaginary person's exciting experience resulting from shifting and colliding plates.

6. Describe and give examples of ways in which the earth's surface is built up and torn down by natural processes, including deposition of sediments, rock formation, erosion, and weathering.

Fossil hunt

 Together, learn about fossils using reference books, such as an earth science book, or online by typing "fossil" into an Internet search engine. Then go on a fossil hunt at http://www.dmns.org/denverbasin2/fossil/. If you don't have Internet access, you can bring your child to a natural history or field museum to look at fossils and how they are excavated. Have your child take "field notes" during your fossil investigation, analyzing the information to summarize in a clear, articulate manner, everything people can learn about the past from studying fossils.

7. Explain and give examples of how physical evidence such as fossils and surface features of glaciation supports theories that the earth has evolved over geological time.

Very old fuel

 Together, with your child, learn why the nonrenewable sources of coal, oil, and natural gas are called fossil fuels at http://www.energy.ca.gov/education/story/story-html/chapter05.html, or use library resources to explore this topic. (The term fossil *comes from the fact that they were formed during the time of the dinosaurs.) Have your child create an illustrated conservation brochure that informs people about the need to conserve these nonrenewable centuries-old resources. Your child's brochure should be persuasive and lively, and all claims should be supported with research. Be sure your child reviews his final version for correct spelling, punctuation, and grammar.*

THE EARTH IN THE SOLAR SYSTEM

8. Recognize that gravity is a force that pulls all things on and near the earth toward the center of the earth. Gravity plays a major role in the formation of the planets, stars, and solar system and in determining their motions.

9. Describe lunar and solar eclipses, the observed moon phases, and tides. Relate them to the earth moon and sun.

 MONTHLY CALENDAR PAGE Because it's hard to see the moon every night through its twenty-eight-day cycle, together research information on the Moon's phases, tides, and eclipses with library resources or an almanac, or visit "Virtual Reality Moon Phase Pictures" at http://tycho.usno. navy.mil/vphase.html. Have your child use the information to draw in that day's phase of the Moon, as well as any relevant eclipse and tide information, on a monthly calendar page for each night. Also, either use the website or resources from previous years to identify the Moon's phase for specific past dates—a household member's birthday, for instance. Have your child reproduce the image on the front of a birthday card as a special greeting.

10. Compare and contrast properties and conditions of objects in the solar system (i.e., sun, planets, and moons) to those on Earth (i.e., gravitational force, distance from the sun, speed, movement, temperature, and atmospheric conditions).

11. Explain how the tilt of the earth and its revolution around the sun result in an uneven heating of the earth, which in turn causes the seasons.

Seasonal rays

FLASHLIGHT, ORANGE, CHERRY TOMATO OR OTHER SMALL ROUND OBJECT THAT CAN BE SKEWERED WITH A TOOTHPICK, TOOTHPICK Explain that together, you will explore how the Sun's direct and slanted rays determine the seasons on Earth. First, hold a flashlight (representing the Sun) directly over a desk or countertop where your child has placed his hand. Hold it just close enough so that your child can feel warmth from the flashlight. Now, have your child switch hands (so that you start from the same baseline for each experiment) and hold the light at the same height, but on a slant. Can your child detect how the heat from the flashlight at this angle feels less warm? From this experience, have your child describe whether North America receives direct or slanted rays from the Sun during the summer (direct). Next, skewer a cherry tomato with a toothpick. Have your child hold it up so that "Earth's" axis (the toothpick) tilts from lower left to upper right (at this angle /). Hold up an orange, representing the Sun, to the right of your child's Earth. Also, hold a pen at the horizontal midway point (attached to the orange and pointing toward Earth) to symbolize the Sun's direct rays. Have your child make small holes in Earth (cherry tomato) for the approximate locations of North and South America. Which location receives direct Sun rays during this representation of the summer position of the continents? Have your child use the first part of this activity to describe why summer is hotter in North America and winter is colder. (The Sun's hot direct rays hit North America in the summer. The slanted, less warm rays hit North America in the winter.) Use science resources /or the Internet for further illustrations of the Sun's relationship to Earth's seasons.

Life Science (Biology)

GRADES 6-8

CLASSIFICATION OF ORGANISMS

1. Classify organisms into all kingdoms according to characteristics that they share. Be familiar with organisms from each kingdom.

World kingdom hunt

 Explain that until the 1960s, scientists classified organisms into just two kingdoms—animal and plant. This proved too limiting, so today scientists typically use five major kingdoms: Animalia,

Plantae, Fungi, Protista, and Prokaryotae. Together, use an encyclopedia, the Internet, or library materials to find the definition of each kingdom. Then, have your child write the name of each kingdom, with its definition, on separate note cards. Distribute one note card, writing paper, and natural history/science magazines to five players, including your child. During each three minute round, players must list on paper as many examples as possible for their kingdom card. If players are stumped, they can look through the magazines for inspiration. Play four more three-minute rounds, switching cards each time so every player writes examples for all five kingdoms. When all of the rounds have been completed, have your child check to make sure everyone's answers are correctly classified. The person with the largest total of right answers wins!

STRUCTURE AND FUNCTION OF CELLS

2. Recognize that all organisms are composed of cells, and that many organisms are single-celled (unicellular), e.g. bacteria, yeast. In these single-celled organisms, one cell must carry out all of the basic functions of life.

Tangible cell basics

WWW **MATERIALS FOR CELL MODEL (DESCRIBED BELOW)** *Explain to your child that cells are the basic units of life. Simple organisms are made of one; humans are made of ten trillion (10,000,000,000,000) cells! Together, bring a cell visually to life, learning about basic cell components as your child follows instructions for making a squeezable model at http://gslc.genetics.utah.edu/basic/cell/index.html. Alternatively, find a reproduction of a cell in library sources. Together, construct a model cell using Jello and other edible items such as miniature marshmallows, licorice, m&ms, and so forth. Have your child use the model to teach the basic elements of the cell to another person in a clear well organized manner.*

3. Compare and contrast plant and animal cells, including major organelles (cell membrane, cell wall, nucleus, cytoplasm, chloroplasts, mitochondria, vacuoles).

The Sun's taste

 ✍ WWW 📕 *OPTIONAL: SAMPLE OF CHLOROPHYLL FROM HEALTH FOOD STORE Using life science or biology reference books (or an encyclopedia), or searching online, explore the similarities and differences between plant and animal cells. Have your child create a chart, with "plant cells" and "animal cells" in columns across the top, and listing the characteristics that they have in common, and the ones that are particular to a certain kind of cell. For instance, in plant cells, chloroplasts, resembling incredibly tiny footballs, contain chlorophyll, which helps make food for the plant. To taste the dark green building block of life, buy an organic bottle of chlorophyll at your local health food store. Enhance half a glass of juice (or water) with a tablespoon a day. Besides its nutrients, chlorophyll helps freshen breath.*

Edible cell comparison

 WWW 📕 *MATERIALS FOR CELL MODEL Have your child construct one model cell for an animal and one for a plant using Jell-O and other edible items, such miniature marshmallows, m&ms, licorice, and so forth to create the cell membrane, cell wall, nucleus, cytoplasm, chloroplasts, mitochondria, and vacuoles. Have your child identify as many of the differences and similarities between the two cells as possible.*

4. Recognize that within cells, many of the basic functions of organisms (e.g., extracting energy from food and getting rid of waste) are carried out. The way in which cells function is similar in all living organisms.

Eating green I

 ✏ WWW 📕 *Can humans make their own food? What organism on Earth can? Green plants can turn sunlight into a meal! Learn all about photosynthesis, its role in food/energy production, and the food chain either online using an Internet search engine, or from reference books. From the research, have your child draw images to illustrate each step along the way in the photosynthesis process. Afterward, move to part II (Standard 14).*

Whose tosis?

WWW *LONG YELLOW STRING BEANS, LONG GREEN STRING BEANS, LARGE DINNER PLATE, TWO SMALL DESSERT PLATES First learn about mitosis, the process of cell division using library resources or online at http://esg-www.mit.edu:8001/esgbio/cb/mitosis.html. To reinforce the concept visually, use string beans (representing chromosomes) and plates to recreate the diagrams in the reference books or on the website. First, have your child place four green string beans and four yellow string beans on a large plate (representing the cell). Continue the mitosis process as illustrated. Pair up the string beans with similar colors (two yellow sets and two green sets), then align them vertically down the center of the plate, and finally divide them up onto two smaller plates—with one set of green and one set of yellow on each. Each "daughter" cell should now look like the original.*

A cell's choppers

WWW *Mitochondria convert the chemical energy contained in food into energy the cell uses to grow, divide, and function. Have your child investigate this cellular "digestion" using reference books or by typing "mitochondria" into an Internet search engine. Ask your child to give a "cell digestion" talk during dinner to household members, explaining the way this process occurs in cells. Your child's discussion should be clear and articulate and presented in a logical, easily understandable manner. Afterward, have your child solicit nicknames from diners for mitochondria, such as "tiny powerhouses" or "mini-power plants," to make sure everyone understands the importance of mitochondria and their function.*

SYSTEMS IN LIVING THINGS

5. Describe the hierarchical organization of multicellular organisms from cells to tissues to organs to systems to organisms.

Flip book inner anatomy

Together, examine the various elements of human anatomy (cells, tissues, organs, and systems). Visit the "Human Anatomy Online" site at http://www.innerbody.com/htm/body.html, type "human anatomy" into any major Internet search engine, or use library resources. (Local natural history museums and science centers are also good places to conduct research.) Ask your child to create individual, simple anatomy diagrams on large note cards, working from small to big—from cells, to tissues, to organs, and then to entire systems (digestive, circulatory, etc.). Have your child place the note cards in a logical order and "flip" through the human body, from small to large. Reverse the order of the cards and then flip from large to small.

6. Identify the general functions of the major systems of the human body (digestion, respiration, reproduction, circulation, excretion, protection from disease, and movement, control, and coordination) and describe ways that these systems interact with each other.

REPRODUCTION AND HEREDITY

7. Recognize that every organism requires a set of instructions that specifies its traits. These instructions are stored in the organism's chromosomes. Heredity is the passage of these instructions from one generation to another.

Cellular commander

Why do nose cells look different from toenail cells, eye cells, and so forth? Together, discover how the nucleus serves as the "control center" of the cell using reference books or by typing "nucleus" into an Internet search engine. Afterward, have your child create a persuasive argument (in a clear and articulate manner) for why the nucleus should be referred to as the "brain" of the cell. Your child should cite her research as support for the argument.*

---

8. Recognize that hereditary information is contained in genes located in the chromosomes of each cell. A human cell contains about 30,000 different genes on 23 different chromosomes.

WWW *Together, begin with the basics about cells and genetics. Information can be found in reference books about life science, or click on the right-hand arrow on the "Cells Are Us" website at http://www.icnet. uk/ kids/cellsrus/cellsrus.html to follow an illustrated story of how we all began from two cells, and the role of DNA and chromosomes. Have your child retell the story of his coming into being in his own words, from the cellular point of view! The narration should be logical, chronological, and engaging, demonstrating a clear understanding of the material studied.*

---

9. Compare sexual reproduction (offspring inherit half of their genes from each parent) with asexual reproduction (offspring is an identical copy of the parent's cell).

EVOLUTION AND BIODIVERSITY

10. Give examples of ways in which genetic variation and environmental factors are causes of evolution and the diversity of organisms.

Interviewing Charles D.

WWW *Have your child study the life and work of Charles Darwin, using library resources (such as an encyclopedia or short biography), or by typing "Charles Darwin" into an Internet search engine. Afterward, you should play the role of a graduate student gathering first-hand history for your thesis, interviewing Mr. Darwin (your child) about his life and scientific work. (Have your child help you come up with a list of relevant and probing interview questions before taking on your roles.) Your child's answers during the interview in the role of Charles Darwin should demonstrate an understanding of his work and life, as well as an ability to speak clearly and articulately.*

11. Recognize that evidence drawn from geology, fossils, and comparative anatomy provide the basis of the theory of evolution.

12. Relate the extinction of species to a mismatch of adaptation and the environment.

Here today, gone tomorrow

WWW 📖 *Together, investigate the causes of extinction and endangered species using reference books, or online at http://library.thinkquest.org/ 25014/english.index.shtml. Have your child select one of the endangered species and cover it from a television reporter's point of view. Your child should research, assemble, and present the information as a "news flash" on a nightly newscast (right before or after dinner to assembled household members), using correct diction and clearly articulated ideas.*

LIVING THINGS AND THEIR ENVIRONMENT

13. Give examples of ways in which organisms interact and have different functions within an ecosystem that enable the ecosystem to survive.

What's a biome?

✏ WWW 📖 *Together, research biomes, either using reference books or by taking a virtual tour with pictures and information about various biomes located on the world map at http://www.cotf.edu/ete/mod ules/msese/earthsysflr/biomes.html. Biomes are distinct ecological communities of plants and animals living together in a particular climate. Next, have your child select two biome examples (such as a desert and a tropical savannah) and conduct further research in order to draw at least two parallels between the similar role different plants or animals play in each environment. (For instance, your child could investigate which animals are the hunters and scavengers in the two types of locales.) Afterward, have your child use her research as the basis for a labeled drawing that reflects an understanding of the environmental and ecological differences and similarities in each biome.*

ENERGY AND LIVING THINGS

14. Explain the roles and relationships among producers, consumers, and decomposers in the process of energy transfer in a food web.

Eating green II

✎ 🖵 📕 *Review "Eating green I" (Standard 4). Now that you have seen how plants make food from the sun's radiant energy, have your child complete a simple food web, which involves the flow of energy from the sun to green plants to animal consumers. Have your child divide a large piece of drawing paper into three horizontal bands. Ask your child to sketch the sun and its radiant energy in the top band, and then have your child sketch plants that grow from the sun's energy in the second band, and finally, animal consumers (including humans) in the bottom band. Ask your child to expand and refine his diagram by referring back to his reference books or with information from http://edu.leeds.ac.uk/~ edu/technology/epb97/forest/fdchn.htm.*

15. Explain how dead plants and animals are broken down by other living organisms and how this process contributes to the system as a whole.

16. Recognize that producers (plants that contain chlorophyll) use the energy from sunlight to make sugars from carbon dioxide and water through a process called photosynthesis. This food can be used immediately, stored for later use, or used by other organisms.

CHANGES IN ECOSYSTEMS OVER TIME

17. Identify ways in which ecosystems have changed throughout geologic time in response to both physical conditions, interactions among organisms, and the actions of humans. Describe how changes may be catastrophes such as volcanic eruptions or ice storms.

18. Recognize that biological evolution accounts for the diversity of species developed through gradual processes over many generations.

Physical Sciences
(Chemistry and Physics)

PROPERTIES OF MATTER

1. Differentiate between weight and mass, recognizing that weight is the amount of gravitational pull on an object.

Mass-weight "diet"

SCALE, CALCULATOR Together, explore the difference between mass and weight. First, have your child weigh himself on a scale and write down the number. Explain that weight is the pull of gravity on an object. If a person weighs 120 pounds, Earth's gravity pulls the person with a 120 force. Ask your child if he would weigh less on Earth or the Moon. (If necessary, remind your child that the Moon is smaller and has less gravity.) The Moon's gravitational pull is about $^1/_6$ as powerful as Earth's. Have your child calculate his weight on the Moon, checking the answer with a calculator. Have your child create two sketches of himself—one on the Moon and one on Earth, labeling each figure with the appropriate weight. Now discuss mass—the amount of material in an object. Ask your child if his mass would be different on the Moon than it is on Earth. As a hint, have your child think about astronauts and space vehicles. Do they gain or loose material (or substance) once they leave Earth? If your child's sketches suggest a different mass (size) on the Moon than on Earth, make sure he revises them to reflect this understanding. Have your child use library resources or websites such as http://www.exploratorium.edu/ronh/weight/ to learn about weight variations on different planets. Have your child ask five people of different ages and sizes if they would like to lose or gain weight, and then have him recommend a planet that would satisfy each person's desire.

2. Differentiate between volume and mass. Define density.

WWW *INGREDIENTS LISTED AT WEBSITE Explain that <u>density</u> is the amount of mass an object has compared to its volume, or size. To gain a better understanding, together try the cool egg, salt, and water experiment to see how density changes using the instructions at http://library.thinkquest.org/11771/english/hi/chemistry/dense.shtml.*

3. Recognize that the measurement of volume and mass requires understanding of the sensitivity of measurement tools (e.g., rulers, graduated cylinders, balances) and knowledge and appropriate use of significant digits.

Together, review the "Mass-weight 'diet'" activity (Physical Sciences Standard 1). Have your child identify how the use of inaccurate measuring tools (scale, calculator) could have thrown off the results. Help your child describe how incorrect results in figuring out mass or volume for everyday events might lead to significant mistakes. Also, discuss with your child how mistakes might occur when significant digits aren't used in making these calculations (such as 2 grams instead of 2.57 grams, and so forth). For instance, the miscalculation of cargo weight might affect an airplane's ability to lift off or land properly. Watch the news or go through the newspaper as inspiration for other circumstances in which it is very important to use sensitive measuring tools.

4. Explain and give examples of how mass is conserved in a closed system.

WWW *CLEAR PLASTIC SODA BOTTLE WITH TOP CUT OFF, GRAVEL, SMALL PLANTS, ROCKS, BRANCHES, MOSS, PLASTIC WRAP Explain to your child that she is going to create a small closed ecosystem at home. If possible, together, first visit a local plant store and examine various terrariums. Then, help your child create an example at home with the simple online instructions at http://www.nsc.org/ehc/kids/terrar iu.htm, or use reference books from the library. (For further information visit the Chicago Field Museum terrarium site at http://www.fmnh.*

org/ua/netterr.htm.) Have your child create an illustrated "viewer's information poster" to display by the container, adding information and observations about the ecosystem of the terrarium over time, and providing examples of how mass is conserved in the system. Your child's poster, with correct spelling, punctuation, and grammar, also should address the living organisms as well as abiotic factors (those without life, such as water, temperature, soil, and so forth).

ELEMENTS, COMPOUNDS, AND MIXTURES

5. Recognize that there are more than 100 elements that combine in a multitude of ways to produce compounds that make up all of the living and nonliving things that we encounter.

Periodic super heroes

Have your child identify which elements in the periodic table are in solid, liquid, and gas form at their normal temperature and pressure. (Examples of periodic tables can be found on the Internet, including http://EnvironmentalChemistry.com/yogi/periodic/.) Ask your child to create a "super hero" with characteristics of two elements, such as the Amazing He-Fe Man (helium-iron), or Au-O Wonder Woman (gold-oxygen). What special abilities will the hero have because of his or her chemical makeup?

6. Differentiate between an atom (the smallest unit of an element that maintains the characteristics of that element) and a molecule (the smallest unit of a compound that maintains the characteristics of that compound).

Edible atom

GUMDROPS, TOOTHPICKS, MINIATURE MARSHMALLOWS Together, learn about protons, neutrons, and electrons in science reference books, or by taking a virtual tour of atoms at http://education.jlab. org/atomtour/. Then, help your child create an edible atomic model.

Have your child select gumdrops to represent protons and neutrons (using a different color to represent each), connecting them with tooth-picks into circular forms. Then add small, lightweight electrons, using miniature marshmallows.

The tiniest substance

WWW *SUGAR, OPTIONAL MAGNIFYING GLASS, PERIODIC TABLE Have your child look at a single grain of sugar (with a magnifying glass, if possible). Ask if this is as small as the substance gets. One tiny sugar crystal is made up of millions of sugar molecules! A <u>molecule</u> is the smallest particle of a sub-stance that retains all the properties of the substance. Molecules themselves are made of atoms. Learn more about molecules and atoms, elements and compounds at http://www.nyu.edu/pages/mathmol/textbook/compounds. html, or by researching the topic in a physical science book or encyclopedia. Then, have your child use a periodic table (online at http://pearl1.lanl. gov/periodic/) to identify the type of atoms and their number in a molecule of sugar when written as $C_{12}H_{22}O_{11}$. (12 carbon atoms, 22 hydrogen atoms, 11 oxy-gen atoms). Also, ask your child how many atoms are in a single molecule of sugar (45).*

7. Give basic examples of elements and compounds.

A substance by any other name

WWW *Learn the chemical names of substances you and your child encounter on a regular basis (salt, sugar, water, etc.) and substitute these names in your regular conversation for a day. So, you would say, "Please pass the NaCl (sodium and chloride) at dinner, instead of asking for the salt, or you might say, "Be sure to turn off the H_2O when you're done with your shower."*

8. Differentiate between mixtures and pure substances.

Sore throat soother

MEASURING SPOON, SALT, WATER, SUGAR OR HONEY, SHORT CINNAMON STICK, LEMON PEEL, STERILIZED BOTTLE FOR LIQUID STORAGE Allow your child to help you make a natural sore throat soother while keeping an eye out for chemical and/or physical changes through-

out the process. First, have your child predict if combining salt and hot water will produce a chemical or physical change. After adding $\frac{1}{4}$ teaspoon of salt to a cup of hot water, what happens to the salt? It dissolves. But what happens chemically? Ask your child to find the elements that make up this new equation using the Internet, library resources, or science books: (Salt/Na + Cl = NaCl (the plus sign means that the sodium and chloride are reacting) + H_2O/ water.) Thus, the salt water is both a chemical and physical reaction. Repeat this investigation for each step, next mixing in one teaspoon of sugar or honey. (This also will be a physical and chemical reaction.) Then add a cinnamon stick and lemon peel for the final touch (physical—softens). Finally, have your child pour the sore throat concoction into a sterilized bottle, label with a descriptive name and illustration, and keep refrigerated until needed. The next time someone has a sore throat, warm the solution and have your child administer the sore throat soother while describing the chemical and physical changes that occurred during its manufacture.

---

9. Recognize that a substance (element or compound) has a melting point and a boiling point, both of which are independent of the amount of the sample.

Boiling hot!

CANDY THERMOMETER, WATER, TWO DIFFERENT SIZE POTS Together, first try this little projection test. Fill a large and a very small pot with water, place on a stove, and set the flame to the same point. Ask your child which one he thinks will boil first. (The smaller amount of liquid.) Now, ask your child to hypothesize whether the boiling temperature of the water in the smaller or larger pot will be hotter. As soon as each one boils, turn the flame off, and then carefully measure the temperature with a candy thermometer. Surprised at the results? The boiling point is the same regardless of the amount of water. Discuss with your child how the results of this experiment can be extended to the melting point of two different-size samples of a substance.

---

10. Differentiate between physical changes and chemical changes.

MOTION OF OBJECTS

11. Explain and give examples of how the motion of an object can be described by its position, direction of motion, and speed.

Arm wrestle

Explain that you will arm wrestle with your child to explore a scientific idea about force. Both take a neutral arm wrestling position. Then, have your child exert a moderate force, which she should keep constant throughout the experiment. Explain that you will change the amount of your own force, from very little to a lot. First, exert just a tiny bit so that your child's hand tips yours over. Then slowly add more force so your hands come into balance, and then, finally, exert more force so your child's hand goes down. Repeat the experience switching roles and having your child speed up the process just a little, noting how much more quickly your clasped hands change location.

12. Graph and interpret distance vs. time graphs for constant speed.

FORMS OF ENERGY

13. Differentiate between potential and kinetic energy. Identify situations where kinetic energy is transformed into potential energy and vice versa.

HEAT ENERGY

14. Recognize that heat is a form of energy and that temperature change results from adding or taking away heat from a system.

Whistle away

TEA KETTLE THAT "WHISTLES" Boil water in a kettle that whistles. From a safe distance, have your child describe what happens as the water heats up. What form of energy makes the kettle whistle? (The heat boils the water—the heat energy makes it move, and the resulting steam makes the kettle "whistle.") Discuss with your child what happens when heat is taken away from the tea kettle (the water stops boiling and eventually returns to room temperature). Together invent silly lyrics for a song about heat as a form of energy, inserting the whistling kettle at appropriate moments for audible emphasis. 📖

Forever changing

✍ PLASTIC BAG, FOOD COLORING OR INK Have your child fill a plastic bag about a third of the way full with water tinted with food coloring or ink for easy observation. Blow some air into the bag and then tie it tightly closed. Have your child describe the water's state within the bag as it sits on the counter (liquid). Next, place the bag in direct sunlight. Have your child periodically check the bag until he can see the vapor that rises from the water when heated. Have your child describe this state too (gas). Finally, place the bag into the freezer and have your child describe the water in this final state (frozen). Afterward, note how all these physical changes occurred without any chemical reaction!

15. Explain the effect of heat on particle motion through a description of what happens to particles during a change in phase.

16. Give examples of how heat moves in predictable ways, moving from warmer objects to cooler ones until they reach equilibrium.

Technology/Engineering

1. MATERIALS, TOOLS, AND MACHINES

Broad Concept: Appropriate materials, tools, and machines enable us to solve problems, invent, and construct.

1.1 Given a design task, identify appropriate materials (e.g., wood, paper, plastic, aggregates, ceramics, metals, solvents, adhesives) based on specific properties and characteristics (i.e., weight, strength, hardness and flexibility).

Handmade mitts

MATERIALS FROM THE HOUSEHOLD Have your child imagine starting a baseball team, but only being able to use ordinary household items to make the mitts, balls, and bats (as many children did in the first part of the twenteth century). Have your child design the sports equipment, selecting the appropriate materials (e.g., rags sewn together for mitts, mop handles for bats, rubber-band balls for baseballs) and describing how the specific properties and characteristics of each make it the right choice for creating particular sports equipment. Have your child make two mitts, and one ball and bat, and then test out the "equipment." Your child should come back to the "drawing board" with revisions and improvements for the equipment after playing.

1.2 Identify and explain appropriate measuring tools, hand tools, and power tools used to hold, lift, carry, fasten, and separate, and explain their safe and proper use.

1.3 Identify and explain the safe and proper use of measuring tools, hand tools, and machines (e.g., band saw, drill press, sanders, hammer, screwdriver, pliers, tape measure, screws, nails, and other mechanical fasteners) needed to construct a prototype of an engineering design.

Kitchen safety

When cooking together, demonstrate appropriate safety precautions for your child, such as wearing oven mitts when handling hot things, turning the handles of pots on the stove inward so no one can accidentally knock them, never leaving an open flame, clearing oven of all items before turning it on, storing foods at proper temperatures, never putting metal in a microwave, knowing the location of the fire extinguisher and how to activate it, and so forth. Make sure your child can articulate the purpose of each safety measure. Have your child create a kitchen safety poster explaining these kitchen safety measures and hang it on the refrigerator for easy reference. Ask your child to describe why safety measures must be taken in science activities as described in the Standard, just as in daily cooking.

2.   ENGINEERING DESIGN

Broad Concept: Engineering design is an iterative process involving modeling and optimizing for developing technological solutions to problems within given constraints.

2.1   Identify and explain the steps of the engineering design process, i.e., identify the need or problem, research the problem, develop possible solutions, select the best possible solution(s), construct a prototype, test and evaluate, communicate the solution(s), and redesign.

Lung savers I

Explain to your child that he is a car designer who has been asked by a client to invent a fabulous looking, energy-saving, alternative-fuel car. Before beginning his design process, your young designer should outline on paper all the steps of the process, as mentioned in the Standard. Move to the next step.

2.2   Demonstrate methods of representing solutions to a design problem, e.g., sketches, orthographic projections, multiview drawings.

Lung savers II

Your young designer must start with some research about the history of cars and fuel and what is being produced currently. Use library materials or type terms such as "alternative fuel," "cars," and so forth into any major Internet search engine. (Or visit "Alternative Fuel Vehicles" at http://www.energy.ca.gov/education/AFVs/index.html. This site provides an overview of the history of the car from gasoline to electric cars of the future.) Continue with the next step.

2.3   Describe and explain the purpose of a given prototype.

Lung savers III

Have your child sketch and revise his own prototype and then present the final car design, clearly labeled with its environmentally sensitive elements to the client (you). Proceed to the next step.

2.4   Identify appropriate materials, tools, and machines needed to construct a prototype of a given engineering design.

Lung savers IV

Now, with the client's approval, your young designer needs to select the appropriate materials, tools, and machines necessary for the car's construction, making a detailed list to show the client. Now for the final step.

2.5   Explain how such design features as size, shape, weight, function and cost limitations would affect the construction of a given prototype.

Lung savers V

Have your child examine and explain the issues mentioned in the Standard—as they apply to his prototype—to the client (you) so the imaginary project can "proceed."

2.6   Identify the five elements of a universal systems model: goal, inputs, processes, outputs, and feedback.

3. COMMUNICATION TECHNOLOGIES

Broad Concept: Ideas can be communicated though engineering drawings, written reports, and pictures.

3.1   Identify and explain the components of a communication system, i.e., source, encoder, transmitter, receiver, decoder, storage, retrieval, and destination.

Communication ins and outs

 PAPER FOR LARGE, LONG TIMELINE Ask your young communications analyst to sketch communication systems through the ages on a wide, long sheet of paper to make a timeline. (Examples include handwritten letters, telegrams, telephones, satellites, e-mail, cell phones, faxes, and so forth.) Next, research each of the different components of a communication system listed in the Standard, online or using library resources. Have your young analyst now identify the applicable components for each of the systems on the timeline and list them underneath the system. Thus, for e-mail, the "transmitter" component would be "modem," so your child should write "modem" underneath "e-mail" on the timeline. Your child also should write each of the words listed in the Standard below the timeline (source, encoder, and so forth) and then draw a line from the word to the corresponding items on the timeline (i.e., a line should connect the word "transmitter" to the word "modem"). After completing the timeline, have your analyst examine all the information and see if there are any observations she can make about technology, complexity of process, and speed of communication systems through the years and the impact of each on society.

3.2   Identify and explain the appropriate tools, machines, and electronic devices (drawing tools, computer-aided design, and cameras) used to produce and/or reproduce design solutions (engineering drawings, prototypes, and reports).

3.3   Identify and compare communication technologies and systems, i.e., audio, visual, printed, and mass communication.

Press agent

✐ ✑ ✎ ▨ 📺 Explain to your child that he has just been hired to develop a thorough advertising campaign for his favorite sports, music, or movie star. Together, first examine the different ways of getting his message across, examining audio, visual, printed and mass communication examples (television commercials, radio spots, ad campaigns in newspapers, posters, billboards, and so forth). Now your child should research his new client. What information will he feature in his ad campaign for the star? Accomplishments? Attractive traits? Fascinating gossip? From his notes, your child should now create an engaging message about the new client in each medium. Written examples must contain correct spelling, grammar, and punctuation as well as short, evocative text. Visual examples also must use color, composition, shape, and lines to communicate the message effectively. Finally, have your young press agent present the campaign to the client (you) for feedback, making sure he includes a comparison of the different media and what each one will help accomplish in terms of reaching different people. After revisions, the campaign is ready to hit the road!

3.4 Identify and explain how symbols and icons (e.g., international symbols and graphics) are used to communicate a message.

In any language game

✑ Have your child draw an easy to understand icon for "Do not enter" and one for "love." (Your child might draw a large "X" and a heart, respectively.) Have your child show her two images to people of various ages and backgrounds, asking them what they think the symbols mean. Did the majority of people understand the icons? Ask your child to list some other international symbols and describe why visual symbols might be useful, say if driving in a country in which you did not speak the language, or in trying to communicate with someone who cannot hear. Finally, when outside, conduct a symbol hunt. Whoever spots and correctly identifies the meaning of the most icons wins!

4. MANUFACTURING TECHNOLOGIES

Broad Concept: Manufacturing is the process of converting raw materials (primary process) into physical goods (secondary process), involving multiple indus- trial processes, e.g. assembly, multiple stages of production, quality control.

4.1   Describe and explain the manufacturing systems of custom and mass production.

4.2   Explain and give examples of the impacts of interchangeable parts, components of mass produced products, and the use of automation, e.g., robotics.

Big business I

FRESH FRUIT, WASHED AND CLEANED, BLENDER, ICE CUBES Have your child make a juice cooler with fresh fruit and ice cubes. After taste-testing and perfecting the recipe, tell your child she is now going into big business. Help your child plan on paper the technology and process necessary to expand into a large-scale company that can serve hundreds of consumers the tasty fruit treat, addressing the Standard, and providing examples. Move to step II.

4.3   Describe a manufacturing organization, e.g. corporate structure, research and development, production, marketing, quality control distribution.

Big business II

Before your child's business is up and running, she will need to out-line a plan for the company's organization, as addressed in the Standard. For instance, what personnel will your child hire (financial officer, mar-keting director, manufacturing employees, and so forth)? Have your child review her plans in part I and integrate the two into one cohesive plan of action to get her thirst-quenching business off the ground. As everyone sips the prototype of the drink, have your child present the plan in a clear, well-supported manner to the board of directors (household members) for feedback and revise it accordingly, if necessary.

4.4   Explain basic processes in manufacturing systems, e.g. cutting, shap-ing, assembling, joining, finishing, quality control, and safety.

5 . CONSTRUCTION TECHNOLOGIES

Broad Concept: Construction technology involves building structures in order to contain, shelter, manufacture, transport, communicate, and provide recreation.

5.1 Describe and explain parts of a structure (e.g. foundation, flooring, decking, wall, roofing systems).

Cross-view architect

WWW *DOLLHOUSE ADVERTISEMENTS IN TOY/CHILDREN'S CATALOGS, HOUSEHOLD OBJECTS TO MAKE A MODEL HOME* Explain that your child is going to build an architectural model for a client who desires a twenty-first century "ideal" home. First, together use the Internet or look for dollhouse advertisements in toy/children's catalogs to find examples of those that provide a cross-section of a house. Now, have your child use ordinary household items (shoe boxes, cardboard, paper, rulers, straws, paper clips, and so forth) to create a cross-section of the ideal "model" home. Your child should present his model to the client (you), explaining in detail what each section represents.

5.2 Identify and describe three major types of bridges (e.g., arch, beam, and suspension) and their appropriate uses (e.g., site, span, resources and load).

Span it!

WWW *MASSACHUSETTS TRAVEL BROCHURES* Together, learn about arch, beam, and suspension bridges either using the "Bridge Basics" page on the PBS "Building Big!" site at http://www.pbs.org/wgbh/build ingbig/bridge/basics.html, typing the related terms into any major Internet search engine, or using library resources. Next, use the Internet or Massachusetts travel magazines and brochures to hunt for pictures of each type of bridge. Have your child create a Massachusetts travel song that captures what it would feel like to travel over the different kinds of bridges. Your child should create, draft, and revise the lyrics and then teach the song to you and other household members.

5.3   Explain how the forces of tension, compression, torsion, bending and shear affect the performance of bridges.

Spanning suspension I

WWW 📖 *ENCYCLOPEDIA OR SCIENCE RESOURCES Together, find pictures of suspension bridges and identify forces of compression (pressing force that squeezes a material together). If necessary, review the information at the "Bridge Basics" page on the PBS "Building Big!" site at http://www.pbs.org/wgbh/buildingbig/bridge/basics.html, or type the related terms into any major Internet search engine. (You can also find more information in encyclopedias or science resources.) Finally, find a picture of one of the country's most famous suspension bridges, the Brooklyn Bridge, and have your child learn about the engineering feats this bridge accomplished when it was built more than a century ago (either online or with library materials). Ask your child to use the research to write a newspaper article as a reporter of the time, giving details on the bridge's technological significance and addressing the items in the Standard. In addition to correct spelling, punctuation, and grammar, you child's evocative article should be well-organized, with a clearly stated main idea. Move to the second step.*

5.4   Describe and explain the effects of loads and structural shapes on bridges.

Spanning suspension II

WWW 📖 *Now, help your child also learn the effect of <u>loads</u> (the way a weight or mass is supported) on bridges using the Internet or library resources. Have your child find a reproduction (online or in art books) of the "futuristic" paintings of the Brooklyn Bridge by Italian-American artist Joseph Stella (1877–1946). Together, identify how Stella depicts the way the bridge deals with loads caused by wind and how gravity distributes the weight throughout its structure. Finally, have your child describe and support with details whether photographs of the Brooklyn Bridge, or Stella's creative rendering, best communicates the idea of the bridge's original modern engineering.*

6. TRANSPORTATION TECHNOLOGIES

Broad Concept: Transportation technologies are systems and devices that move goods and people from one place to another across or through land, air, water, or space.

6.1 Identify and compare examples of transportation systems and devices that operate on each of the following: land, air, water and space.

Here-to-there on land and in air

Have your child examine a Massachusetts map and select two locations that are far away from one another. Ask your child to plan a travel itinerary for someone who loves different modes of travel. Have your young travel agent devise a trip that will include as many forms of transportation as possible, routing each stage using specific areas on the map, and describing why each selection was chosen over the alternatives for that particular leg of the trip. (Options include, bus, car, train, boat, helicopter, small plane.) Have your child legibly write up the itinerary and present it to the client (you), supporting his selection for a specific transportation mode on each leg of the trip.

6.2 Given a transportation problem, explain a possible solution using the universal systems model.

Boston rush hour

What a headache your young transportation director has! Rush hour traffic in downtown Boston has become unbearable. Using a map of downtown Boston, available online or from tourists bureaus, have your child devise solutions to the clogged road systems, proposing wider roads, alternative routes into and out of the area, or new, alternative methods of transportation. Have your child discuss each solution with the "authorities" (household members) who can express their concerns.

6.3 Identify and describe three subsystems of a transportation vehicle or device, i.e., structural, propulsion, guidance, suspension, control, and support.

6.4   Identify and explain lift, drag , friction, thrust, and gravity in a vehicle or device, e.g., cars, boats, airplanes, rockets.

Model forces of flight

MODEL AIRPLANE Together, learn about the four forces of flight: lift, weight, thrust, and drag on NASA's "Planetary Flight" page at http://quest.arc.nasa.gov/aero/planetary/atmospheric/forces.html, or by using any major Internet search engine or library resources. Then, buy and construct a model airplane, having your child identify which parts are involved in which of the four forces of flight as you work; alternatively, ask your child to draw one of the vehicles described in the Standard and have her label the four forces.

7. BIOENGINEERING TECHNOLOGIES

Broad Concept: Bioengineering technologies explore the production of mechanical devices, products, biological substances, and organisms to improve health and/or contribute improvement to our daily lives.

7.1   Explain examples of adaptive or assistive devices, e.g. prosthetic devices, wheel chairs, eyeglasses, grab bars, hearing aids, lifts, braces.

Helpful devices

Help your child make simple sketches of each of the devices mentioned in the Standard. Next, have your child write the function of each under the related image. Finally, have your child list what everyday activities he does (sees movies, reads signs, hears music, runs in a sport) that these devices make possible for other people with physical disabilities. Research the "Special Olympics" online or with library resources to discover amazing stories of powerful athletes who participate in all sorts of sports with the aid of adaptive or assistive devices.

7.2   Describe and explain adaptive and assistive bio-engineered products, e.g. food, bio-fuels, irradiation, integrated pest management.

MASSACHUSETTS

History and Social Science

Grades 5-8

Strand One: History

Learning Standard 1: Chronology and Cause

Students will understand the chronological order of historical events and recognize the complexity of historical cause and effect, including the interaction of forces from different spheres of human activity, the importance of ideas, and of individual choices, actions, and character.

Learning Standard Components
(Core Knowledge and Skills)

GRADES 5-8

■ Students understand multiple causes, how forces from different spheres of life can cause or shape an event.

Examples

Students explain the economic, social, cultural, and political causes for the American Revolution.

Patriotic flick

WWW 📺 *Rent the movie of the highly entertaining musical 1776, based on the proceedings of the Second Continental Congress as it decided whether to declare independence from Britain. Actual statements made in the debates of the Continental Congress, or in the letters and other writings of the historical figures portrayed in the film, have been inserted into the dialogue. Helpful background information and ideas for how to use the movie as a learning tool appear at http://www.teachwith movies.org/guides/1776.html. After watching the movie, ask your child to identify some of the economic, social, cultural, and political causes for the American Revolution.*

They explain the various factors that shaped the main compromises in the writing of the U. S. Constitution.

They compare and contrast the causes for the decline and fall of the Han and Roman empires.

They explain the causes of our Civil War, both long term and short term, and the several reasons for the defeat of the Confederacy.

■ Students understand the power of ideas behind important events.

Examples

They explain why John Adams said the American Revolution was "made in the minds and hearts of the people" before hostilities commenced.

They explain why democratic revolutionaries from 1776 to Prague and Beijing in recent times have repeatedly quoted Jefferson's words in the Declaration of Independence.

They discuss how the ideas of Moses, Jesus and Muhammed could motivate entire peoples to action.

Documentary view

Together, read about Muhammad, the founder of Islam, using library resources or by typing his name into any major Internet search engine. Have your child imagine being a film director planning a documentary about Muhammad and his ability to motivate entire peoples to action and belief. What pertinent information will your child (the director) include in her documentary to convey the impact of one of the world's most important religions? Have your child sketch a storyboard (quick sketches for key scenes) for the film documentary, demonstrating a grasp on the narrative of Muhammad's life and his impact on the rise of Islam.

They describe historians' views of the effects on Northern opinion of Harriet Beecher Stowe's Uncle Tom's Cabin.

■   Students recognize the importance of individual choices, action, and character.

Examples

They explain the reasons that guided Jefferson's decision to undertake the Louisiana Purchase, despite his doubts about its constitutionality.

They explain the significance of the choices of career made by Horace Mann, Dorothea Dix, and Frederick Douglass.

Freedom lovers

Have your child research the career choices of the individuals listed in the Standard by typing their names into any major Internet search engine or using library resources. (Horace Mann was a leader in education, Dorothea Dix was a nurse who campaigned for better treatment for prisoners and the mentally ill, and Frederick Douglass was a newspaper publisher, writer, and orator who was a leader for the aboli-

tionist cause.) Each of these individuals had a powerful impact on society through his or her chosen career. Have your child choose one of these individuals and conduct additional research to create a "before and after" list to illustrate how the individual changed society. For example, if your child chooses Dorothea Dix, his "before" list should include details about the way prisoners and the mentally ill were treated prior to her reform efforts, and should describe medical conditions on battle-fields prior to the introduction of female nurses. The "after" list should cite specific examples of the reforms Dorothea Dix introduced in jails and hospitals. Ask your child to imagine how the individual would react to the current state of his or her chosen field. What would Horace Mann think of American schools today? What would Dorothea Dix think of the treatment received by the incarcerated and the mentally ill? What would Frederick Douglass say about the state of race relations in the United States? Ask your child to imagine what new reforms these distinguished reformers would recommend to us today.

Learning Standard 2: Historical Understanding

Students will understand the meaning, implications, and import of historical events, while recognizing the contingency and unpredictability of history—how events could have taken other directions—by studying past ideas as they were thought, and past events as they were lived, by people of the time.

Learning Standard Component (Core Knowledge and Skills)

GRADES 5-8

■ Students understand how people in the past could believe themselves justified in excluding others from their community or privileges.

Examples

Students explain the reasons why the citizens of Athens, under the circumstances of their time, could convict Socrates of impiety and corrupting the young and put him to death. They contrast freedom of religion in the United States with governmentally sanctioned religion in ancient Athens and contemporary theocracies such as Iran; and they discuss current Massachusetts laws and regulations against educational malpractice.

They explain why, in the 18th century, despite the fact that by 1789 the United States was the most democratic large nation in the world, most political leaders believed it was reasonable to exclude women, Native Americans, slaves, and men without property from voting and public office. They discuss the power of the Declaration of Independence to show the injustice of slavery, oppression, and discrimination; and they discuss reasonable contemporary qualifications for voting, including age, citizenship, and absence of felony convictions.

Everyone can vote!

Ask your child to write and perform a rousing patriotic song defending the right of every United States citizen to vote, regardless of race, creed, or color. Ask your patriotic songwriter to incorporate phrases from the Declaration of Independence (available online at http://www.law.ou.edu/hist/decind.html or in library resources) into her song. Your child can borrow the tune from an existing patriotic song (for example, "America the Beautiful," "The Star Spangled Banner," "This Land is Your Land," "My Country 'Tis of Thee," "You're a Grand Ole' Flag," "I'm a Yankee Doodle Dandy") or create a new musical composition for her lyrics. Your child's verses should be persuasive, demonstrate an understanding of the issue, and contain correct grammar, spelling, and punctuation. Have your young composer teach the song to the rest of the household for a group performance.

■ Students recognize the contingency of history and how it must have taken into account when passing judgement on people and actions of the past.

Examples

They explain references to historical contingency in Lincoln's Second Inaugural Address, and how his words demonstrate both empathy and strict moral judgement.

WWW 📖 *Have your child read Abraham Lincoln's Second Inaugural Address at http://www.bartleby.com/124/pres32.html (or type the term into any major Internet search engine or use library resources). Afterward, have your child imagine being a newspaper reporter for a Southern journal. How would the reporter (your child) respond to Lincoln's words? Then, have your child assume the role of a Northern journalist. How would that reporter respond to the speech? Have your child write two brief newspaper articles, one to represent each reporter's point of view, and then ask your child to compare and contrast their positions. Your child's newspaper articles should include correct grammar, spelling, and punctuation, and convey a keen understanding of how Lincoln's ideas would have been received differently in the North and South.*

They explain both the intended and the unintended consequences of Radical Republican activism in the defeated South, early in Reconstruction years.

Learning Standard 3: Research, Evidence, and Point of View.

Students will acquire the ability to frame questions that can be answered by historical study and research; to collect, evaluate, and employ information from primary and secondary sources, and to apply it in oral and written presentations. They will understand the many kinds and uses of evidence; and by comparing competing historical narratives, they will differentiate historical fact from historical interpretation and from fiction.

 WWW 📖 *Review the "Patriotic flick" activity together, and then ask your child to conduct additional research on the Second Continental Congress and the individuals and events covered by the movie 1776, using the library and Internet resources. As your child conducts his research, ask him to draw upon both primary sources (actual letters, documents, and other first hand records of an event) and sec-*

ondary sources (summaries or accounts of an event created at a later date). Based on his research, ask him to identify which elements of the film were invented for entertainment purposes, and which elements are based on fact. When your child has demonstrated an ability to differentiate historical fact from interpretation, select several newspaper and magazine articles and ask him to look for examples of fact and interpretation in each story. Have him circle facts with a red pencil and circle interpretations with a blue pencil. Review his selections together and suggest additions or corrections where appropriate.

Learning Standard Components
(Core Knowledge and Skills)

GRADES 5-8

■ Students explain differences in the points of view in historical accounts of controversial events.

Complex connection

WWW 📖 Help your child understand the complex relationship between native peoples and the first English colonists in Massachusetts by reading the successive pages at http://www.pilgrimhall.org/nativep. htm or visiting the reference section at your local library. Have your child try to understand the perspective of both the native peoples and the settlers. How might their respective experiences and expectations have differed and contributed to the complicated nature of the relationship between them? (For instance, the colonists believed they were coming to a new, unsettled world while in fact, native peoples' ancestors had inhabited the lands for thousands of years before.)

Examples

Students explain how Americans and the British gave differing accounts of the Boston Massacre, and how portions of each might be used to reconstruct the event as it most likely happened.

They describe conflicting views of pre-Civil War Northern and Southern authors and statesmen on slavery as an institution and its effects on the lives and thoughts of slaves.

■ **Students understand ways of finding and testing evidence from societies leaving no written records.**

Examples

They explain methods of archaeologists, and what may be learned from their discoveries of human remains, artifacts, and cave paintings.

Virtual archaeology

WWW *Together, take a virtual tour of the cave of Lascaux, one of the most important Paleolithic archaeological sites in existence, with more than 1500 paintings on the walls at http://www.culture.fr/culture/arc nat/lascaux/fr/. First click on "Discover" to explore the find itself and view the images. Then click on "Learn" for fascinating archaeological information and techniques. Have your child take notes while visiting the site to discuss what information the archaeological find reveals about early human civilization. What do the images indicate about eating and hunting habits? (People hunted bison.) What do the art, and also its location (in a cave), reveal about uses of natural resources? (People would have used fire to illuminate the dark cave when painting. Also, the pigment for the artwork came from plants and animals.) Finally, have your child imagine being an archaeologist in the distant future who uncovers your home. Walking around the house, discuss what observations the archaeologist could make about contemporary culture—particularly in terms of food, clothing, and work.*

■ **Students recognize relationships between primary and secondary sources, and the uses of each.**

First-hand history

PRIMARY SOURCE MATERIAL SUCH AS FAMILY MEMORABILIA, LETTERS, GOVERNMENT RECORDS, PHOTOGRAPHS, NEWSPAPER CLIPPINGS, CERTIFICATES Have your child study the history of a relative (yourself, a grandparent, or an aunt or uncle) up close by examining primary sources (those created during the time period being studied, including photographs, letters, and personal memorabilia). Help your child assemble a variety of primary sources and create a mini-exhibition of the individual's life on a table, counter, or other open flat space. Your child should carefully label each item in the exhibit to help viewers understand the significance of each item. When the exhibit is complete, discuss the difference between studying history with primary sources and secondary sources, which are materials prepared later by people who studied the primary sources. (Secondary sources include textbooks, biographies, and documentaries.) Have your child create her own secondary source by writing an introductory essay to the exhibition.

Examples

They explain the conflicting views of historians on the reasons for the decline and fall of the Roman Empire, and how some Roman writers viewed the major dangers and identified major problems facing the Empire.

Be the historian

WWW Together, read the outlined version of factors leading to the fall of the Roman Empire at http://www.republic.k12.mo.us/high school/teachers/tstephen/romemp-7.htm. Have your child investigate the social, political, and economic causes further, using the Internet or library materials. Ask your child to "be the historian," deciding from her investigations which two or three conditions were the most important factors in the empire's decline. Have your child present her conclusions to a conference of other historians (household members and friends), supporting her case with specific information presented in a clear, articulate, and persuasive manner.

Learning Standard 4: Society, Diversity, Commonality, and the Individual

As a vast nation, the overwhelming majority of whose population derives from waves of immigration from many lands, the United States has a citizenry that exhibits a broad diversity in terms of race, ethnic traditions, and religious beliefs. The history of the United States exhibits perhaps the most important endeavor to establish a civilization founded on the principles that all people are created equal, that it is the purpose of government to secure the inalienable rights of all individuals, and that government derives "its just powers from the consent of the governed." It is also true, however, that federal, state, and local governments, as well as the people themselves, have often fallen short in practice of actualizing these high ideals, the most egregious violation being the acceptance of slavery in some states until the Civil War. Students should be expected to learn of the complex interplay that has existed from the beginning of our country between American ideals and American practice in the pursuit of realizing the goals of the Declaration of Independence for all people. While attending to the distinct contributions that immigrants from various lands and of various creeds, along with Native Americans, have made to our nationhood, students should be taught above all the importance of our common citizenship and the imperative to treat all individuals with the respect for their dignity called for by the Declaration of Independence.

Democratic contributions

 ✍ 🖥 📖 *Together, read how the Haudenosaunee (Iroquois) and other Native American confederacies helped shape the ideas of democracy in the early United States online at http://www.fee.org/education/ lessons/9909/sturgis.html or using library resources. Learn about connections between United States political systems and rights, and those developed earlier by native people with whom the early founders of the United States had contact. Have your child draw a line down the middle of a sheet of paper and place "Native American Institution" as the header in the left column, and "United States Institution" in the right. Then, have your child note parallels between the two societies, such as The Great Law of Peace, which included a section similar to the U.S. Bill of Rights, both of which protect the individual's rights to the freedom of worship, speech, and assembly.*

Learning Standard Components
(Core Knowledge and Skills)

GRADES 5-8

■ Students learn the nature of stereotyping, commonly from racial, ethnic, religious identifications; they learn the reasons stereotypes are logically and factually mistaken, and the reason stereotyping is morally wrong. They consider the capacity of determined individuals sometimes to achieve success even amidst adversity and in the face of unjust treatment.

Mistaken stereotypes

 Help debunk the common mistaken belief that all Native American peoples are the same—or that they live today just as their ancestors did, frozen in the past. Today, there are more than 500 individual nations of Native Americans. Although there are commonalties among the tribes (such as a respect for the land), each people's traditional clothing, language, and social and religious beliefs are unique. Thinking that all Native people are the same, or that they only live in past traditions, is like someone from another country visiting your hometown and deciding that everyone in the entire United States lives exactly as you do—both now and centuries ago. Have your child investigate various Native American tribes using library resources or websites such as "First Nations Histories" at http://www.tolatsga.org/Compacts.html and "The First Americans" at http://www.germantown.k12.il.us/html/intro.html. Help your child develop a chart for at least five different nations, displaying information about each tribe's traditional food, clothing, shelter, social customs and first European encounter. To understand that native people live just as we do today, eating the same foods, working at the same jobs, and watching the same movies, have your child also use the Internet or library resources to identify contemporary Native Americans who are athletes, doctors, writers, lawyers, and so forth. Excellent information on how to avoid stereotyping is available on the "ERIC Digest" website at http://www.ed.gov/databases/ERIC_Digests/ed394744. html.

Examples

Students read "The Education of Frederick Douglass" and write essays on Douglass' success in covertly learning to read and write, despite all efforts to prevent literacy among slaves.

■ Students explain the importance of our common citizenship in the United States and imperative of the Declaration of Independence to treat all individuals as equals and with respect for their dignity and rights.

July 4th sing along!

✍ *Discuss the rich variety of cultural, social, and religious beliefs in the United States with your child as reflected by the abundance of different cuisines, holiday observances, religious institutions, and the like. Next, ask your child to summarize the rights of United States citizens, reviewing the Declaration of Independence and the Bill of Rights, if necessary. Ask your child to compose lyrics for a Fourth of July song that celebrates the ways the diverse United States populations also are threaded together by common beliefs, such as life, liberty and the pursuit of happiness.*

Examples

Students write essays explaining both the meaning of "all men are created equal" and the reasons this proposition does not mean or imply that everyone is equal to everyone else in every respect.

■ Drawing on studies in history, geography, and economics, students learn of religious, ethnic, gender, and class persecution, of individual and group achievements despite adversity, of unjust laws and their reform, and of patterns of emigration from other lands in search of liberty and equality.

Roots

🌐 📺 *Together watch a videotape of the 1977 miniseries Roots, based on Alex Haley's Pulitzer Prize winning book that details the generations of a black family, starting in Gambia, Africa in 1750 through Emancipation and Reconstruction. Helpful background information and*

*viewing questions are available online at http://www.teachwith
movies.org/guides/roots-vol-i.html (with additional questions for each
of the six episodes on related pages). After viewing the series, have your
child conduct addition research on the African-American experience in
the United States using library resources or online at the History Channel
website at http://www.historychannel.com/exhibits/index.html. Ask
your child to use his research and the series to identify some of the obstacles faced by African-Americans and examples of African-American
achievement in the face of adversity. Have your child write a poem about
the African American experience that includes specific details about the
challenges and achievements he has learned about. Your child's edited
and revised poem should feature evocative imagery and descriptive language as well as correct spelling, punctuation, and grammar.*

Examples

Students memorize the inscriptions on the Statue of Liberty and the Iwo Jima
Memorial ("Uncommon Valor Was A Common Virtue"), explain the meaning of each,
and consider each in the light of E Pluribus Unum. Students consider the unifying
bonds of American citizenship appealed to by James Madison in Federalist 14.

Learning Standard 5: Interdisciplinary Learning: Religion, Ethics, Philosophy and Literature in History

Students will describe and explain fundamental tenets of major world religions; basic ideals of ethics, including justice, consideration for others, and respect for human rights; differing conceptions of human nature; and influences over time of religion, ethics, and ideas of human nature in the arts, political and economic theories and ideologies, societal norms, education of the public, and the conduct of individual lives.

Learning Standard Components
(Core Knowledge and Skills)

GRADES 5-8

■ Students learn and compare basic tenets of world religions and their influence on individual and public life as well as the course of history.

Monotheistic mobile

WWW 📖 *NOTE CARDS, STRING, TAPE, SCISSORS, WIRE HANGER*
Explain to your child that in ancient times virtually all religions worshipped numerous gods—those of war, love, fertility, protection, and so forth. Judaism, one of the oldest major religions, was the first to teach the belief in one God who prescribes moral laws for people. Help your child visualize Judaism's significance as a "monotheistic" religion out of which both Christianity and Islam developed. These religions accept the Jewish belief in a single deity and the moral teachings of the Hebrew Bible. Have your child write the word "monotheism" on a note card and tape it to the center of a wire hanger. Then, have your child write "Judaism," "Islam," and "Christianity" on separate cards and attach short strings to each card. Together, use reference materials or the Internet to research information about all three major monotheistic religions. Have your child add notes to the appropriate card as you gather your research. Hang the Judaism card in the middle of the monotheism card, and hang the Christianity and Islam cards on either side of the Judaism card to create a monotheistic mobile.

Islam basics

✎ ꝃꝃꝃ 🗐 *Together, explore the fundamental beliefs of Islam using library resources or online at http://www.ifgstl.org/html/basics/belief snf.htm. Have your child take notes during her research, and then ask her to use her notes to help her describe, in her own words, the five pillars of Islamic belief and their importance: Shahada (the oath), Salat (prayers), Siyam (fasting), Zakat (alms), Hajj (pilgrimage).*

Buddha image

ꝃꝃꝃ 🗐 *Together, read about Buddhism in reference materials or online. (Type "Buddhism" into an Internet search engine.) Then, look at images of Buddha online (at http://www.prs.k12.nj.us/~ewood/World _History/buddha/index.html) or in library materials. Have your child write a poem, using evocative words (correctly spelled and used) to describe Buddha's personality. What makes him appear calm, peaceful, and serene?*

Examples

Following a three-part lecture in which the teacher a) identifies the major religions in world history; b) describes the research and scholarship on which the lecture is based; and c) explains the criteria for a religion, and for a world religion, students form small study groups. Each group selects a religion to study and conducts research on its basic tenets, spiritual leaders, and sacred documents. The groups prepare reports for other students to read. The class as a whole then discusses the meaning of the word "religion" and identifies similarities and differences in the tenets of the religions studied.

Learning Standard 6: Interdisciplinary Learning: Natural Science, Mathematics, and Technology in History.

Students will describe and explain major advances, discoveries, and inventions over time in natural science, mathematics, and technology; explain some of their effects and influences in the past and present on human life, thought, and health, including use of natural resources, production and distribution and consumption of goods, exploration, warfare, and communication.

Printed word

 Have your child search your home and make a list of all the written material produced by printing technology (books, newspapers, comics, magazines, junk mail, instruction manuals, food labels, CD and videotape covers, and so forth). Discuss how printing, something your child probably takes for granted, is essential to daily contemporary life. Remind your child that printing did not always exist. Together, explore the history of its development using library resources or online at http://www.digitalcentury.com/encyclo/update/print.html. (Information about the long-range effects of the Gutenberg Press are available at http://bbms.bigbear.k12.ca.us/historyday/Effects.html.) Have your child describe what school would be like if printing technology had not been invented and developed. Every book would have to be written and illustrated by hand! How might this affect the number of books available and their cost? (In earlier times only the rich could afford hand-made books and only they knew how to read.) How would people share important news on a daily basis if there were no newspapers?

Learning Standard Components (Core Knowledge and Skills)

GRADES 5-8

■ Students understand the importance of technological advances for the spread of literacy in the Republic, and for citizen access to information.

Examples

Students read Abraham Lincoln's 1858-59 address, "Discoveries and Inventions"; reconstruct his arguments about the effects of printing and literacy on the aspiration of members of the broad public; and assess his view on fundamental purposes of education of the public.

■ Drawing on their studies in geography, students learn of inventions that have revolutionized exploration—such as the compass, the mechanical clock, the sextant, the telescope—and how they are used.

Examples

From accounts of voyages of explorers and traders, students explain the uses of navigational instruments.

Navigating the open seas

Ask your child how early explorers from other lands might have navigated the open seas in their voyages to North America before the invention of modern technology. Discuss <u>sextants</u> (instruments for measuring altitudes of celestial bodies from a moving ship), <u>astrolabes</u> (instruments for observing the position of celestial bodies before the invention of the sextant), and <u>chronometers</u> (instruments for measuring time with great accuracy). Why were these instruments so important in traveling over great distances of water without being able to see land? Encourage your child to create a sea shanty—a work song whose rhythms helped sailors as they hauled lines. (Traditional shanties can be found online at http://www.delweb.com/andrew/shanty/.)

■ Students understand the effects of inventions and discoveries that have altered, for better or worse over time, working and safety conditions in agriculture, mining, manufacturing, and transportation; and discoveries and inventions that have transformed medicine, education, daily life, and free time.

Examples

Students study the effects of technology on the availability and uses of free time and consider the extent to which they use free time for self improvement as distinguished from mere amusement.

Strand Two: Geography

Students will describe earth's natural features and their physical and biological characteristics; they will be able to visualize and map oceans and continents; mountain chains and rivers; forest, plain, and desert; resources both above and below ground; and conditions of climate and seasons.

Mapping the world

LARGE SHEET OF TRACING PAPER *Together, thoroughly explore a comprehensive atlas with your child. Study the symbols for landscape features, bodies of water, and elements such as cities, airports, railways, historic sites, and so forth, and find examples of their use throughout the atlas. Have your child trace one continent in the atlas, create his own legend for different land, water, and man-made features, and fill in the map accordingly. Conduct additional research (online or using library resources) to learn about the animal and plant life present on the continent, create symbols for them, and add them to the map in appropriate locations. Display the map in a prominent location so that other members of the household can learn about the variety of physical and biological characteristics on the continent.*

Learning Standard Components
(Core Knowledge and Skills)

GRADES 5-8

■ Students learn and locate the principal ocean currents and wind patterns.

Examples

Students trace the Gulf Stream and the Jet Stream on a globe.

■ They learn and locate the watersheds, ecological regions, and resources of the United States.

Origin "super" detective

MAP OF THE UNITED STATES, POST-IT NOTES At the supermarket, have your child check the labels on a wide variety of products (including the labels on produce such as bananas, oranges, and so forth) to determine the state of origin. Ask him to find as many different states as possible during his search, and to keep a list of the products for each state. For example, he may find fruits from Florida, vegetables from California, cheese from Wisconsin, maple syrup from Vermont, and so forth. When you return home, place a Post-it Note for each product on a map of the United States to illustrate its point of origin. Encourage your child to add additional Post-it Notes after future shopping trips. Display the map in a prominent location so other members of the household can see where some of their favorite foods originate.

Examples

Students trace the Great Divide, the Great Lakes, and the areas where iron ore, coal, and oil are found.

Learning Standard 8: Places and Regions of the World

Students will identify and explain the location and features of places and systems organized over time, including boundaries of nations and regions; cities and towns; capitals and commercial centers; roads, rails, and canals; dams, harbors, and fortifications; and routes of trade and invasion.

Silk road journal

Explore the importance and lucrative allure of long-distance trade between the East and West. Together, read about and follow the "Silk Road" on the map at http://library.thinkquest.org/ 13406/sr/ or by typing the term into any major Internet search engine. (You can also research this topic using library resources.) Tell your child to imagine being a merchant traveling the 7,000-mile route, which spanned China, Central Asia, Northern India, and the Parthian and Roman Empires. Have your child research information (online or at the library)

about each of the major countries he would have passed through. As you travel virtually from one location to another, have your child keep a detailed written and illustrated travel log about what she would sell or buy in each location. Your child's writing should contain correct grammar, punctuation, and spelling as well as capture the spirit of the trading journey during this time. 📖 🖋

Learning Standard Components (Core Knowledge and Skills)

GRADES 5-8

■ Students map the historical migrations of the American people.

Examples

Students compare patterns of immigration in eastern and western states during the 19th century.

Charting United States growth

 🖋 **WWW** 📖 *Have your child explore the U.S. Territorial Growth maps from 1775–1920 at http://www.lib.utexas.edu/Libs/PCL/Map_collection/histus.html or find them in reference books. Study the maps chronologically and ask your child to describe the changes in settlement patterns in North America during the course of the nineteenth century. Then, for each map period, have your child use the Internet or library resources to research the circumstances and events that contributed to the country's expansion (e.g., the discovery of gold in California drew thousands to the area in the mid-1800s). Have your child take notes while conducting this research, and ask him to share his findings with other household members at dinner.*

■ They map the growth and decline of empires.

Rome falls

 WWW 📺 📖 *WORLD MAP Together, watch the 1964 movie, The Fall of the Roman Empire, starring Sophia Loren, Stephen Boyd, and Alec Guinness. Then, have your child use library resources or the Internet to explore the geographic expansion and eventual contraction of the Roman Empire. (Information is available online at http://www.roman-empire.net/maps/map-empire.html or by typing the term into any major Internet search engine.) Then, read the outlined version of factors leading to the fall of the Roman Empire at http://www.republic.k12. mo.us/highschool/teachers/tstephen/romemp-7.htm, or use library resources to learn more about this topic. Ask your child to use his research and the movie (keeping in mind that the movie is historical fiction, not fact) to identify some of the social, political, and economic factors leading to Rome's demise. After discussing a variety of factors leading to Rome's fall, ask your child to select the two or three most significant factors. Have your child present his conclusions to household members and friends. Prior to his presentation, remind him to include facts from his research to support his conclusions, and to address his audience in a clear, articulate, and persuasive manner.* 📖

Examples

Students map the conquests of Alexander the Great and of the Romans.

What made Alexander great?

 WWW 📖 *Together, read about Alexander the Great in reference books or at http://www.mrdowling.com/701-alexander.html, or by typing his name into any major Internet search engine. Have your child use the information to explain why the leader is referred to as Alexander the Great. Look at a map of Alexander the Great's empire together. (You can find one online at http://library.thinkquest.org/10805/alexmap.html.) Ask your child to identify the locations of Alexander's exploits as the empire grew. Finally, have your child create a mime of one of Alexander's exploits, using gestures to convey the actions and events.* 🎬

■ They map the diffusion of ideas across regions of the globe.

Examples

> Students make maps of the spread of Judaism, Christianity, Islam, Hinduism, and Buddhism from their origins to the present.

Religion around the world

✎ WWW 📖 POST-IT NOTES, WORLD MAP Have your child conduct research about the geographic reach of Judaism, Christianity, Islam, Hinduism, and Buddhism, using the Internet or library resources. (Geographic information is most likely to be found in books and on websites focusing on the history of these religions.) As he learns about the countries in which each religion is practiced, have him annotate a world map with Post-it Notes recording this information. When he is finished annotating the map, ask him to share his observations about the presence of these major religions around the world.

Learning Standard 9: The Effects of Geography

Students will learn how physical environments have influenced particular cultures, economies, and political systems, and how geographic factors have affected population distribution, human migration, and other prehistoric and historical developments, such as agriculture, manufacturing, trade, and transportation.

Prehistoric survival manual

✎ ✐ WWW 📖 Ask your child to travel back in time to the hunter-gatherer societies that lived about 2 $\frac{1}{2}$ million years ago. Have your child imagine learning to survive by using only natural materials from the environment, and then write a "survival manual" with tips appropriate to the time period. First, help your child create a chart that will serve as an outline for the manual. Tell your child to write "food," "clothing," and "shelter" in separate columns on a sheet of paper and then under each heading write ideas and methods for supplying each the way the hunter-gatherers would have done (e.g., animals and plants for food, animal skins for clothing, wood for shelter). Explain that one of the most important implements for survival was sharpened stones. Have your child list how stone tools would help in each of the three categories. For instance, spearheads for hunting would go under "food" or "clothing," axe heads to cut trees under shelter. Next, have your child read more about the Stone Age (lasting until about 8000 B.C.E.), typing the term into a major Internet search engine or using library resources. Your child should search for more information pertaining to the three survival areas. Finally, ask your child to use the research and chart as the basis for an illustrated survival manual that, with correct spelling, punctuation, and grammar, explains how to exist in prehistoric times.

Learning Standard Components
(Core Knowledge and Skills)

GRADES 5-8

■ Students understand how physical characteristics, transportation routes, climate, and specialization influenced the variety of crops, products, and industries and the general pattern of economic growth in Massachusetts.

Examples

Grades 5-6: Students describe how the geography of Massachusetts influenced the location of communities, the forms of shelter, and the economic life of Native Americans and English settlers in the 17th century.

Geography and early Colonial life

COLLAGE MATERIALS *Ask your child to consider the influence of Massachusetts's geography (as outlined in the Standard) when researching state history during the seventeenth century, using library resources or websites such as http://www.kidinfo.com/American _History/Colonization_Colonial_Life.html. Ask your child to use the information from her research to create a collage to represent the various geographical factors (climate, natural resources, soil for farming) that shaped the experience of English settlers and Native Americans.*

Using maps, climate data, narratives, pictures, and archaeological data, students explain how geography shaped continental movements of Native American groups, 1600-1800.

■ **Students recognize the settlement patterns, migration routes, and cultural influence of racial, ethnic, and religious groups.**

Examples

By interviewing parents, older friends, and relatives, and by reading primary sources such as newspapers, students gather information on how and why the ethnic composition of some neighborhoods in their city or town has changed since the 1940s.

Here, now, and then

Visit your local historical society or library and together, look at early photographs of your community's environment. Then, have your child explore primary sources by interviewing parents, older friends, and relatives, as suggested in the Standard. Interviews can be used to learn how and why the composition of your community has changed since the 1940s. Have your child write a letter to an imaginary child from an earlier era, describing to him or her how the community has changed. Ask your child to add "before and after" illustrations to her letter to highlight the most significant changes. Your child's edited and revised letter should make specific use of the information she gathered during her research, and should use correct grammar, spelling, and punctuation to describe the changes in the area over time.

■ **Students understand the reasons for the distribution of cities over a region.**

Examples

Students locate the major cities in ancient history on a map of the Mediterranean, and hypothesize reasons for their locations.

WWW *Have your child find the Mediterranean Sea, the Red Sea, and the Nile River on a map of ancient Egypt, which can be found using library resources or online at http://www.virtual-egypt.com/newhtml /maps/index.html. Have your child imagine being a trader in ancient Egypt, and ask him to identify the areas in which potential clients could be found. Which countries would your child be able to do business with because of Egypt's location and access through its waterways? Have your child use the map to explain why this powerful civilization was a major force in the ancient world.*

■ Students understand how technology has increased human capacity for modifying the environment and acquiring resources, and analyze the impact of increased technology on the environment.

Examples

Students show how water was managed in Egyptian and Mesopotamian civilizations, in prehistoric Pueblo cities of the Southwest, and in modern agriculture.

Learning Standard 10: Human Alteration of Environments

Students will describe the ways in which human activity has changed the world, such as removing natural barriers; transplanting some animal and plant species; and eliminating others; increasing or decreasing natural fertility of land; and the mining of resources. They explain how science, technology, and institutions of many kinds have affected human capacity to alter environments.

WWW *WORLD MAP Where were potatoes first cultivated? Your child will learn the answer to this question, along with the history of this popular vegetable, by visiting http://www.potatohelp.com/pota to101/facts.asp. Ask your child to use the information on this site to illustrate the potato's journey on a map, drawing lines to indicate how the potato traveled and labeling the lines with relevant dates. (For instance,*

draw a line from Peru to Spain and write "sixteenth century," to represent the potato's transportation from South America to Europe by the Spanish Conquistadores.) After completing the mapping process, help your child find potato recipes from a variety of cultures, in cookbooks or online. Potatoes are an ingredient in bangers and mash (Ireland), curries (India), and soufflés (France). Help your child hone his math skills by having him mentally halve, double, and triple the measurements for the ingredients for a few of the recipes found in your research. (For example, $^1/_2$ teaspoon of salt would be $^1/_4$ teaspoon if it was halved, one teaspoon if it was doubled, and $1\,^1/_2$ teaspoons if it were tripled.) Have him practice these mental calculations with several recipes to help him increase his speed and accuracy. **1₂3**

Learning Standard Components (Core Knowledge and Skills)

GRADES 5-8

■ Students recognize the intended and unintended consequences of technological advances on the environment.

Examples

Students examine social and environmental changes brought about by the technological advances in transportation, food production, and preservation in the 19th century.

Strand Three: Economics

Standard 11: Fundamental Economic Concepts

Students will understand fundamental economic concepts, including choice, ownership, exchange, cooperation, competition, purposive effort, entrepreneurship, incentive, and money.

Learning Standard Components
(Core Knowledge and Skills)

GRADES 5-8

■ Students name, define, and use correctly the common terms of economic life.

Examples

Students show practical use of terms such as goods and services; natural human, and capital resources; scarcity, production, distribution, consumption; consumer, buyer, producer; product, seller, labor, wage, salary, competition, money, wealth, capital, income, profit, loss, supply, and demand.

Keeping stock

Explore the concept of supply and demand on your next trip to the grocery store. Together, study the inventory at your local supermarket, paying special attention to categories where a lot of merchandise is displayed—peanut butter, breakfast cereal, ice cream, bread—and categories where very little merchandise is displayed—specialized gourmet foods. Ask your child what would happen if everyone in the neighborhood stopped eating peanut butter sandwiches and started eating anchovy paste sandwiches instead. What would happen to the store's inventory of these products? If your child was the store manager, would he change the number of supplies previously ordered for each of these goods? Ask the store manager if there has ever been a situation where customer demand exceeded store supply—rock salt during a snowstorm; batteries and candles during an electrical blackout; charcoal briquettes during cookout season, etc. Now, ask your child to consider the opposite scenario: Would he stop shopping at this store and shop elsewhere if it no longer sold certain products?

Who's the consumer?

SMALL BOWLS FOR ICE CREAM, CARTON OF ICE CREAM WITH NUTS OR CHIPS Make the idea of businesses being both producers and consumers tangible for your child. At dessert time, have her imagine owning

an ice cream store. Customers (household members) are coming in for ice cream. Stop and ask, "Who is the producer and who is the consumer?" After serving the customers (household members), have them complain that this product is "defective." It has much less nuts (or chips) than usual. Your child realizes that this is right! What will she do to save the business and get the product she has paid for (the carton of ice cream)? Ask your child to outline, draft, edit, and revise a complaint letter, with correct spelling, punctuation, and grammar, to the ice cream supplier, explaining why she, as the consumer, is unhappy with the product. Make sure she addresses the topics in the Standard. For example, does she willingly pay more for this ice cream than others on the market because it is a superior product? Are her consumers happier with this product than with other varieties that she has sold in the past? Is this product with less chips/nuts going to cause her to lose business?

- Students understand basic ideas of financial record keeping.

Examples

Students keep track of their expenses in a one-month period, compare it to their income, and project a monthly budget in which their expenses will not exceed their income.

- They understand how financial record-keeping is applied by business.

Tax time

TAX FORMS Together, visit the U.S. Department of the Treasury kids' site "Simplified Wage and Tax Reporting System" at http://www.employers.gov/stawrs/kids/ to learn about the tax responsibilities of starting a new business. Have your child discover what taxes are used for and the job of different government agencies. Then, have your child start his own virtual business from the three ventures offered at http://www.employers.gov/stawrs/kids/business.htm. The interactive experience will take your young entrepreneur through sales, hiring employees, and filing the correct forms. When tax season rolls around, show your child the different local, state, and federal forms that you use to determine income tax on earnings from salaries and/or investments.

Examples

They analyze simple profit and loss statements to see that profits are earned when total revenues exceed total costs.

■ Students understand that individuals or organizations working separately—in competition with one another—lower costs and prices, encouraging producers to produce more of what consumers are willing and able to buy.

Examples

Students explain how the opening of a second pizza shop in a small community or neighborhood affects prices, service, and quality.

Be the producer

 Review with your child the ideas of market price and supply and demand, either using reference books or the Internet. (Information can be found at http://pittsford.monroe.edu/jefferson/cal fieri/economics/SupDemand.html.) Then, have your child imagine that she runs a farm and is about to plant two new crops. Visit your local supermarket or fruit and vegetable store to conduct "market" research to see which items appear to be in the highest demand. Ask to speak to the store manager and have your child inquire, taking detailed notes, which fruits or vegetables have risen in price recently. Then, have your child ask which produce moves most quickly off the shelves. Afterward, have your child select two crops she will plant this season, supporting her decision and reasoning with specific information from the interviews. Make sure she considers how much competition there is, and how much she will have to charge to cover her costs and make a profit. To extend this activity, keep track of the market price and supply and demand of your young farmer's crops over the next few months.

- They understand differences between individual and institutional aims of economic activity; they understand differences between private and government interests in economic activity.

Examples

Students explain why government prohibits some behavior which would be profitable to individuals.

Learning Standard 12: Economic Reasoning

Students will demonstrate understanding of supply and demand, price labor markets, the cost of capital, factors affecting production, distribution, and consumption, relations among such factors, the nature of goods and services, incentives, financial markets, cost-benefit (including marginal cost-benefit) analysis, fairness, and the value of trade.

What the market commands

Help your child understand the idea of the market clearing price of a good or service, in which the supply price leaves no surplus or shortage. Have your child describe a business he might like to run— lemonade stand, dog walker, newspaper delivery, and so forth. Before beginning the venture, your young entrepreneur will need to do some research. Help him begin by listing all the costs for the good or service (tools, transportation, materials, etc.). Then, help your child decide how much profit he expects to make per unit of good or service. Using the research from cost and profit, help your child decide on a price to charge per service or product. Now, before opening for business, have your young entrepreneur survey at least five potential customers, asking if they would pay the price he has designated. Help your child adjust the price accordingly to find the correct market clearing price, so that the supply price leaves no shortages or surpluses. Finally, have your young entrepreneur design an evocative illustrated poster advertising (with correct spelling, punctuation and grammar) for his business, including the "just right" price, based on his research.

Lemonade for sale

MATERIALS FOR SETTING UP A LEMONADE STAND Use the creation of a lemonade stand to explore the issues of production and consumption. Ask your child to fully consider how the weather, location of the stand, price, and resources—such as number of lemons, glasses, and so forth— will affect her business. After the venture, discuss what further insight your child gained about production and consumption from the experience. How might she amend the endeavor next time to make it more successful?

Starting up

YELLOW PAGES, WANT ADS Together with your child, use the Yellow Pages and newspaper want ads to make a list down the side of a sheet of paper of as many businesses as possible that your child might want to operate. Then, next to each one, have your child explain the incentive for starting this business. For instance, the incentive to open a computer supply store might be that your child is interested in technology; for an ice cream shop, it could be that your child is an "expert" and can run the store easily; for a child care center, it could be the desire to provide a service to the community, and so forth. After running down the list and thinking of as many incentives as possible, have your child select just one business she would like to start. Ask your young entrepreneur to put together a simple business plan—outlining the materials, resources, personnel, and location necessary for starting such a venture.

Learning Standard Components
(Core Knowledge and Skills)

GRADES 5-8

■ Students explain law of supply and demand.

Examples

Students explain how an increase in the supply of wheat can cause a decrease in the price of bread.

■ Students explain how labor markets work.

Examples

Students analyze the "help wanted" pages in the newspaper.

■ Students explain why it costs money to borrow money.

Examples

Students discuss the various ways a bank might use the money it holds.

■ Students explain how someone running a business thinks about the cost of money.

Examples

They explain why the purchase of a car to use for delivering pizzas may be less attractive when interest rates are higher.

■ Students evaluate the advantages of different kinds of distribution channels.

Examples

Students discuss advantages and disadvantages for a producer of selling door-to-door, to a retail shop, through the mail, to a distributor, locally, across the country, and overseas.

Learning Standard 13: American and Massachusetts Economic History

Students will describe the development of the American economy, including Massachusetts and New England, from colonial times to the present.

Learning Standard Components
(Core Knowledge and Skills)

GRADES 5-8

■ Students describe the stages of economic change in New England from the 1600s to the present.

Examples

Students draw timelines of New England industries: fishing and farming in 17th century; textiles and whaling in 18th century; large-scale manufacturing in 19th and early 20th centuries; and recent emphases on technology, education, tourism, and health care.

Industrial revolution/urban growth

✍ WWW 📖 Together, read about the Industrial Revolution in reference books or online at http://tqjunior.thinkquest.org/4132/info.htm. Then, explain that with the growth of factories during the American Industrial Revolution, increasing numbers of young people, including women, migrated to urban areas. Together, explore the life of a "Mill Girl" working in Lowell, Massachusetts at http://www.fordham.edu/hal sall/mod/robinson-lowell.html. Have your child use information from the site to write a journal entry from the point of view of a young working girl in the mill, describing her typical day and feelings about it—doing repetitive work, being far from home, but also having the new freedom to live with other single females in an urban setting. Give your child feedback on the journal entry, and then have him revise it, responding to your comments and double-checking for correct spelling, punctuation, grammar, and evocative tone. 📖

■ Students describe effect of changing modes of transportation and communication on the distribution of goods and services.

Examples

Students trace connections between coastal, road, canal, railroad, and air transport and rise and fall of Massachusetts towns and industries.

■ Students describe differing views of how government may affect an economy.

Examples

Students explain conflicts between Jefferson and Hamilton on the relation of government to the economy.

■ Students analyze the effects of American inventions on the U.S. economy in the 18th and early 19th centuries.

New-fangled contraptions

 Using library resources or the Internet, have your child research the major inventions of Thomas Edison, Alexander Graham Bell, and Orville and Wilbur Wright. Have your child identify and draw the items each person's invention replaced or improved. For instance, the light bulb replaced oil and gas lamps, airplanes made long distance travel faster than by horse, and so on. Then, ask your child to write a story from the perspective of someone living in the industrial age who experiences one of the inventions for the first time, conveying, with correct grammar, spelling, and punctuation, his or her response to the new-fangled contraption and its effect on his or her daily life. Finally, have your child consider and discuss how these inventions affected of the economy in the country during the eighteenth and nineteenth centuries. In what ways did they help the economy grow? (For example, which invention(s) helped speed up business communication and transactions?)

Examples

Students examine the effect of the cotton gin and interchangeable parts manufacturing on American trade and the development of New England industry.

Learning Standard 14: Today's Economy

Students will describe the distinctive aspects of the contemporary economy of the United States and the world.

Learning Standard Components (Core Knowledge and Skills)

GRADES 5-8

■ Students describe international trade in Massachusetts.

Examples

Students describe Massachusetts' trade with foreign countries in the 18th and 19th centuries.

■ Students describe the role of information in the contemporary economy.

Examples

Students discuss how the Internet, newspapers, and television affect business decisions.

Business plan

 Invite your child to open her own imaginary sporting goods store that will sell goods nationwide and internationally. Your young entrepreneur will need to make use of various forms of information to set up a sound business plan. Have her use the Internet, newspapers, television, sports journals, and so forth to research the competition (other sporting goods stores). Who are they, what do they sell, and how do they market themselves? Then, have your young retail mogul use this information to decide what she will sell (for example, she may decide to specialize in tennis or ski equipment), how she will attract loyal customers (for example, she could offer "the lowest prices in town," or she could carry exclusive merchandise), how she will market her business (for example, she could opt for an innovative online campaign or a contest for consumers), and so forth. As you and your child

discuss each of her important business decisions, ask her which media source (the Internet, newspapers, magazines, or television) provided her with the information that enabled her to reach each conclusion about her business venture. When her business plan is complete, ask your child to present it to an imaginary group of financial backers (household members or friends), explaining the plan and supporting it with details from her research. Have your child use charts and diagrams to enhance the presentation and win the backers' endorsement.

■ Students describe how the pace of economic transactions has quickened.

Examples

Students discuss how many transactions take less time today than in the past.

■ Students explain differences and similarities between producing for local and for international markets.

Examples

Students discuss changes a Massachusetts computer manufacturer might make in products to be sold in Vietnam.

■ Students describe the changing role of labor in the global economy and the rise of service industries.

Examples

Students discuss the rise and fall of membership in American trade unions in relation to new technology and global markets.

Learning Standard 15: Theories of Economy.

Students will describe and compare the major theories of economy, and will identify the individuals and historical circumstances in which these theories were developed.

Learning Standard Components
(Core Knowledge and Skills)

GRADES 5-8

■ **Students distinguish between money and barter economies.**

Examples

Students read about societies without money and discuss what Americans would have to give up if they had to barter for all their needs.

■ **Students explain the relationships among the elements of the United States economy.**

Examples

Students examine how private property, banking, contracts, labor agreements, federalism, and environmental regulations interact.

Strand Four: Civics and Government

Learning Standard 16: Authority, Responsibility, and Power

Students will explain forms of authority in government and other institutions; explain purposes of authority and distinguish authority from mere power, as in "a government of laws, but not of men"; and describe responsible and irresponsible exercise of both authority and power.

Learning Standard Components
(Core Knowledge and Skills)

GRADES 5-8

Drawing on Core Knowledge in History, students:

■ identify elected and appointed officials and their authority and responsibilities;

Who's on first?

 When you read the local newspaper, show your child photographs of elected officials—the mayor, a congressman, and so forth—and discuss his or her job. Encourage your child to create a gallery of politicians by cutting out newspaper photos, labeling them with each individual's name and position, and displaying them together. Over the next few days, see if your child can begin to identify the pictures of these individuals in the paper herself and recall their role in government. Ask your child which of these offices she might want to run for personally and why. How might your child want to affect the political life of your state or community?

■ learn laws that specify duties and limits to authority of public servants;

■ learn the nature, purposes, and limits of majority rule;

■ describe and compare legitimate exercise of authority, abuse of office and power, historical effects of and public responses to each.

Examples

Students correspond with elected or appointed officials, asking how and why they have applied their authority to specific problems.

Question authority

 Have your child apply the Standard to one of the individuals he is familiar with from the "Who's on first?" activity. Your child's edited and revised letter (containing correct spelling, grammar, and punctuation) should demonstrate a clear understanding of the issue addressed and pose a specific question about why the official acted in a particular manner.

Students research the differences between a government of laws and a government of men and assess the reasons historically given for each.

Learning Standard 17: The Founding Documents

Students will learn in progressively greater detail the content and the history of the Founding Documents of the United States including the Declaration of Independence, United States Constitution, and selected Federalist papers (as required by the Massachusetts Education Reform Act of 1993). They will assess the reasoning, purposes, and effectiveness of the documents; and, similarly, elements of the Constitution of the Commonwealth of Massachusetts.

Historical detective

 Explain to your child that he is going to be an historical detective, searching for the influences on the political ideas that helped shape the Declaration of Independence. Together, first read The Declaration of Independence at http://lcweb2.loc.gov/const/declar.html or find it in a reference book. Have your child summarize in his own words the key points, making a list with plenty of blank space in between each one (e.g., government by and for the people, inalienable rights of people, all men are created equal). Then, rent the movie of the highly entertaining musical 1776. (Helpful background information and questions for discussing the movie appear at http://www.teachwithmovies.org/guides/1776.html.) As you watch, have your young detective pause at any event depicted in the movie that he believes is related to the shaping of the Declaration of Independence. Your young detective should write down the event under the related key point. Ask your young detective to support his detective work with strong "clues." For example, your child could use a character's lines as support for the right to self-government or the end of tyranny. At the end of the movie, have your detective review his "clue" sheet to see how many ideas in the Declaration of Independence he can trace back to specific historical influences.

Declaration theater

 Together, read the Declaration of Independence in a reference book or online at http://lcweb2.loc.gov/const/declar.html. Search for and discuss portions that pertain to the government as a means of ensuring individual rights. Help your child rewrite the Declaration of Independence with an emphasis on personal rights, to put this important document in language that might be used by the authors

if they were writing today. Help your child edit the work for clarity and correct spelling, punctuation, and grammar. Then, have your child present a reading of the work, speaking slowly and clearly, and stressing important words.

Learning Standard Components (Core Knowledge and Skills)

GRADES 5-8

■ Students identify authors and other key figures in drafting and signing the Declaration of Independence, and in drafting and ratifying the United States Constitution:

Founding dads

Together, explore the biographies of the delegates to the Constitutional Convention of 1787 using library resources or online at http://www.nara.gov/exhall/charters/constitution/confath.html. Ask your child to focus her research on Elbridge Gerry, Nathaniel Gorham, Rufus King, and Caleb Strong, the delegates from Massachusetts. Together, use the information to create a skit in which the delegates from Massachusetts present the United States Constitution to people at home, convincing them to support the document. Rehearse the skit, practicing clear delivery of lines and effective gestures.

■ They describe the circumstances in which each was written and the basic content of each document.

■ They explain the meaning of "all men are created equal," the differences between granting rights and securing them, the relations between "just powers" and "consent of the governed," and the principle of separation of powers and checks and balances.

Examples

As they learn the elements of the Declaration of Independence, students study John Trumbull's painting, "The Declaration of Independence" (reproduced on the reverse side of the two- dollar Federal Reserve Note or "two- dollar bill"); explain that the painting does not depict the signing of the Declaration; and identify the persons depicted in the painting and their respective parts in the drafting and adoption of the Declaration of Independence.

As students memorize the Preamble, they explain the meaning of each reason given for ordaining and establishing the Constitution.

Preamble Scramble

WWW *Together, play the fun "Preamble Scramble" game on "Ben's Guide to U.S. Government for Kids" at http://bensguide.gpo.gov/9-12/games/preamble_scramble.html.*

Learning Standard 18: Principles and Practices of American Government

Students will describe how the United States government functions at the local, state, national, and international levels, with attention to the Constitution of the Commonwealth of Massachusetts, its Declaration of the Rights of the Inhabitants, and the basic elements of its Frame of Government; analyze the background and evolution of constitutional and democratic government in the United States to the present day; and explain the place of institutions of government in securing the rights of citizens.

Driving age

WWW *GRAPH PAPER Help your child understand that certain rights are determined by state government, not federal (e.g., driving age, highway speed limits). Have your child chart the age at which people can apply for their driver's license in ten states across the country on a bar graph. Draw a large box on graph paper. List ages sequentially, starting with the youngest age on the bottom and moving up along the left side. Across the bottom horizontal line, mark off ten columns for the states your child has researched, drawing a vertical line from the bottom to the* *top of the graph. Label each column with a state. Then fill in a "bar" for each, stemming from the bottom line to the point on the graph that correctly indicates the state's driving age. As an extension, have your child chart the age allowance of all the states and then find the median (the middle value of a group of numbers arranged in order) for the age at which people can apply for their driver's license in the United States. Discuss with your child the reason why a law like the driving age might be left to the states, while other laws are created by the federal government.* ¹₂₃

U.S. interests hunt

 Have your child read and then summarize the day's newspaper headlines and the first paragraphs of the major news stories involving the United States and other nations. Have your child clip each one and tape it to a sheet of paper. Ask your child to identify the reason for United States involvement in each case (territory, environment, trade, use of technology), marking it on the related sheet of paper. Continue the activity over the course of a week, helping your child understand the range and depth of concerns of the United States on the international level.

Learning Standard Components (Core Knowledge and Skills)

GRADES 5-8

■ Students describe how the ideals expressed in key documents relate to the structures, functions, and powers of national, state, and local governments, including:

■ the division of powers among levels of government;

■ the units of Massachusetts government cities, towns, counties, and regional authorities;

- the election and appointment of officials;

- the history and practice of the town meeting form of local government.

Examples

Students debate opposing arguments of the Federalists and Anti-Federalists during the struggle for ratification of the Constitution.

Let's party!

Ask your child to name the two major political parties in America today. Now, explore their origin together, learning about the Federalists, led by Alexander Hamilton, and Thomas Jefferson's Democratic-Republicans using reference books or online at http://gi.grolier.com/presidents/nbk/side/polparty.html (scroll down to the section "Parties Begin in the U.S."). Have your child use the information to identify the differences of opinion and approach to government between the two parties and then design campaign posters, using evocative images and text (with correct spelling, punctuation, and grammar) for both parties, defining and supporting the political stance of each. Finally, have your child imagine hosting a fundraiser (at which the posters will be hung) for the Federalists and one for the Democratic-Republicans. Given what your child has learned about the interests of each party, what types of people should your child invite to each party's bash to raise campaign funds? Which party would someone who wants strong state government likely support and why? How about someone concerned with the country staying out of foreign affairs?

Students read portions of the Massachusetts Constitution and explain their applications in state government today.

Massachusetts Constitution

Examine various articles of the Massachusetts Constitution at http://www.state.ma.us/legis/const.htm or using library resources. Ask your child if the Massachusetts Constitution covers any areas that are surprising to her—labor relations or transportation, for example. Ask your child to suggest some reasons why it might be important for each state, rather than the federal government, to regulate certain issues. For instance, are there unique issues for each state that might affect labor relations? (Types of industry, labor supply, and other issues might vary from state to state and might require different state laws.)

■ Students describe the establishment of the judicial system in the United States and Massachusetts Constitutions, including:

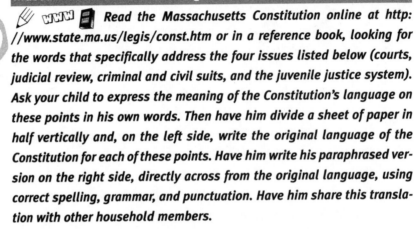

Massachusetts Constitution game

Read the Massachusetts Constitution online at http://www.state.ma.us/legis/const.htm or in a reference book, looking for the words that specifically address the four issues listed below (courts, judicial review, criminal and civil suits, and the juvenile justice system). Ask your child to express the meaning of the Constitution's language on these points in his own words. Then have him divide a sheet of paper in half vertically and, on the left side, write the original language of the Constitution for each of these points. Have him write his paraphrased version on the right side, directly across from the original language, using correct spelling, grammar, and punctuation. Have him share this translation with other household members.

■ the organization and jurisdiction of the courts;

■ the process of judicial review;

■ the process of criminal and civil suits;

■ the process of the juvenile justice system in Massachusetts.

■ Students compare the election process at the national, state, and local levels of government.

Examples

Students visit a local court and interview judges and lawyers about their authority and responsibilities.

■ They describe the process of:

■ nomination and promotion of candidates for elective office;

- the role and functioning of the Electoral College;
- similarities and differences among the major political parties

Separate sides

Use the Internet, newspapers, or magazines to help your child select a political issue of interest to him (education, the space program, minimum wage, the environment, cloning). ("Time for Kids" at http://www.timeforkids.com/TFK/ is an excellent resource for this activity.) Have your child research the positions of the Democratic and Republican parties on the topic and chart the similarities and differences. Ask your child to describe what he agrees with and disagrees with on both sides (and why), and then ask him if his position is more similar to the Democratic or Republican view. Tell him that you are going to play "devil's advocate" for this activity and argue the opposing point of view. Ask him to use specific details from his research in his debate with you, to effectively defend his point of view.

Examples

Students hold a mock election in their school and compare the results with those of their community.

Home Oscars

Have your child create his own ballots when Hollywood announces nominations for the year's top movie, best actor, and best actress (or conduct this same activity for another awards program, such as an All-Star sports team). Have your child distribute the ballots to at least ten people and then tabulate the results. The day after the awards are announced, compare the actual awards results to your child's mock election.

- Students describe and evaluate data and materials related to voter turnout, media coverage and editorializing, campaign advertising, campaign financing.

Examples

Students collect data on campaign financing in the nation, state, city, and town and estimate how much money is spent nationally on political campaigns in a presidential election year.

- They compare the policy-making process at the national state, and local levels.

- They describe and compare:

  - the basic legislative process at all levels; ≥

  - the interaction between chief executives and legislative bodies;

  - the role of political parties;

  - how lobbyists, academics, individuals, private foundations, cultural, ethnic, and other interest groups, and the media can influence policy-makers and legislative agenda;

  - effects of the media on public opinion and public policy;

  - the function of departments, agencies, and regulatory bodies.

Examples

Students in a school district governed by a town meeting study that form of government. They participate in a mock town meeting in which they prepare, debate, and vote on warrant articles. They interview town meeting members and local government officials about the process, and attend town meeting sessions to document how issues are presented, debated, and resolved. They then compare this local process with descriptions and analyses of the legislative process at the state and national level.

- Students understand tensions over the Constitution and the Bill of Rights in history.

Changing constitution

Together, read the Thirteenth, Fourteenth, and Fifteenth Amendments of the United States Constitution in a reference book or online at http://www.ilstu.edu/class/hist136/lectures/13-15amend.html or http://bensguide.gpo.gov/6-8/government/state/index.html. Have your child rewrite them (using correct spelling, punctuation, and grammar) in her own words and discuss their relationship to the aftermath of the American Civil War. Why was it necessary to amend the Constitution after the war? Then, have your child be an historian and research what life was like for people affected by these before the amendments became part of the Constitution. (For instance, prior to the amendments did enslaved blacks have the right to a fair trial, to own land, or to vote?) Ask your child to summarize in her own language, the change in the Constitution because of these specific amendments (e.g., the Constitution spells out the rights of all citizens more clearly).

Examples

Students explain the degree to which the provisions of the Constitution and the Bill of Rights were overridden during the Civil War, and the degree to which they were respected under dangerous conditions.

Learning Standard 19: Citizenship

Students will learn the rights and duties of citizens and the principle of equal rights for all; consider the nature of civic virtue in a school, a community, a nation; and identify major obstacles and threats to civil rights.

Learning Standard Components (Core Knowledge and Skills)

GRADES 5-8

■ Students learn the ways in which individuals participate in the political process and in civic life.

Citizen influence

WWW 📖 **PHONE BOOK** *Ask your child how citizens in the United States can influence government. Most likely, your child will mention elections. But together, explore other ways to make a difference, such as through political parties and special interest groups. Have your child select a topic of concern, such as saving an endangered species, preserving the rain forest, or protecting animal rights. Use the Internet, phone book, and library services to find out more about groups involved with the cause and how they take political action. Ask your child to devise a plan*

so he can make an impact, even before reaching voting age (e.g., through canvassing, educating those of voting age about the topic, and making contributions to organizations working for the cause). Encourage your child to become involved and to involve other young people in political action.

Examples

From their experience in classroom and schoolwide deliberations, students explain the needs, both practical and principled, for rules of order in group discussion and for parliamentary procedure in legislative debate and votes.

They practice skills necessary for participatory citizenship, such as respecting the rights and privacy of others, using the school library properly, deciding when compromise is appropriate and when not, and doing homework to prepare for discussion of a problem to be solved.

■ Students understand the relationship between rights and responsibilities in a democratic society.

Citizen rights and responsibility game

TIMER Write each of the following on separate note cards: "Freedom of Religion," "Freedom of Assembly," "To Keep and Bear Arms in Common Defense," "Freedom of Speech," "Freedom of the Press," "Protection for Those Accused of Crimes." On the back of each card, write "citizen right," without letting your child see the words. Then, write these categories on individual note cards: "voting," "serving on jury," "obeying laws," "respect other people's rights," "paying income tax." Write the term "citizen responsibility," again without your child seeing, on the back of each of these cards. Turn over all the cards, text up, and shuffle the "deck." Now, time your child as she sorts the cards into two piles for rights and responsibilities, respectively. Your young player can refer to the information on Ben's Guide to US Government for Kids about citizen rights (at http://bensguide.gpo.gov/3-5/citizenship/rights.html and citizen responsibilities at http://bensguide.gpo.gov/3-5/citizenship/responsibilities.html. Afterward, have your child check her answers by turning over the cards to see if they are in the correct pile. Your child should compute five points for each correctly categorized card. Then, in

successive rounds, your child also gets five bonus points if she can beat the time of her previous round. If your child plays against another player who is also learning about rights and responsibilities (instead of against herself), then the bonus points go to the person with the shortest time in each round. The highest total score wins! **1 2 3**

Examples

Students hold a debate about the meaning and implications of specific Amendments in the Bill of Rights for laws against public nuisances, regulation of controlled substances, and gun control legislation.

■ Students trace the development of the idea of citizenship, with a focus on ancient Greece and Rome, and the American Revolutionary period, and the history of opposition to universal suffrage.

■ They identify the contributions of leaders and people who made a positive difference in the community, state, nation, or world.

Examples

Students examine the courage, conviction, and works of women in the anti-slavery movement, focusing on the life of Sojourner Truth.

"Ain't I a woman?"

WWW *Together, learn about Sojourner Truth using library resources or by typing her name into any major Internet search engine (such as Yahooligans at http://search.yahooligans.com). Explore the many sites dedicated to this formerly enslaved woman who fought against slavery in the United States. Afterward, have your child study and then read aloud Truth's famous "Ain't I a woman?" speech given during the Akron, Ohio women's rights convention of 1851. (The text of the speech is available at http://www.hartford-hwp.com/archives/45a/170.html.) Before performing the speech in a clear and passionate voice, your child should determine what Truth meant to convey—how she wanted to affect the audience. Have your child present the speech to others playing the audience at the nineteenth century convention. Afterward, have your child ask people how they felt after hearing Truth's words and discuss her impact on American history.*

Learning Standard 20: Forms of Government

Students will study, compare, contrast, and analyze diverse forms of government; the ways of life and opportunities they permit, promote, and prohibit; and their effects on human rights. They will evaluate forms of government in terms of justice, ordered liberty, efficiency, public safety, educational opportunity, and economic and social mobility.

Learning Standard Components (Core Knowledge and Skills)

GRADES 5-8

■ Drawing on Core Knowledge in History for this and earlier grade spans, students identify the characteristics of a democratic government.

My democracy

✍ *Ask your child to devise his own democratic society. What characteristics will it include and why? Have your child check to see if his government plan is missing any key elements by reviewing the U.S. Constitution. Your child can omit any of the characteristics of the democracy in the United States if there is sound reason for support. (For example, he may want to create a new system for voting that takes advantage of technologies that didn't exist when the founding fathers created the Constitution.)*

Examples

Students explain Aristotle's classical formulation of the six forms of government, and explain why he held "polity" best, and what social conditions he believed necessary to maintain it.

Students discuss the Confucian view of the virtues necessary in rulers and their people to make any form of government stable, just, and effective.